Life and Work

LIFE AND WORK

WRITERS, READERS, AND THE CONVERSATIONS BETWEEN THEM

TIM PARKS

Yale

UNIVERSITY PRESS

New Haven and London

Published with assistance from the foundation established in memory of
Amasa Stone Mather of the Class of 1907, Yale College.

Yale University Press books may be purchased in quantity for
educational, business, or promotional use. For information, please e-mail
sales.press@yale.edu (U.S. office) or sales@yaleup.co.uk (U.K. office).

Set in Gotham and Adobe Garamond types by IDS Infotech, Ltd.
Printed in the United States of America.

Library of Congress Control Number: 2015951353
ISBN 978-0-300-21536-6 (cloth : alk. paper)

A catalogue record for this book is available from the British Library.

This paper meets the requirements of ANSI/NISO Z39.48-1992
(Permanence of Paper).

10 9 8 7 6 5 4 3 2 1

Contents

Introduction   vii

Charles Dickens   1
Feodor Dostoevsky: Crime or Punishment   24
Thomas Hardy   48
Anton Chekhov   67
James Joyce   81
Samuel Beckett   102
Georges Simenon   124
Muriel Spark   138
Philip Roth   150
J. M. Coetzee   163
Julian Barnes   174
Colm Tóibín   183
Geoff Dyer   194
Peter Stamm   206
Graham Swift   219
Dave Eggers   233
Haruki Murakami   247

CONTENTS

Peter Matthiessen   260

Stieg Larsson   271

E. L. James   286

Acknowledgments   299

Credits   301

Index of Names   303

Introduction

How to write about literature? Or rather, how to write about reading and writing? Would that be the same thing?

At school and university our teachers taught us how to talk about literary texts but not about our experience of reading them. We were given the tools to analyze rhythm and assonance and imagery and metaphor, to spot ambiguity and polysemy, lexical fields and onomatopoeia, but never invited to pin down the exact nature of our response to the work. The text has an objective existence. Things can be demonstrated. Your reaction to it is personal. It is not the same as my reaction. It might not be the same today as it will be tomorrow. Best not to talk about it. Yet when we read, we do so for our personal response, and if literary criticism is so little read, it is because it has so little to say to the ordinary reader.

This exclusion of our personal response went hand in hand with a disdain for biographical information about the author. The critic is not supposed to reflect on the relationship of a writer's life to his or her work. The expression "biographical fallacy" was coined: it was a mistake and an insult to the sacred powers of the imagination to reduce a text to a series of elements taken from the author's life. Yet literary biographies, unlike literary criticism, are widely and avidly read, and not in order to discover which bits of *David Copperfield* or *Middlemarch* came from which experiences. Readers want to know who this person is whom they have met through his or her novels. The meshing of life and work in literature is infinitely more complex than a mere identification of where this or that idea might have come from.

So critical orthodoxy eliminated both writer and reader and focused on the text. This way it was safe from the muddle of psychology, from subjectivism, from mere chatter. It was free to be serious, solemn even. Considered aside from both maker and consumer, the text assumed a near sacred importance, as though it had value and substance of its own, regardless of any traffic with mere human beings. Paradoxically, the "objective," "scientific" approach was supported by an unspoken mysticism that placed literature beyond our immediate experience of it. A breed of acolytes grew up: those who ministered to the work, indeed, to the Word. And they are still around. As a rule these professors keep their backs turned toward the people, and in general one can only suppose that the people, though they never read what the acolytes write, are happy with that. The very fact of all this worshipful industry confirms for the mere consumer of literature that his habit is noble and important.

Twenty years ago I had the good fortune to be invited to contribute to the *New York Review of Books,* then some years later to the *London Review of Books.* As a result I have now written perhaps a hundred literary essays. Clearly the *New York Review* and the *London Review* are not publications where one writes the kind of academic assessments I had been taught to concoct at university. Given the proper decorum, personal responses and even some reflection on the author's relation to the work are permitted. From the start, however, the challenge was how to prove the tradition wrong; how to give form to a discussion of the whole experience of reading without falling into the *merely* personal, above all the *merely* speculative.

One of the distinguishing characteristics of the *New York Review* is that one rarely writes about a single novel, but about an entire oeuvre, or at least a number of works by the same author. So the reviewer has the experience of entering into another's world of thought and feeling over an extended period of time. Developing as they do from book to book, style and content suggest a pattern of communication typical of this author, as if the writing of novels were part of, or at least in relation to, the author's behavior in general. In that case, a reader's reaction to that pattern might not be unlike his or her reaction to this kind of behavior in general, whether in books or out.

Developing this line of reflection, I established the habit of always reading a biography or autobiography of the author under consideration, or any biographical material I could find. I also began to draw on recent work in systemic psychology and positioning theory. Valeria Ugazio's book *Semantic Polarities and Psychopathologies in the Family: Permitted and Forbidden Stories* proved particularly useful. Ugazio considers the construction of identity in terms of a number of "semantic polarities" (fear/courage, good/evil, success/failure, belonging/exclusion) and suggests that in each family of origin one criterion of value will tend to be hierarchically more important than others in the way people talk about and assess each other. As a result, it becomes a matter of urgency for each individual in the group to find a stable and comfortable position in relation to this dominant polarity. Is it, for example, more important in this family to be seen as independent and courageous, or as pure and good, or as a winner? Wherever and for whatever reason an individual is unable to find a stable position—perhaps he or she wishes to be good but simultaneously yearns for transgression, or desires intensely to belong but then feels diminished by inclusion in the peer group—this can lead to the kind of conflicts and oscillations we associate with mental illnesses, or again with the tensions and ambiguities we find in creative art.

Without becoming schematic, I began to explore the possibility of using this kind of approach to experience as a way of reading novels and getting a sense not just of what they are about but of why readers react to them as they do. Let me give a simple, or rather simplified, example. All Thomas Hardy's novels present characters who take risks in career and above all love, seeking to free themselves from the limitations of their origins and the constrictions of social convention. The language is packed with references to fear and courage, rashness and cowardice, boldness and timidity. Wisdom is always seen as a form of caution. Increasingly, novel after novel, the protagonist's struggle toward freedom is more and more severely, even grotesquely punished. So *Tess of the D'Urbervilles* and *Jude the Obscure* have tended to be read, as is convenient for liberal thinkers in the twentieth century, as attacks on Victorian bigotry, but as D. H. Lawrence pointed out, Hardy seems to be deliberately loading the dice against his characters as if he needs to prove to himself that any courageous attempt to achieve personal freedom is doomed to failure. Courageous in themselves, in the subjects they tackle, his novels seem to suggest that courage is a mug's game. And in fact, if we look at Hardy's life, a desire for freedom and with it a need to see himself as courageous is constantly contrasted by a crippling fear of exposure, criticism, and public disapproval. The novels allow him to be brave on paper while remaining cautious in his actual life, always in church though quietly atheist, never actually betraying his wife while constantly planning to do so.

An awareness of this conflict helps us to understand many elements of the style, but more important, it raises interesting questions about the way we react to Hardy's stories. If courage and independence are crucial to us and the way we construct our self-esteem, these books will speak to us more directly or perhaps just differently than to others for whom issues of belonging or goodness are more urgent. Lawrence, whose own work also revolved around questions of courage, independence, and confrontation, reacted quite differently to Hardy from those critics who were used to thinking of his stories in terms of right and wrong.

The ideas that lie behind my approach in these essays are never declared or systematically elaborated—something I have tried to do in the book *The Novel: A Survival Skill*—nor do I adhere to them slavishly; but I have found over the years that they do offer a way to understanding what is at stake in a work of fiction and in people's reactions to it. Essentially, each essay is seeking to establish what values, or rather what tensions between competing values, are most important in the novels under consideration, then to show how these tensions shape the relationship between reader and writer that forms through the work.

One implication should be obvious. Each reader's response will have largely to do with where he or she is coming from, how he or she positions him- or herself in regard to the issues that matter most for the author. The idea that there is an absolute text or a correct reading of a book begins to break down. But that does not mean we have a free-for-all. Rather, we can begin to understand ourselves and our relationship with the writer and indeed with other readers by how we all respond to the work that lies between us. The underlying claim, though this was never my starting point, is that literature offers us an immensely rich, ramified, and nuanced series of "conversations" or "encounters" in reaction to which are constantly discovering and reconstructing our own identities.

Charles Dickens

In 1850 Charles Dickens invented a little game for his seventh child, the three-year-old Sydney, tiniest boy of a family of short people. Initially, in fun, Dickens had asked Sydney to go to the railway station to meet a friend; innocent and enterprising, to everyone's amusement, the boy had set off through the garden gate into the street, upon which someone had to rush out and bring him back. The joke was then repeated, sending the five-year-old Alfred with him; but when the boys had got used to being rescued, Dickens changed the rules, closed the gate after they had gone out, and hid with some of the older children in the garden. In *Great Expectations: The Sons and Daughters of Charles Dickens,* Robert Gottlieb quotes the letter in which Dickens explains to his wife what happened: "Presently we heard them come back and say to each other with some alarm, 'Why, the gate's shut, and they are all gone!' Ally [Alfred] began in a dismayed way to cry out, but the Phenomenon [Sydney], shouting 'Open the gate!' sent an enormous stone flying into the garden (among our heads) by way of alarming the establishment." "This," Gottlieb remarks of the anecdote with a warmth that he sustains throughout his book "was a boy after his father's heart."

Gottlieb's *Great Expectations* brings together in simple, almost schematic fashion, the lives of Dickens's ten children. There is a brief introduction to remind us of the main events of Dickens's life, followed by accounts of his dealings with each child before his death and then of how each fared afterward. The strange thing is that despite its unambitious, unassuming approach—often it seems this short book was written simply for the pleasure of contemplating a man whom Gottlieb admires to the point of worship—*Great Expectations* is more intriguing and revealing than many weightier works, perhaps because it allows us to observe, as we might not in a long and dense biography, certain patterns of behavior, certain obsessions, that we soon realize are absolutely central not only to the plots of Dickens's novels but to his whole approach to writing and being read. Dickens spoke of his readers as his extended family; to understand our response to him, it isn't a bad idea to see how he dealt with his children.

The game with Sydney, for example—where infant enthusiasm is first encouraged, then thwarted, the child spurred on to believe he is performing a useful task for the family only to find himself frighteningly excluded, father and siblings gone, the gate shut—can all too easily be connected to the two crucial events in Dickens's life that inevitably frame any discussion of his representation of family, poverty, and Victorian endeavor. The first we all know about from school days, since it constitutes the Dickens legend: his having been sent out as a child to work in a factory. Those drawn to write popular rather than academic books about Dickens like to get this story in early. Gottlieb gives it on page one:

> Charles had endured a difficult childhood: When he was eleven, his father, a well-meaning but improvident clerk in the navy pay office, was sent to debtors' prison, with young Charles put to menial work in a blacking factory—a social disgrace that demoralized him and from which he never fully

recovered, keeping it a secret from the world (even from his children) until his death.

The desire to have this experience authenticate Dickens's adult concern for the urban poor and explain his later depiction of any number of child waifs (one critic has counted 318 orphans in Dickens's fiction) tends to obscure the real nature of the young Charles's suffering as he later and very emotionally recalled it for his friend and biographer, John Forster. He was not beaten, starved, or ill-treated in any way. The factory was run by an acquired cousin, the son of a widower who had married Charles's aunt. Charles worked there for a year or less before returning to school and normal middle-class life. What upset the boy was that he was the only member of the family to be sent off to earn his keep in demeaning circumstances. His elder sister Fanny continued to study at the Royal Academy of Music, where the fees were thirty-eight guineas a year (at the factory Charles was earnings six shillings a week). Apparently the girl had a bright future while he did not. His younger siblings lived together with their mother and father in Marshalsea Prison. For Charles, then, alone in cheap lodgings, "utterly neglected," the experience was one of unnecessary, even vindictive exclusion from the family circle—the gate inexplicably shut, the father hiding—and what he begged for initially was not to be spared the factory, but to be lodged nearer Marshalsea so he could share his meals with his parents. There was also the shame, as this ambitious middle-class child saw it, of being obliged to consort with "common men and boys" and worst of all of being seen among them by friends of the family who came to the factory shop. Charles was meant for better things and better company.

All the same, if one is singled out for exclusion, it isn't unreasonable to fear that there might be grounds for it, that one might indeed be unworthy in some way, or again that simply by being excluded one might become unworthy, at least in the eyes of one's peers. Dickens later referred to himself at this time as "a small Cain," though he had "never done harm to anyone." One can well imagine that a response to this experience might be a determination to demonstrate one's worthiness at all costs in order to regain a secure position inside the domestic circle and the community at large. What Dickens so admired in little Sydney's reaction to exclusion was his ferocious determination to get right back into the garden where he belonged, with the help of a big stone. The moral of the story, which Gottlieb happily chuckles over, is that Sydney, but alas not crybaby Alfred, is the worthy son of a combative father.

The second unhappy event is directly related to the first, though this is rarely pointed out. Those who write enthusiastically about Dickens never seem to regret that he had to work in a factory as a boy, since there is a consensus that without this experience he might not have become the novelist we admire; but they do very much regret that thirty-four years later he excluded his wife (and the mother of his ten children) from the family, not only separating from her, but keeping the family home and custody of the children for himself (the youngest was six at the time) and frowning on every contact between them and her. In *Charles Dickens: A Life,* Claire Tomalin remarks: "The spectacle of a man famous for his goodness and attachment to domestic virtues suddenly losing his moral compass is dismaying"; to the point, Tomalin writes, "You want to avert your eyes." Gottlieb is equally uneasy about "the callous way he treated her," making it clear over and over again that however much he loves Dickens, he has to distance himself from this.

So again, together with an act of exclusion—one member of the family cast into darkness—comes the question of blame and worthiness. In letters to his friend Forster, Dickens admitted he was not without blame for the deterioration of his marriage, but when he actually forced the separation he put all the blame on his wife, accusing Catherine in private and public of not being fit for her role, of laziness and lassitude, "weakness and jealousy," of "not caring" for the children, whom she "was glad to be rid of." She was not worthy of him or them. She doesn't even have the grit to heave a big stone and fight for her place. Her defeatist acceptance of banishment is part of her crime.

The uneasiness of biographers suggests how contagious, when reading Dickens, is his constant and emotional taking sides over matters of worthiness, inclusion, and exclusion. Tomalin and Gottlieb feel obliged to let us know that in this case they stand, dismayed, on the side of the wronged wife. Thus the whole fraught question of belonging and not belonging, of being deserving or undeserving, inside a respectable group around the merry fire or outside in the damp dark, a question that recurs obsessively through Dickens's novels, also colors the reader's response to the writer himself. We feel we have been invited into the happy family, only to be disappointed with the man who wrote it into being. Conversely, disappointment, as Gottlieb repeatedly tells us, was Dickens's defining and constant experience with his children, great expectations coming to nothing. "I never sing their praises," he remarked, "because they have so often disappointed me."

Dickens married Catherine Hogarth in 1836 when he was twenty-four and she twenty. He had only recently got over an earlier love for a well-to-do girl whose family rejected him because he was young and without good career prospects—another exclusion. The eldest of nine children, Catherine was better placed socially than Dickens; her father was an editor on a newspaper Dickens was writing for.

Marrying her, Dickens was gaining entry to more respectable society. The move was not entirely distinguishable from his urgent project of becoming part of the literary world and being loved and accepted by readers. Serialization of *The Pickwick Papers* was under way, inviting everyone to become involved in the droll Pickwick Club. In 1837 the book's success won Dickens election to the rather more real Garrick Club.

The marriage took place on April 2 and the first child was born on the following January 6. Nine months almost to the day. From then on the Twelfth Night of Christmas would always be an occasion of rumbustious family celebrations and elaborate theatricals of which Dickens was both creator and main performer. Over the next fifteen years nine other children would follow, plus miscarriages. So although Dickens would show more and more unease about the numbers of his children, at one point claiming he'd only ever wanted three and even regretting he'd ever had any at all, there was a willfulness in this rhythm of production, again not entirely distinct from the enormous effort of will that must have been involved in writing *Pickwick* and *Oliver Twist* simultaneously, then beginning *Nicholas Nickleby* nine months before *Oliver Twist* was finished, obliged to meet deadline after deadline for relentless monthly serialization schedules. By the time the tenth and last child was born, Dickens was publishing his ninth novel. He was also editing a magazine, *Household Words,* had briefly edited a newspaper, published highly popular Christmas stories every festive season as well as scores of essays and articles throughout the year, and ran a home to rehabilitate fallen women: all activities that put him at the center of other people's attentions and (great) expectations. His children vied constantly for his affection; his readers eagerly awaited their monthly fix from his pen; other writers sought inclusion in his magazine (the name

Charles Dickens appeared in the header on every page); destitute women presented themselves for admission to the home, where they were interviewed personally by Dickens, who decided whether to grant them entry or not. He was involved in society in every possible way, by far the most popular author in the land. He belonged. No one could exclude him, though there was always the possibility that he might isolate himself, as someone now too worthy and remarkable to demean himself with the group, or immerse himself in it for too long, setting out on long walks and trips alone, as his alter ego *David Copperfield* often does in moments of depression when society seems to offer only disappointment. A year after his admission to the Garrick Club, Dickens resigned from it. In each of the following three decades he would rejoin the Garrick and resign again in protest over this or that issue, moving dramatically in and out of the community it offered.

The sense of ambitious expectation is evident in the names of the Dickens children. Charles alone chose the names, Gottlieb writes. Catherine was given no say in the matter. The first was Charles Culliford Boz Dickens. Charles after himself, of course, and Boz too, since that was the pen name he had used for his early work. Culliford was the second name of Charles's maternal uncle, Thomas Barrow, a cultured man who had forbidden Dickens's father ever again to come in his house after the latter failed to honor a loan of two hundred pounds. Dickens identified with this more respectable side of the family and often visited the house from which his dishonorable father was permanently excluded.

The second child, a girl born in 1838, was named not after Catherine but after her mother's younger sister Mary, who had died some months before. The child's second name, Angela, reflected the fact that Dickens had always and rather extravagantly considered Mary "an angel." Here one has to pause to mention that Dickens never lived—and only rarely spent time with his wife—alone. From the beginning he had invited the seventeen-year-old Mary to live with them, and after she died another younger sister, Georgina, was brought in to take her place, becoming so attached to Dickens that she would stay with him years later when Catherine was banished. But even at moments when one might have expected exclusiveness and intimacy—wedding anniversaries, for example—Dickens generally invited a third to the party, often his close friend Forster. It was conviviality rather than intimacy that interested him, a conviviality in which Dickens, flamboyantly dressed in colored silks and velvets, played the role of animator and entertainer. It is curious how many of his famous characters are actually double acts; in *David Copperfield* there are the Murdstones, brother and sister, Steerforth and his mother, the Micawbers, man and wife, Uriah Heep and his mother, Aunt Trotwood and Mr. Dick, Dora and her friend Julia, Agnes and her father; but David himself, like other alter egos, is never quite locked into any relationship. It is as if the most natural meeting Dickens can imagine is himself alone in the presence of at least two others, who draw him in, or repel him. When David does marry and form a couple, we are aware at once that it's a terrible mistake and that Dora isn't worthy of him. He was better off alone. She can't keep house, she has no intellectual conversation. Only at the end of the novel does David surrender his solitariness to become one with his soul mate Agnes, but at that point Dickens can no longer continue the story, as if the fusion of one's destiny with another's were unimaginable, a kind of death even.

After Charles Culliford Boz Dickens and Mary Angela Dickens, the next child, Catherine Macready Dickens, took her mother's name followed by that of a leading male actor, William Macready, a close friend of Dickens's. From this point on the names grow ever grander: Walter Landor Dickens (after the poet, a friend), Francis Jeffrey Dickens (after the founder of the *Edinburgh Review,* another friend), Alfred D'Orsay Tennyson Dickens (after the French artist and dandy and the English poet, both friends), Sydney Smith Haldimand Dickens (after the famous wit and the philanthropist, both friends), Henry Fielding Dickens ("in a kind of homage," Forster had been told, "to the style of the novel he was about to write"). An exception is the ninth child, Dora Annie Dickens, named after the brainless girl David Copperfield loves and whom Dickens, at the moment of the child's birth, was about to "kill off" in print, thus giving his hero an easy way out of his inappropriate marriage. Annie came from Annie Thackeray, the novelist's daughter and a friend of the newborn's older sisters. In the event, baby Dora died only months after her fictional namesake. The last boy was Edward Bulwer Lytton Dickens, named after the aristocrat and hugely popular novelist, who, needless to say, was a friend of Dickens and who was published in Dickens's *Household Words.*

With the one exception of Dora, then (a tribute to his own genius perhaps, since he felt that Dora was one of his best characters), Dickens was creating a thick web of worthy belonging for his family, placing them at the heart of contemporary cultural life, and making them constantly aware of the ideal of artistic achievement. Along with the official names, however, Dickens also gave his children nicknames, often more than one, usually in cartoon contrast to the grandeur of the baptismal name. So Charles, who soon became Charley, to distinguish him, but also diminish him, was also Flaster Floby, or the Snodgering Blee. Mary was Mamie or Mild Glo'ster. Catherine was Katey, but also the Lucifer Box. Walter was Young Skull. Francis was Frank, but also Chickenstalker (after a comic character in Dickens's *The Chimes*). Alfred was Skittles. Sydney was Ocean Spectre, or just Spectre. Henry was the Jolly Postboy and the Comic Countryman. Edward, having been extravagantly announced in Twelfth Night home theatricals, aged three, as Mr. Plornishmaroontigoonter, became Plornish and then simply Plorn for all his life, to the point that he was hardly referred to by his baptismal name at all.

In Dickens's fiction, giving nicknames is an indication of one character's power over others, for good or ill. In *David Copperfield* David's peremptory Aunt Betsey insists on calling him Trotwood (her surname), then just Trot, as a condition of his being accepted into her household; Dora she calls Little Blossom. David allows the sinister Steerforth to call him Daisy, a name that immediately asserts the inequality and ambiguity of their relationship. But for Dickens's grandly named children, we can imagine that their inane nicknames created a sense of extremes, of moving between the sublime and the ridiculous: invited to aim high, among poets and artists, they were actually accepted into their father's effusive affections mainly as figures of fun.

No sooner was Charley born than Dickens was sending lavish descriptions of the boy in letters to friends, a practice that would be repeated with each successive birth. Dickens had learned in adolescence that exaggerated imitation was always popular; it was the way he won the admiration of his fellow clerks when he worked in law firms in his teens (and the way David Copperfield establishes a place for himself among his companions at school). Dickens was a talented mimic and saw how people were always excited to recognize another's foibles. He had developed this talent on the page in his *Sketches by Boz* and again in *The Pickwick Papers,* where a happy complicity between reader and writer is fostered through relishing caricatures from a world both share. Now, as Gottlieb points out, the author's children too were rapidly transformed into comic sketches to amuse his friends and impress upon them the Dickens family's domestic happiness. Nicknames to the fore, tales were told of the children's prodigious abilities and infant achievements; Dickens himself is present throughout as boisterous master of ceremonies. The thrust of almost any act of writing was to conjure the world through imitation, compelling the admiration of the reader and creating a sense of shared, celebratory belonging.

Biographers too, it seems, take pleasure recounting this festive and much documented aspect of Dickens's fatherhood, as if they had a personal investment in his exuberance: "He was a magical father," Gottlieb tells us, "loving, generous, and involved. . . . He romped with them, took them on long walks—sometimes exhausting them with his preternatural energy. Every Christmas he took them to the famous toy store in Holborn to shop for their presents. He had a special voice for each of them. How could they not adore him?"

Inevitably, Charley was the first to appreciate that this jolly relationship might be difficult to grow out of. As a child, you could prove yourself a worthy member of the Dickens household simply by satisfying your father's rigid rules regarding tidiness and punctuality (Dickens inspected his children's bedrooms every morning, exacting punishment if anything was out of place); but as one got older it all became rather confusing. Charley was sent to Eton at the age of twelve, but despite his doing well there Dickens withdrew him three years later. He didn't want a son with a sense of entitlement, but a worker and fighter like himself; Charley must be "pampered in nothing." Dickens had begun to marvel that his children were not as determined and hardworking as he was. Charley had "less fixed purpose and energy than I could have supposed possible in my son." Indeed, "he inherits from his mother . . . an indescribable lassitude of character." It never seems to have occurred to Dickens that a certain passivity on the part of wife and children might be a natural response to his own energetic monopoly of the domestic stage, to the point of ordering the family groceries himself and insisting on the exact arrangement of the furniture. "For twenty years," Gottlieb writes, without quite seeing the sad comedy of the situation, Dickens "exhausted himself trying to strengthen" his children's "willpower and forward their careers."

How much like himself did Dickens really want his children to be? Great mimic as he was, he frequently referred to himself as "the Inimitable One." Charley composed a play at eight and showed some talent for translating and writing, but Dickens decided that his future was in business and sent him off to Germany to learn German, which he supposed was the business language of the future. After some modest success as a bank employee, and a far from shameful failure in business deals with China, Charley would eventually be allowed to become Dickens's assistant in *All the Year Round,* the magazine that replaced *Household Words.* Later it would be the second son, Walter Landor, who enjoyed writing but was discouraged from continuing. With the indulgence Dickens inspires, Gottlieb quotes Lucinda Hawksely, a Dickens biographer and descendant, explaining that the author was probably aware that Walter "did not have the aptitude or ambition to work at" writing "as hard as he would need to in order to succeed financially." It must be confusing to be named after a poet yet discouraged, at a very early age, from writing. But then Walter's older sister Katey, who took her second name from a great actor, would later be forbidden by her father from taking up a career in acting. These activities risked imitation of the Inimitable One.

In his essay on Dickens, remarkable for its combination of admiration and perplexity, George Orwell points out that for all the author's generous involvement in social issues and endless speeches at charity dinners, there's little representation or understanding of the world of work in his novels, or of the working class; the characters are intensely and immediately striking, but the melodramas they are involved in muddled and forgettable; "crossword puzzles of coincidences, intrigues, murders, disguises, buried wills, long lost brothers," allowing for no real mental life or character development. In particular, Orwell complains, "there is no objective except to marry the heroine, settle down, live solvently and be kind," after which "everything is safe, soft, peaceful and above all domestic . . . the children prattle round your feet . . . there is the endless succession of enormous meals, the cold punch and sherry negus, the feather beds and warming-pans . . . but nothing ever happens except the yearly childbirth. The curious thing is that it is a genuinely happy picture, or so Dickens is able to make it appear."

Dickens was indeed able to make it look like that, but in describing this weakness of the novels, Orwell also touched on a genuine problem in Dickens's life. The happy family was the be-all and end-all, but Dickens didn't reckon on the children growing up, the childbirths coming to an end, and his depressive, often sick wife proving less than a cheerful and admiring companion. He was disappointed, and his assessments of family and children began to oscillate rapidly as he switched between exuberantly performing father, delighted with his adoring offspring, and depressive long-range walker disgusted with a tribe of hangers-on. "You don't know what it is," he wrote of his sons to one friend, "to look round the table and see reflected from every seat at it (where they sit) some horribly well-remembered expression of inadaptability to everything." Of Walter, he remarked: "I don't at all know how he comes to be mine or I his."

Daughters were less of a problem; they merely had to be appropriately accomplished and prepare themselves for marriage, though it was never clear who could possibly replace their father in their lives. Mamie, the eldest girl, was his favorite, supporting her father and remaining with him when he left her mother, and years later, after a spinster's life, declaring it "a glorious inheritance" to have Dickens's "blood in my veins. I'm so glad I never changed my name." To gain some attention, the younger Katey, when ill, would insist that her father look after her, something that pleased Dickens immensely. There is no record of any of the children competing for their mother's affections.

With the boys Dickens was increasingly at a loss, and when at a loss his solution was to send people as far away as possible. He had tried this with his embarrassing parents, renting them a house in Devon, a form of exclusion without infamy (in *David Copperfield* the impossible Micawbers, modeled on his parents, are dispatched to Australia). Walter, who had enjoyed writing, was prepared for an army life in India, leaving for the subcontinent, never to return, aged sixteen; all the younger boys were sent to a cheap, gloomy boarding school in Boulogne, and came home (to be entertained by their father) only once or twice a year. Eventually, Francis Jeffrey (Frank) departed for India aged nineteen; Alfred for Australia aged twenty; Sydney joined the navy and sailed on his first three-year mission aged fourteen; Plorn, the saddest and shyest of the troupe, sailed for Australia, never to see his parents again, aged sixteen. Only the eighth child, Henry, managed to convince his father he was worthy of bearing the Dickens name in London and got himself sent to Cambridge and trained in the law at great expense.

Expense was now a crucial issue, since the children who had left England, or whom Dickens had sent away—Walter, Frank, Alfred, Sydney, and Plorn—all suffered from what Gottlieb calls "the fatal family weakness of financial irresponsibility," tacitly accepting Dickens's notion that once again there was a hereditary trait, this time on his side of the family, for falling into debt. Walter borrowed heavily in India, writing home frequently to ask for money; Alfred liked the same kind of fancy clothes his father wore and ran up debts accordingly; in the navy Sydney spent heavily in every port, giving his father's famous name as security. At this point, Dickens had no real financial problems but complained bitterly and eventually cut both Walter and Sydney off, forbidding the erstwhile Phenomenon to return home and remarking of him, in a letter to his brother Alfred: "I begin to wish he were honestly dead." Ashamed, Walter said he wouldn't write home again until he was out of debt. He died of an aneurism in Calcutta in 1863, aged twenty-two. On his tombstone, ordered and paid for by Dickens, he appears as the son of Charles Dickens; his mother's name is excluded.

The boys at home, Charley and Henry, didn't run up debts, though Henry at Cambridge was freely given far more than the boys in exile ever spent. It didn't occur to Dickens that using one's wealthy father's name to run into debt was a way of insisting on kinship from a distance, as if to say: "You can't get rid of us so easily." Arriving on Dickens's desk from Bermuda or Vancouver, Sydney's bills were another manifestation of the same spirit that had thrown that stone into the garden when the gate was shut. After Dickens's death, the faraway boys continued to borrow from the stay-home boys without paying back, Plorn in particular refusing to return eight hundred pounds to Henry. If his reasoning was that the money was a fraction of what had been spent on Henry's education, he had probably got his sums right.

If we summarize the central plot of the avowedly autobiographical *David Copperfield* with an awareness of the patterns of exclusion that galvanize the author's life, we have: Young David grows up with his kind, weak mother, deprived of his father who lies, excluded by death, in the graveyard close to their house. His mother's maid, Pegotty, gives David the chance to observe a happy working-class family among whom he will frequently take refuge, but which he never actually joins, having higher aspirations. Remarrying, the mother introduces the home-wreckers, Murdstone and his sister, into David's family. The Murdstones pronounce David unworthy and send him to the brutal Mr. Creakle's school, where David fears exclusion by his fellow pupils but manages to win the affection of the supremely worthy (he believes) Steerforth. After his mother's death, David is more radically excluded from his family and sent to work in a factory, where others, however friendly, are below him. He escapes and tracks down his father's sister Aunt Trotwood (the search for family members is a constant Dickens trope), who includes him in her household and pays for his education at Doctor Strong's school, allowing him to lodge with the Wickfield family, honorable people who share his class and aspirations, but whose weaknesses make them vulnerable to another home-wrecker and social climber, Uriah Heep. Thanks to hard work and talent, David shines first at the law courts, then as a writer, taking his rightful place in society and justifying all those who believed in him, but makes the mistake of marrying Dora, who, despite her higher social class, is not intellectually or spiritually worthy of him. David falls into a conflicted state; he has invested everything in the idea of domestic bliss but is increasingly frustrated that Dora is holding him back. Sadly, but fortunately, Dora dies and though David isolates himself for a year or two in proud depression, traveling all over Europe, he eventually sees that the person he should have married was Agnes, because she is beautiful, loyal, and above all worthy of him. There is no mention of sexual attraction.

Like all Dickens's fiction, the novel is attractively inclusive of a wide range of classes, language habits, and accents, as if drawing readers in to one vital and bustling society, but it also makes clear which villainous members (Heep, Steerforth, Murdstone) should be excluded from that society, if possible killed off or imprisoned. Another search for a family member has Mr. Pegotty traveling as far as Italy to look for his niece Little Em'ly, who, having fallen into disgrace through her relationship with Steerforth, isolates herself from the family, not realizing that her uncle is more than ready to take her back. When Em'ly is found, the two are allowed to emigrate to Australia, where her disgrace will not be known.

Orwell and many other critics are no doubt right to point to an absence of character development, or the kind of inner life we find in George Eliot, but the plot, like other Dickens plots, is far from being a melodramatic mess. What we have is every permutation of exclusion and inclusion, with many characters alternating between being in and out, worthy and unworthy, rich and poor, though without actually developing and without much explanation, as if both sides of the coin were constantly possible. One example: the aging, academic, absentminded Doctor Strong asks for the poor but beautiful young Annie's hand in marriage. Although she already has a sweetheart, Jack, she allows herself to be persuaded by her social climber mother to marry. To preserve propriety, Doctor Strong's friend Wickfield has Jack removed to army service in India. Annie wilts; Dickens allows us to feel the pathos of the young woman who has sacrificed her natural sexuality to her mother's social aspirations. But many hundreds of pages later, when Jack has returned from India and is again frequenting the Strong household, Uriah Heep tells the good doctor what every reader is thinking, that his wife is unfaithful. Both the doctor and Annie fall into depression. Feeling sorry for them, the affably unhinged Mr. Dick persuades Doctor Strong to write a will leaving everything he owns to Annie, and this supreme gesture of trust and inclusion (in other books Dickens uses the will as an instrument of exclusion) prompts Annie to fall on her knees and offer not a confession but an explanation of her behavior that shows her to have been pure throughout. Aware that others thought her involved with the despicable Jack, she felt too disgraced to speak of the matter to her husband, whom she honored to the point that she felt he could have made a "worthier home" with another woman. The speech, made in the presence of David and others, is unrealistic and wildly sentimental. In particular it denies the possibility that the young woman's character might have developed over the years, slowly changing her position with regard to her husband and Jack. On the other hand, the improbable turnaround (made easier by serialization, in the sense that many months would pass before anyone would read the later scenes) exposes and intensifies the polarized values that obsess Dickens and electrify the domestic atmosphere his characters move in. In that sense the scene is true to what Raymond Williams called the unified "structure of feeling" in Dickens's work.

Having expelled his wife from his worthy home, Dickens didn't go to his son Charley's wedding because the boy was marrying the daughter of an ex-publisher who had been critical of his treatment of Catherine. Charley was also the only child to defy his father and choose to live with the mother. Soon afterward, Dickens voted against the young man's admission to the Garrick Club. He also frowned on Katey's wedding to Wilkie Collins's brother Charlie because, as Gottlieb puts it, "no one was worthy enough for his beloved daughter." The marriage was childless, and it seems sexless; there were suggestions that Charlie was homosexual.

With the extravagant performance of the happy family now over, Dickens's life split into two parts. Theatricals with his children were replaced by dramatic readings to a much larger family of public audiences all over Britain and the United States. Here was a new, exciting, and extremely profitable form of belonging, and Dickens went for it with all his usual willfulness, traveling interminably, reading energetically and exhaustingly for hours, celebrating with pints of champagne and sherry. But the adoring public who substituted for his children, and who brought money in rather than sucking it out, could not be allowed to know that he now had a very young mistress, the actress Ellen Ternan; were they to find out, the risk of disgrace and ostracism would have been far greater than being known to have worked in a blacking factory.

Supporting Ellen's mother and two sisters financially, while denying loans to his sons in the far-flung empire (Mrs. Ternan and her girls were extremely worthy), Dickens hurried back and forth between readings, his official home with his wife's sister Georgina and daughter Mamie at Gad's Hill and the various places—Paris, London, Slough—where at different times he hid Ellen. He had forbidden her to go on with her acting, making her entirely and expensively dependent on him. His restless traveling over the next decade, as documented in Tomalin's biography, shows a man whose life has no center, obsessively driven and deeply divided, with no plan for achieving any kind of stability in the future, as though the only life he had really believed in was already over. That he wrote two more wonderful novels in these circumstances, *Great Expectations* and *Our Mutual Friend,* the latter a kaleidoscope of exclusions and inclusions, is a tribute to his genius and energy. But his eventual collapse and death in 1870, aged just fifty-eight, was something many had foreseen. Mamie wrote up a version of it that excluded the presence of her brothers and awarded herself the role of closest child. Katey was furious.

Gottlieb includes a brief chapter, "The Eleventh Child," drawing on declarations left by Henry and Katey, combined with much research by Claire Tomalin, suggesting that Dickens had a son by Ellen, born in France in 1863 but dying some months later. "We can only speculate," Gottlieb writes, "how Dickens that master tactician would have handled either keeping him or hiding him." It is odd that biographers don't wonder whether this story of the death mightn't have been fabricated, to win sympathy and avoid investigation, and the child given out for adoption. Such behavior would be perfectly in line with Dickens's habit in this period of excluding from his immediate life anyone who weighed on him, or might cause a loss of honor and prestige. He never had a plan that involved setting up a family with Ellen. That he had no children (or further children) with her suggests how willed the family with Catherine had been.

"We can be gratified," Gottlieb writes, ever concerned to guide our emotional response to his story, "that Dickens died knowing that at least this one of his worrisome children," Henry, "was worthy of his father's approbation." It is fascinating how the emotional atmosphere that drove the author's life and writing continues with his children after his death and today still continues among his admirers. Not long after the funeral Charley astonished and infuriated the other family members, Georgina in particular, by turning up to the auction of the Dickens home and buying it himself at a price others were too respectful to bid against. Having established his role as chief child, but wildly overspent, he then sold the small prefabricated conservatory Dickens wrote in. Aghast, Georgina and the girls sought to buy it back, Georgina cutting Sydney out of her will because he refused to make a contribution. "So many unworthy sons of their great father," she lamented. Biographers tend to share her opinion.

In the following years all the children at some point wrote about their father or did public readings from his works. Some isolated themselves in distant parts; the others went looking for them, or rejected them. Henry, all of whose seven children's names, boys *and* girls, included a Charles immediately before the Dickens, became involved in setting up the Boz Club and the Dickens Fellowship, whose purpose was "to knit together in a common bond of friendship lovers of the great master of humour and pathos." The Inimitable One had become a focus of community and belonging. Mamie wrote a memoir and edited her father's letters (another book from "the dear dead hand"). Alfred D'Orsay Tennyson Dickens, who spent much of his life rearing sheep in the Australian outback, eventually gave a series of successful lectures and readings in England and the United States. "I never forget my father for a moment," he declared. Henry omits to mention the readings in his family memoirs. Mamie said she held her father "in my heart of hearts as a man apart from all other men, as one apart from all other beings." Charley's elder son disgraced himself by marrying a barmaid and was disowned and excluded by the entire family.

"I'm glad my father never wrote anything that was harmful for young or old to read," Frank Dickens said shortly before he died. Frank had been one of the more melancholy children, abandoning his army career in India and squandering the money he inherited from his father. Rescued after a long search by Georgina, he allowed himself to be banished abroad again, this time to serve with the Mounties in the Canadian wilds. It was a curious thing to say of his celebrated father. Did it mean that he thought Dickens had done harm in life, but not in his writing? Or that writers can do harm and he was glad his father hadn't? Shortly before Dickens died, he had worked up the scene from *Oliver Twist* where Sikes kills Nancy; he wanted to terrify his audiences, he said. First he read the part where Nancy meets the benefactor Brownlow on a remote foggy river bridge and tells him she will never denounce Fagin, however evil, because their lives are bound together. In the version edited for the reading she says the same of her lover Sikes. She is "chained" to her past, bound to her community. Brownlow tells her, "You put yourself beyond the pale," suggesting that society is still ready to welcome her as it has welcomed Oliver if only she would stop isolating herself. Later, Sikes is not impressed when she protests that she has been loyal to him and brutally clubs her to death. Having killed his woman, he wanders alone out of London, but is oppressed by the solitariness. At least if he returns there will be "somebody to speak to." Trapped in an accomplice's house surrounded by his pursuers, he dies trying to escape.

Dickens read the piece with frightening energy. He expressed the pathos of isolation, he made the gestures of the murderer. His heartbeat (which he counted afterward) raced. There was collective hysteria in the air. Perhaps reading Dickens's novels quietly alone does not have this immediate effect, but great writing is never innocuous. It initiates a real relationship that urges us to think and feel as the author does and to organize our lives accordingly.

Discussing families obsessed by issues of belonging, the psychologist Valeria Ugazio, in her book *Permitted and Forbidden Stories,* speaks of conflicted members of such families who find themselves "oscillating between two equally unacceptable alternatives": they have to belong and remain at the center of the family, indeed can see no life for themselves outside it, but at the same time they feel that other family members dishonor them and are unworthy of them. They need to move on. Reflecting on this while reading Gottlieb's account of Dickens's dealings with his children, I began to wonder whether, as with all his relationships, there doesn't come a moment when Dickens suddenly begins to worry that his readers too are not entirely worthy of him. Most critics have noted how, at a certain point in Dickens's novels, the story, instead of developing, becomes stymied in a back-and-forth of positive and negative revelations, unlikely reversals and coincidences. In some books—*Dombey, Our Mutual Friend*—the energy and creativity of the opening chapters falls off so drastically it seems the Dickens we know has disappeared from the text to be replaced by a journeyman under instructions to finish the job. "Everyone who reads it feels that something has gone wrong," Orwell says of the end of *David Copperfield.* No one could read "the latter half of *Dombey,*" Wilkie Collins said, "without astonishment at the badness of it." Perhaps, having already secured our respect and awe in the earlier part of the book, the author's mind was already withdrawing, moving on to his next, more important project. Meantime, we are left wondering, as Dickens's children so often must have, why this "magical father" has lost interest in entertaining us.

Feodor Dostoevsky: Crime or Punishment

"You cannot take *a man who was all struggle*," wrote Tolstoy of Dostoevsky, after his great rival's death, "and set him up on a monument for the instruction of posterity."

To which struggle exactly was Count Tolstoy referring? Certainly not the liberal/revolutionary cause that had condemned Dostoevsky to spending four years in a Siberian labor camp and six more as a simple soldier in the army. In his mid-twenties Feodor Mikhailovich had spoken with great animation at the literary soirees of St. Petersburg. He had fallen under the charismatic influence of the determined revolutionary Nikolay Speshnev and joined his secret society. Immediately he was anxious: Speshnev had lent him a large sum of money. How could the young writer ever repay his "very own Mephistopheles" and escape this compromising situation? Three days after being arrested and placed in solitary confinement, Dostoevsky tells us, he felt an enormous sense of relief and serenity. He had a great respect for authority. Later he would remark: "Penal servitude saved me."

Such moments of relief, of internal conflict resolved in extreme well-being, feature prominently in Dostoevsky's life and work. Often they follow a dramatic surrender of pride on the part of a powerful personality, a murderer's confession, a complete loss of liberty. Or the great man kneels before the simple peasant, the holy hermit, the innocent prostitute, though never before having passed through agonies of uncertainty and rebellion. Paradise, Dostoevsky surmised—and he firmly believed in its existence—would be a place, above all, of contradictions resolved, "fully synthetic," the selfish ego at last in harmony with everything that was not itself. Indeed, "the highest use man could make of his ego," he commented elsewhere, "was to annihilate that Ego, to give it totally and to everyone undividedly and unselfishly." With such thoughts in mind he planned an epic work, ("longer than War and Peace") to be called *The Life of a Great Sinner,* in which the hero's greatness would be confirmed not so much by the enormity of his sins as by the dramatic and total nature of his repentance and consequent selfless dedication to the welfare of the Russian people. Even the novelist's account of the onset of his epileptic fits speaks of a sensation of extreme well-being, of "history arrested," before convulsions and unconsciousness followed to remove him from life's ordinary fray. Dostoevsky's fits, it might be worth noting, became less frequent when he abandoned literary polemics and the responsibilities of married life in St. Petersburg for the travel and transgressions of western Europe, though he never ceased to denigrate the West for its rabid individualism, materialism, and nihilism. He told neither of his wives about his medical condition before they married him, then suffered a severe fit in the presence of each spouse very soon after the wedding. The marriage bond was not something he took lightly.

But this still hasn't pinned down the nature of Dostoevsky's struggle, nor the role it plays in the writer's work. The escape from internal conflict into convulsions, or prison camps, suggests that the resolution of mental tension need not always be entirely positive. *Notes from the Underground* is unique among Dostoevsky's writings in that it *begins* with a description of struggle resolved, albeit in the worst possible way, and proceeds to give us, without any of the complex and often obfuscating machinery of the writer's usual plotting, an account of what exactly it might mean to live a life that is "all struggle." It is the ruthless directness with which this relatively short work confronts the author's most intimate themes, together with the stylistic revolution such directness entailed, that was to make *Notes from the Underground* so important for later generations. For though Dostoevsky will always remain a very special case, the mental condition he dramatizes here is central, even structural, to the modern experience. Anticipating our conclusions, we might say that the price of a world where individualism has triumphed over the commune, where man is, as Dostoevsky describes it, "cut off from the soil," is a background noise of guilt, a constant fizz of anxious unease.

"I am a sick man . . . I am a wicked man," our anonymous "underground" narrator begins his monologue in the 1993 translation from Richard Pevear and Larissa Volokhonsky. "I am a spiteful man," Jane Kentish translated for the Oxford World's Classics edition. "I am an angry man," offers Jessie Coulson in the Penguin edition. Very soon the reader will appreciate that all three descriptions are appropriate and none, alone, quite adequate. In any event, both the sickness and the angry, spiteful wickedness seem to have to do with the problem of "intellectual activity," which, we hear, is always and in every form "a disease" (Coulson), one that has led our narrator to be acutely sensitive to the good and the beautiful while interminably choosing to act in an ugly and repulsive fashion. It is that painful contradiction, the distance between the narrator's apprehension of the beauty of a moral life and his interminable choice of the immoral, that lies behind years of unhappy struggle. But at last this minor civil servant, having retired early on the back of a modest inheritance, is worn out. He has "lost even the desire to struggle" (Coulson). More conscious and intellectually feverish than ever, he gnashes his teeth in obscurity, consoling himself only with the thought that "it had to be so," that "this was really my normal state" (Coulson).

The circumstances in which Dostoevsky sat down or, as we shall see, perhaps stood up to write this disturbing incipit are worth keeping in mind. Almost ten years earlier, in 1854, after labor camp and during his forced service in the army, he had begun a relationship with a married woman, then, when her husband died, moved heaven and earth to overcome both economic difficulties and a more suitable suitor in order to marry the lady. On regaining his liberty, he had brought his wife to St. Petersburg and, after a year spent reestablishing his literary reputation, begun publishing, together with his faithful older brother Mikhail, a political and literary magazine, *Time*. This was 1861 and Dostoevsky was forty-one years old. The magazine was successful, the writer's career on the rise, but his marriage was unhappy. The neurotic, aggressive Maria Dimitrievna suffered from tuberculosis and had a habit of accusing her husband of being "a rogue, a rascal, and a criminal." She did not get on with his family and was rarely seen by his friends. Perhaps to be worthy of her accusations, Dostoevsky began an affair with a twenty-three-year-old and took time out to travel in Europe, where he discovered the joys of roulette.

In 1863 the censors closed *Time* when one of its contributors was misconstrued as taking an anti-Russian position over the Polish revolt of 1863. The closure was an economic disaster for the Dostoevsky brothers. While waiting for permission to reopen, Feodor Mikhailovich again set out to travel in Europe, despite the fact that he was now desperately short of money and his wife was entering the final phase of her disease.

Dostoevsky's excuse for the trip was that he must consult Western doctors about his epilepsy; the secret plan, however, was to meet his young mistress in Paris. But first the writer paused to throw his money at a roulette table in Wiesbaden. When he won it was a sign that God forgave him, and he could repay his debts. When he lost, heavily, he could get down on his knees in abject confession for having "committed a crime" and beg for loans to play some more. Intriguingly, Dostoevsky was convinced that the distance, at the gambling table, between immediate divine reward and immediate divine punishment was self-control. He had an infallible system, he claimed, for winning at roulette; the only problem was to keep control of himself and stick to his system in the excitement of the game. Unfortunately, this was something quite beyond the extremely excitable Feodor Mikhailovich. Of *Notes from the Underground* we can say that whenever its narrator sets out to engage in life in any way, to risk contact with the world and other people, he always warns himself to keep strict control over his behavior, and is painfully and simultaneously aware that he will not be able to do so.

On arriving in Paris, Dostoevsky discovered that while waiting for him his beloved Apollinaria Suslova had had an unhappy fling with a young Spaniard. Suslova had always been afraid that the writer she so greatly admired for his moral and intellectual qualities was after her only for her body. Now she agreed to travel with him to Italy, but only on the condition that there be no more sex. Holier than the average adulterer, or more concerned with being so, Dostoevsky went along with this frustrating proposition, while making constant attempts to get his girl back between the sheets. She refused, but generously lent him money to get home when the gambling bouts left him penniless.

Dostoevsky thus returned to a Russian winter after almost three months away. His wife was at death's door, his brother desperate to gather enough material for the new magazine that the censors had at last given them permission to publish. Feodor Mikhailovich must absolutely stop indulging himself, buckle down to being an attentive husband, and above all write something, *at once*. But away from the corrupt West, the writer's epilepsy had returned, and now he had a bladder infection too that prevented him from sitting or even lying down in comfort. Thus he may well have been standing up when, with only two months to his publication deadline, he put pen to paper and wrote those words, "I am a sick man . . . I am a wicked man." Only a few pages in, he would be reflecting, "The main thing is that, however you look at it, it always turns out that you are chiefly to blame for everything . . ." (Coulson).

It should be clear now that for Dostoevsky the disease of consciousness meant a tormented struggle to reconcile compelling appetites, enormous ambitions, and a huge personal vanity, with a belief that any real spiritual superiority could come only through renunciation and sacrifice. And what was the hallmark of a great writer if not spiritual superiority? But simultaneously, how could one, as a writer, convince the censors, the critics, and above all the purchasing public, without engaging in constant and ruthless self-promotion? Written after a long spree, in a period now of suffering, sacrifice, and renunciation ("yet I write with enthusiasm," he told his brother), *Notes from the Underground* is remarkable for the way the polarities of good and evil are simultaneously present, even superimposed, throughout, but without any apparent hope of reconciliation or any middle ground other than the narrator's wildly oscillating thoughts: "Remarkably, these influxes of 'everything beautiful and lofty,'" our narrator tells us of his more noble thoughts, "used also to come to me during my little debauches [with prostitutes]; precisely when I was already at the very bottom, they would come just so, in isolated little flashes, as if reminding me of themselves, and yet they did not annihilate the little debauch with their appearance; on the contrary, it was as if they enlivened it by contrast and came in exactly the proportion required for a good sauce. The sauce here consisted of contradiction and suffering, of tormenting inner analysis and all these torments and tormenticules lent my little debauch a certain piquancy, even meaning—in short, they fully fulfilled the function of a good sauce. All this was even not without some profundity" (Pevear).

But while the unhappy narrator imagines his monologue as an entirely private matter, a long exercise in solipsism that, a priori, declares his failure to establish any relationship with anyone else, Dostoevsky's work, of course, was to be published and, like it or not, to publish narrative fiction in Russia in the mid-nineteenth century meant to enter into an ongoing and highly polarized public discussion. For, given the strict censorship that made direct statements on many issues impossible, fictional characters were invariably used and inevitably interpreted as spokesmen and exempla for political ideas. There could be no question of Dostoevsky's avoiding this debate, nor would he have wanted to. To engage in public discussion was simultaneously a noble thing, an outlet for the aggressive ego, and essential for a magazine looking for a readership. So no sooner has the narrator of *Notes* established his perverse and even scandalous psychology than the fact of this perversion is being used by Dostoevsky in the public arena as an attack on the recent and sensationally successful novel *What Is to Be Done?* by the revolutionary theorist Nikolay Chernyshevsky. This attack takes up the whole first part of *Notes from the Underground.*

A word must be said here on Dostoevsky's decidedly idiosyncratic style when entering the political fray. Throughout the nineteenth century a fierce debate was raging between liberal westward-looking reformers on the one hand and staunch tsarist conservatives on the other. At issue above all were the condition of the serfs and the authority of the tsar. As the century progressed the positions hardened, particularly on the left, with philanthropic liberalism giving way to Bakunin's more ruthless and systematized communism. In his editorial for the opening issue of *Time* in 1861 Dostoevsky had made the rather bizarre claim that what would distinguish his paper from others was that he was really convinced of what he was saying, even if it might seem the ridiculous product of "copybook maxims," while others in the debate were not really convinced of their positions but were merely seeking to convince themselves. In the following editorials he would, on the one hand, attack the political ideas of the westernized liberals while sympathizing with the generous spirit of the young men who mistakenly upheld such revolutionary views, and on the other support the conservative ideas of the tsarist camp while attacking the meanness of spirit that often lay behind them. The public debate was thus psychologized and undermined. Nobody was really right or wrong. No idea could be judged without consideration of the mentality that defended it. The only thing that inspired the writer's wholehearted approval was the great Russian people, who, while containing much evil, were overall a force for good, indeed the main force for good on this earth, and with a mission, Dostoevsky believed, to save the world. And he declared that his magazine was launching a movement called Pochvennichestvo, Native Soil. The Russian soil, it seemed, offered, in some marvelous and above all unconscious chemical compound, the yearned-for reconciliation between good and evil.

Needless to say, this strange approach to public debate won Dostoevsky no friends, exercised no real political influence, completely confused the censors, and was at least partly responsible for the decision to close down *Time* in 1863. So as he embarks on *Notes,* his first piece for the new magazine, *Epoch,* on which the economic welfare of his family is riding, he is determined that there be no mistake: he absolutely and implacably opposes the revolutionary Nikolay Chernyshevsky, who, at the time of writing, was interned in a Siberian labor camp, as Dostoevsky had once been.

Basically, Chernyshevsky was an idealist proposing an ethics of rational, utilitarian egoism. Far from struggling with irreconcilable and unrenounceable opposites, the characters in *What Is to Be Done?* show how a person's real self-interest, when properly and rationally understood, is always compatible with the general good. Utopia is possible. We can know "what is to be done." Thus the two young heroes of the novel, who are in love with the same woman, are able to sort out their problems without any pain or conflict. Thus, if everybody acts *selfishly and in his or her own interest* (properly understood) society can be entirely reorganized to the benefit of everyone.

At first, it would seem, the target is really too easy to be interesting. The narrator of *Notes* launches into it thus: "Tell me, who was it who first declared, proclaiming it to the whole world, that a man does evil only because he doesn't know his real interests, and if he is enlightened and has his eyes opened to his own best and normal interests, man will cease to do evil and at once become virtuous and noble, because when he is enlightened and understands what will really benefit him he will see his own best interest in virtue, and since it is well known that no man can knowingly act against his best interests, consequently he will inevitably, so to speak, begin to do good. Oh, what a baby! Oh, what a pure innocent child!" (Coulson).

The narrator then proceeds to break down this position by raising the obvious objection that if one's best interests can be determined by reason and if one then inevitably acts in accordance with those interests, all one's actions can be predetermined, a state of affairs man instinctively resists. He himself, the narrator claims, frequently and deliberately acts against his own best interests, since the highest good is not happiness or material wealth but simply this instinctive desire to act as and how one wishes in spite of everything. As a result of this argument, the first part of the *Notes* is often taken, most particularly by Dostoevsky's exhaustive and exhausting biographer Joseph Frank, as a staunch defense of free will over determinism, even if that means accepting unhappy and unattractive phenomena like our sick and spiteful narrator in preference to the radiantly rational creatures of *What Is to Be Done?*

But *Notes* is a much more radical and disturbing document than that. For Dostoevsky had the immense good fortune that the enemy of the moment provided him with exactly the stimulus he needed for an exploration of the very possibility of speaking of selfhood and self-interest at all, something that must have been much on the author's mind after his own erratic and tortured behavior of recent months. Here the monologue form is crucial. "I am a wicked man," the narrator introduces himself. But only a few moments later he claims: "but as a matter of fact, I was never able to become wicked" (Pevear). Indeed: "I never even managed to become anything: neither wicked nor good, neither a scoundrel nor an honest man, neither a hero nor an insect" (Pevear).

One observes here, as ever, Dostoevsky's tendency to see only opposite and mutually exclusive characteristics, all equally impossible for our narrator, since whichever way he leans his brain is "swarming" with "opposite tendencies" (Pevear). At the same time, one begins to understand why he must remain anonymous. Because he has no stable self in the way Chernyshevsky or indeed all the political polemicists think of such imponderables. "An intelligent man of the nineteenth century," the narrator warns us with the usual mixture of complacency and despair, "must be and is morally obliged to be primarily a characterless being; and a man of character, an active figure—primarily a limited being" (Pevear). When we see this word "must," how can we imagine the text as a simple homage to free will? The very idea of free will is predicated on the notion of an integral self.

But why can't the narrator achieve a recognizable self? Because the corrosive nature of intellectual thought constantly undermines the basis of action so that the potential actor is invaded with a sense of futility and effectively denied any meaningful role in the world. Imagining someone who *is* able to act, to take revenge, for example, because he doesn't think things through, the narrator remarks: "Well, sirs, it is just such an ingenuous man that I regard as the real, normal man, the way his tender mother—nature—herself wished to see him when she so kindly conceived him on earth. I envy such a man to the point of extreme bile. He is stupid, I won't argue with you about that, but perhaps a normal man ought to be stupid, how do you know? Perhaps it's even very beautiful. And I am the more convinced of this, so to speak, suspicion, seeing that if, for example, one takes the antithesis of the normal man, that is, the man of heightened consciousness, who came, of course, not from the bosom of nature but from a retort (this is almost mysticism, gentlemen, but I suspect that, too), this retort man sometimes folds before his antithesis so far that he honestly regards himself, with all his heightened consciousness, as a mouse and not a man. A highly conscious mouse, perhaps, but a mouse all the same, whereas here we have a man, and consequently . . . and so on . . . And, above all, it is he, he himself, who regards himself as a mouse, no one asks him to; and that is an important point" (Pevear).

Such obsessive, self-deconstructing reflection not only dismisses centuries of Enlightenment optimism (the unthinking man is beautiful;

only he really exercises free will), but it opens a wound in the reader's relationship with narrative voice. Who is it really who is speaking? How am I to take him? Since the "retort man" or "mouse" has no real relationship with anyone (he admits that the listeners he is addressing are fictitious, required for the sake of rhetoric), since he constantly contradicts himself (later he will claim that he is worth far more than the man of action), we begin to feel that he is no more than a voice stretched across time, something akin to the constantly receding and superimposing identities of Beckett's long monologues in *The Trilogy*. Frequently the narrator claims that he is not sure himself whether he is lying or not. At moments of ellipsis (and there are many such moments), he simply ceases to exist.

Dostoevsky's style reinforces our doubts. *Notes from the Underground* is dense with references to scenes, slogans, and rhetoric from well-known novels and thinkers of the recent past. This is taken from Gogol, that from Pushkin, another thing from Turgenev. The narrator begins to dream, but then realizes that he is merely fantasizing something he read somewhere. He refers endlessly to his bookish imagination, constantly suggesting that his mind can inhabit well-worn but contradictory positions with equal ease and detachment, or get carried away by a certain kind of rhetoric without having any real investment in what is being said. Or, worse still, without *knowing* whether he has any investment in it or not. The statement reminds us of Dostoevsky's perception that his political opponents often put forward positions without believing in them, hoping to convince themselves, while he himself insisted on believing in a position that sounded like a "copybook maxim." At this point, as with the Hollywood habit of quoting interminably from previous movies that the public may or may not know, we have the growing and very modern concern that every statement put before us comes wrapped in a sticky layer of parody. Nothing can be taken seriously except the general absence of a convincing seriousness consequent on the disappearance of a recognizable and reliable identity.

Alternatively, when not falling into quotation, Dostoevsky's underground voice invents neologisms and syntactical tics all its own. Language is thus either private to the point of excluding the listener (and why not, if the listener is a rhetorical construct?) or so worn out and public as to mean nothing, just chunks of quotation thrown together. Needless to say, this puts the translator under considerable pressure. In his introduction to the new Everyman translation Pevear attacks the tendency of other translations to normalize the book's style, claiming that he and Volokhonsky have had the courage to reproduce its idiosyncrasies. Our problem is that the idiosyncrasies of the original arose from the Russian language and in a Russian literary context and were in intimate relation with both. Their meaning, or undermining of meaning, depended on the readers' recognition of a quotation, on the perceived distance between a particular idiosyncrasy and a normal usage, and, more generally, on ordinary habits of speech and journalism. They need context. Pevear's aims are admirable, and the new text is always intriguing, but there are times when this translation seems merely clumsy, its oddly shifting registers more to do with literal translation than creative prose. If nothing else, however, this problem alerts us to the text's anticipations of modernism. When a writer's prose could be complacently public without seeming parodic, as in the traditional nineteenth-century novel, such difficulties did not arise.

Aside from the roulette table, another form of gambling Dostoevsky indulged in was that of the anomalous and dangerous publishing contract. Two years after finishing *Notes from the Underground* and while working on *Crime and Punishment,* he took a small advance to write a novel of more than 160 pages. If he didn't deliver by November 1 of the same year, he must pay a huge fine, and if he didn't finish by December 1, the publisher could have all his work for the next nine years completely free. Why had Dostoevsky agreed to such mad terms? Why did he wait till six weeks before the deadline to begin writing, a point where ruin was staring him in the face?

The answer, as with the roulette, seems to have been his need to feel that he was chosen, that he was a great and not an ordinary man. This, after all, is Raskolnikov's obsession in *Crime and Punishment.* If he finished his book in time, then he must be a great writer. If not, then he could cease to struggle. The book he wrote, or rather, in desperation and for speed's sake, dictated, was entitled *The Gambler.*

The narrator of *Notes from the Underground* also dreams of being a writer. Once, he tells us, he actually wrote a story, but "satire was not then in fashion and my story was not published. I was bitterly disappointed.—Sometimes my rage positively choked me" (Coulson). Denied this recognition, his dreams became vaguer: "The fact is that at that time I blindly believed that by some miracle, through some outside influence, all *this* [his squalid, debauched life] would be drawn aside like a curtain, and a wide horizon would open out before me, a field of suitable activity, philanthropic, noble, and above all ready made (I never knew exactly what, but the great point is that it was all ready for me), and I would emerge into God's sunlight, practically riding a white horse and crowned with laurel" (Coulson).

It's worth noting here that a purposeful and positive role in the world is given religious overtones. Dostoevsky is a nostalgic. But the great transformation never occurs. Unlike his creator, the narrator of *Notes* is not chosen—indeed, this is the key difference between them—not published, not granted God's sunlight. There is no ready-made role or identity for him. He remains underground, unknown, secret, multiple. And the question that the second part of the *Notes* poses is: in the world of free individuals, cut off from the soil, which is to say from the obvious roles offered by traditional communal relationships, what becomes of the proud and ambitious ego if denied the redemption of celebrity? What will his relationships with others be? "I couldn't even conceive of playing a secondary part," the narrator tells us, "and that is why in actuality I quite contentedly filled the last of all. Either a hero or dirt, there was nothing in between" (Coulson).

While the first part of the *Notes* is all argument, the second is all narrative. We are taken back to a moment when the narrator was twenty-four, a formative and humiliating moment that he can never forget, the moment, we suspect, that marked the beginning of his final retreat into the underground of willful solitary confinement. The story is so simple and schematic that it is impossible not to see in it the seeds of the existential theater of a hundred years later. One by one we are given the narrator's relationships with an unknown army officer, with his boss, with his contemporaries (old school friends), with his servant, and with a woman. In each case, our anti-hero tries to establish a relationship that would offer the gratification of recognition, or, failing that, at least of the exercise of power.

The army officer, a man of superior social status, casually shoves the narrator out of his way at a billiard table without speaking or paying him any attention. Terribly insulted, the narrator seeks to create a situation where he can bump into the man, insult him, and force him to fight a duel, something that would amount to a recognition of their equality. Comically, he buys a new coat, both to be smart enough for the encounter and to show how aware he is of Gogol's story "The Overcoat." Dostoevsky himself had been obsessed with having sufficiently smart clothes when he was at military college, borrowing large sums of money from a father who could ill afford them. Finally the narrator manages to bump into the officer, who still doesn't notice him, but at least our anonymous sufferer can pride himself on not having given an inch.

Unable to live in a completely solipsistic world "for more than three months at a time," the narrator goes to visit his boss, who "lived in four tiny low-ceilinged rooms, economically furnished and jaundiced looking. He had two daughters, and their aunt poured out tea for him. . . . The host usually sat in his study, on a leather sofa in front of the table, with one of his elderly guests, an official from our Ministry or even from one of the others. . . . The talk was about excise duties, arguments in the Senate, salaries, promotion. . . . I would sit there dumb, almost paralysed, and sometimes breaking into a sweat; but it did me good. Returning home, I was able to lay aside for a time my desire to embrace all mankind" (Coulson).

This is barely more satisfactory than the encounter with the officer. But the narrator has an old school acquaintance, Simonov, whom he sees and occasionally borrows money from (having an acquaintance in Dostoevsky's world almost always meant borrowing money from him and thus never quite being sure of the nature of the relationship). One day at Simonov's he meets two other old schoolmates, who are arranging a small farewell dinner party at a hotel for a fourth acquaintance, Zverkov. Irritated that he hasn't been invited, the narrator insists on inviting himself, and paying his share.

The evening is a comic masterpiece and, for the narrator, an unmitigated disaster. Zverkov, in his small way, is one of the chosen, an army officer with a modest fortune. Despite his mediocrity, his three friends worship him. Together they present a world of easy indulgence, absolutely free from tortured moral struggle. This is the world that Dostoevsky himself hated. The biographies are full of his instant dislike of the presumptuous, relaxed vanity of the army officer type who could enjoy life without tying himself up in knots. Immediately, the only relation that the narrator of *Notes* can imagine with the celebrated Zverkov is one of competition; he must force his friends to grant him the same recognition. He gets drunk, insults them, becomes frantic and ridiculous, challenges Zverkov to a duel, and is laughed at and finally ignored. When the others set off to end the evening in a brothel, the narrator borrows money to chase after them, alternating fantasies of self-abasement where he begs forgiveness and is admitted into their company with equally crazy plans to slap Zverkov's face and force him to a duel. At the same time, he is perfectly aware of the sheer ugliness and self-destructive stupidity of it all. Arriving at the brothel, he finds that his friends have disappeared. At once it's clear that this development was just an excuse to bring our narrator into the presence of a woman.

One day, recounts Leonid Grossman in his biography of the author, while Dostoevsky was dictating *The Gambler* to his young copyist Anna Grigoryevna Snitkina, he told her that he was at a crossroads in life and had three choices: "To go east, to Constantinople or Jerusalem and remain there for ever; to go abroad for roulette and give himself up entirely to gambling; or to seek happiness in a second marriage. Anna advised him to take the last course." Not long afterward, having finished dictating a book that largely dealt with his relationship with his young ex-mistress, Dostoevsky proposed to the girl.

What do these three choices signify? Threesomes are fairly common in Dostoevsky. There are three Karamazov brothers: the eldest a drunken sensualist, the youngest a saint, the middle one, Ivan, Dostoevsky's classic intellectual, oscillating between good and evil, at once more interesting than his pious younger brother and more wicked in his convoluted consciousness than the elder.

In the case of the three roads that Dostoevsky posited to young Anna, it's easy to see in "Constantinople or Jerusalem" the way of renunciation and sainthood, in gambling abroad (Dostoevsky did not gamble in mother Russia) the way of debauchery. But this time, in the middle, for the man who could choose neither of those extremes, was a form of salvation, another way of being chosen, at once both finer than celebrity and more widely available: the love of a woman. Our narrator, having failed to achieve recognition with his boss or his contemporaries, finds his last chance of a meaningful relationship with the world in his meeting with the prostitute Lisa. The story is heading for a hysterical climax.

The reader is now given a distressing instance of the right ideas coming from the wrong mouth. Waking from a drunken stupor beside the young and inexperienced girl whom he has paid for and used, the narrator proceeds to persuade her that she must get out of the brothel at once. Immediately we sense that all he wants to do is make her unhappy. She is a beautiful woman, he insists; she could have love and respect and marriage and children. Instead, what awaits her as a prostitute are contempt, disease, poverty, death by consumption. Using trite and hackneyed words that "sound just like a book" (Coulson), as the girl, in a moment of lucidity, has the courage to object, the narrator nevertheless creates a terrifying and heartbreaking picture of a prostitute's future that all too soon has his victim sobbing with regret. "It was the game that carried me along," the narrator tells us, "the game itself, but not only the game . . ." (Coulson).

Dostoevsky is interested in the way ready-made visions adhere, or fail to adhere, to the fertile mind. The narrator has spoken of his trip to the brothel as "my encounter with reality at last" (Coulson). But how can one have an encounter with reality if one is not, in a certain sense, really there to confront it? The narrator plays a hideous trick on the young prostitute, exercising those powers of persuasion that so abysmally failed with his friends. But his "game" is successful only because he starts to believe in it. He is attracted to the girl. Or is he? Does he know? The rhetoric, the hackneyed idea of saving the prostitute, has got the better of him. He gives her his address . . . Somebody is now in a position to step into his solipsistic world and make it real.

The denouement is as painful as it is farcical. Some days later, the narrator is engaged in a wonderfully comic argument with his servant when Liza arrives. He is refusing to pay the servant his salary, trying to force him to recognize a relationship of subservience that goes beyond the exchange of cash. In short, he is seeking the recognition of a real superiority. The servant is having none of it. He will work only if he is paid. Into the room steps the woman who has been selling herself for money but is now presenting herself for a relationship and recognition that go beyond money. The narrator is terrified. He derides her. He tells her he was only fooling her. He breaks down in hysterics. Despite his disgraceful behavior the girl responds to his evident suffering. She comes to comfort him. She is offering love. He has been *chosen*. This is his moment. He can come out from the autism of the underground. But the narrator is not equal to the responsibilities of reality. He has sex with the girl, then thrusts money into her hand in exchange, pushes her out. She rejects the money and leaves. Totally confused, he runs after her to beg forgiveness. "Never before had I endured so much suffering and repentance; but could there have been even the slightest doubt, as I went running out of the apartment, that I would turn back halfway?" (Pevear).

In any event, Liza has gone. And the narrator's mind is doomed to raking back and forth across these moments for decades to come. In a conclusion that is distinctly Beckettian, he tells us he has had enough, he must stop these pointless reflections. In his own authorial voice Dostoevsky adds the postscript: "This is not the end, however, of the notes of this paradoxical writer. He could not help going on . . ." (Coulson).

But if the narrator of *Notes* is in an ugly, perverse, and potentially dangerous relationship with the fantasies and the rhetoric he practices on others, what about Dostoevsky himself? His wife died of consumption in the apartment the couple shared while he was writing the second part of *Notes*. What were his thoughts as he penned the following passage where the narrator is terrifying Liza with the vision of her inevitable destiny in the brothel:

> No, Liza, it will be lucky, lucky for you if you die quickly of consumption, someplace in a corner, in a basement. . . . In a hospital, you say? If they take you there, fine, but what if your madam still needs you? Consumption is that sort of illness; it's not a fever. A person goes on hoping till the last moment, saying he's well. It's just self-indulgence. But there's profit in it for the madam. Don't worry, it's true; you've sold your soul, you owe money besides, so you don't dare make a peep. And when you're dying, they'll all abandon you, they'll all turn away from you—because what good are you then? They'll even reproach you for uselessly taking up space and not dying quickly enough. You'll have a hard time getting a drink of water, they'll give it to you with a curse: "Hurry up and croak, you slut; you're moaning, people can't sleep, the clients are disgusted." It's true; I've overheard such words myself. They'll shove you, on the point of croaking, into

the stinkingest corner of the basement—dark, damp; what will you go over in your mind then, lying there alone? You'll die—they'll lay you out hurriedly, strangers' hands, grumblingly, impatiently—and no one will bless you, no one will sigh over you, all they'll think is how to get you off their backs quickly. (Pevear)

"I'm in a frightening state," Dostoevsky wrote to his brother, six days before Maria Dimitrievna coughed her last, "nervous, morally ill." He then goes on to outline the story of these last chapters of the *Notes* . . .

Is there a sense in which writing fiction, for Dostoevsky, allowing himself to be carried away by various kinds of rhetoric, to describe all sorts of ugly crimes, involves perverse indulgence, sin? Or is all this rather a form of expiation? "I've felt ashamed all the while I've been writing this *story:*" the narrator of *Notes* tells us on the penultimate page, "so it's no longer literature, but corrective punishment" (Pevear). Or, assuming that Dostoevsky thinks in these terms, and he rarely thinks in any other terms, is it that he doesn't really know which it is, crime or punishment, or even, given its implied moral condemnation of the narrator's perversions, a moral act, perhaps? Could it be that, as with gambling, self-control is the key, the ability to indulge, to enjoy expressing the narrator's tortuous lucubration (and it's clear that Dostoevsky is enjoying it) but then to detach himself, to show condemnation? Does the reader too feel something of the same ambiguity about his own engagement with fiction that flaunts negative behavior, that is dense, as Turgenev put it, with "smelly self-laceration"? There are few works that combine laughter and disgust as powerfully as *Notes from the Underground.*

As a rule, one remembers, Dostoevsky liked to finish his novels with the dramatic and instructive redemption of his sinful heroes.

Everybody remembers Raskolnikov reading the Bible with his prostitute girlfriend and getting down on his knees to confess in the public street. The initial, exciting nihilism is absorbed into a reassuring reaffirmation of faith. But this isn't the case with *Notes*. It is decidedly not reassuring. Dostoevsky claimed that there had been "a Christian message in the book, only that. . . . Those swinish censors: in passages where I mocked at everything and sometimes blasphemed for the sake of appearances—that is let by, and where I concluded with the need for faith and Christ—that is censored. What are the censors doing? Are they conspiring against the government, or what?"

It's interesting here that an attack on the faith is understood to be dangerous for the Russian government. If Christianity goes, everything goes with it. The abyss opens. For the man who formed the Native Soil movement, political, moral, and metaphysical authority are all linked. But why would the censors cut a Christian message and why would Dostoevsky not take the trouble to reinsert it later in life when the work was republished? Is his protest just a cover for a lingering guilt that he had offered no Christian solution? Certainly there is no such solution in the trajectory of the story. Or did he instinctively feel that to make the problem of the hideous narrator's disintegrated selfhood disappear by waving the wand of a religious alternative would damage the integrity of the book? The point is that here, more than in *Crime and Punishment* or *The Brothers Karamazov,* the abyss *does* open. That is the power of *Notes from the Underground.*

If the nineteenth century was the time when it became clear to most that the political future lay in the collective choice of the people, it naturally became necessary to discover who all those people really were. This was one of the great tasks of the novel of the period. Yet the more people were losing, in the throng of the impersonal and industrialized city, those traditional hierarchical roles imposed on them by the old rural communal life, the more the suspicion arose that perhaps character was not so easily defined at all, that perhaps it was infinitely malleable. From the rented tenement rooms of the big European and American cities the most disturbing texts began to appear. In Berlin in 1845 Max Stirner wrote *The Ego and His Own,* in which he taught that there was no need to be morally bound by old promises if you no longer wished to adhere to them, nor rules if you didn't agree with them: the only thing that mattered was how much power you had. In 1853 Melville invented a character who took power by simply responding to every order and invitation with the refrain, "I would prefer not to." Dostoevsky's narrator retires from even the most minimal contact with society the moment he has enough money to do so. In 1868 the nadir of negativity was attained (it has never been surpassed) when Lautréamont published his *Chants de Maldoror,* which celebrates with utter complacency the atrocious crimes of a serial killer. Like *Notes from the Underground,* the text is disconcerting for its juxtapositions of pastiches of quite different styles and voices so that it becomes hard to grasp the relationship of any one mind or attitude to the overall production. This is *Pulp Fiction* more than a century before Tarantino.

But it was in the monologue Dostoevsky created for *Notes from the Underground* that the characterless character found his proper literary form, the man who talks endlessly of himself because there is no self, who imagines his listeners because he has none, internalizing the whole world and fantasizing impossible successes from the safety of complete nonengagement. Imitations, adaptations, and ambitious developments of this voice in monologue produced some of the finest works of the twentieth century, from Céline to Beckett and Bernhard. But at the time *Notes* was written few were impressed. There is a reflection to be made here on a profound split in modern consciousness. "I am proud," Dostoevsky wrote in a notebook with the vanity of one of his great sinners, "to have been the first to have portrayed the real man of the Russian majority and to have exposed the ugly and tragic side of his nature. . . . I alone depicted the tragedy of the underground . . ." Why did critics and public not immediately accept the truth of this?

To take on board the implications of *Notes from the Underground* is to undermine any political debate predicated on the existence of people with stable selves who can make mature decisions in line with a vision of their own and society's interests. It is thus to question the very premises of democracy. Officially, such ideas must never be accepted. In reality, the amount of money spent pushing people from one camp to another with inane slogans and meaningless manifestos suggests that the chosen ones who enjoy power and celebrity know these facts all too well. In any event, we can take the date of the publication of *Notes* as the moment when ready-made visions and ideals have been declared absolutely necessary, but only as a form of mental comfort, entirely sheared off from any consequence:

> Even then I comforted myself with these ideas, as I do still. That's why we have so many generous spirits who even in the last degradation never lose their ideals; and although they won't lift a finger for their ideals, although they are declared thieves and gangsters, they are still tearfully devoted to their original ideals and extraordinarily pure of heart. (Coulson)

If a world of the "pure of heart" who behave exactly as they choose is in any way recognizable to the modern reader, then the polarities that tense Dostoevsky's narratives are still very much with us, even if the struggle against this state of affairs was long ago abandoned.

Thomas Hardy

What a pleasure to return to Thomas Hardy. For about a hundred pages. Then the torment begins, the distress. And we're not even halfway through. From now on each turn of the page will seem an act of courage, exposing the reader to greater and greater unhappiness. There is a moment in *The Return of the Native* where the main character, Clym, already deeply troubled by his mother's mysterious death, goes out of his way to find a little boy who may be able to tell him exactly what happened. When he asks the boy's mother for permission to speak to the child, she "regarded [Clym] in a peculiar and criticizing manner. To anybody but a half-blind man it would have said, 'You want another of the knocks which have already laid you so low.'" As the boy then tells his tale, stringing together facts that will destroy Clym's life, the same woman "looked as if she wondered how a man could want more of what had stung him so deeply." At this point many readers may realize that the same question is on their minds too: why am I persevering with a novel that is so painful to me? Eventually this will become the central issue in all Hardy's mature fiction, above all *Tess of the D'Urbervilles* and *Jude the Obscure;* why are these stories so much more painful than anything else I have read, painful *in the reading,* that is, even more than the actual content, in the agonizing unfolding of events. Why did Hardy insist on making them so? Why do people have an appetite for this?

The novel is set on Egdon Heath, fictional name for a desolate area near Dorchester in Hardy's imagined parallel world of Wessex. A "vast tract of unenclosed wild," infertile and intractable, its community left behind by nineteenth-century progress, without even a church, "the Egdon waste" is at once overwhelmingly real and a place of the mind, a landscape of ancient burial mounds and prehistoric remains, "unaltered as the stars," subject to the most intemperate weather, seething with plant and insect life of the most resilient and unprepossessing varieties. Hardy is second to none in conveying the atmosphere of such a place and above all in intimating how remorselessly it belittles human experience, how hard it will be for the heath's inhabitants to create any emotion or community that is not overshadowed by the timelessness of this implacable landscape. Anyone who wants to make anything of him or herself in the modern world *must* leave Egdon. But as our title tells us, the novel is about someone who has come back.

Against this all-conditioning backdrop, complete with its rustic chorus of those happy to live on the heath and accept its limitations, their peasant lives absolutely submissive to its seasons and rhythms, the novel presents six characters who, in seeking to lift themselves above it, will contrive to make each other as miserable as people could ever. The bland young orphan Thomasin, "a pleasing and innocent woman," is timid and sensible in all things except her determination to marry the shifty Mr. Wildeve, almost the only eligible bachelor on the heath. Wildeve is a qualified engineer who for reasons never explained has fallen back on running the heath's only inn and is looking to bring either security or excitement into his life through marriage. Thomasin would bring security; the more striking, passionate, raven-haired Eustacia, another orphan, living alone with her carelessly cantankerous grandfather, is infinitely more alluring; but her inflexible determination to leave the heath for a fashionable city life would require Wildeve to abandon his safe economic base and take a risk in the world.

Thomasin's cousin Clym is the native whose return to Egdon is so inexplicable to the others and above all to his widowed mother, Mrs. Yeobright, who is also aunt and guardian to Thomasin. Clym has been working in the diamond business in Paris, at the very heart of modern fashion and culture, but having deemed this world superficial and unsatisfying he now wishes to set up a school for the poor people of Egdon; he thus returns to the heath in order to put others less advantaged than himself in a position to leave it; or rather, since the peasant folk are very much one with the landscape, to change the nature of the heath itself, manifestly an impossible task.

Initially unhappy that her niece wants to marry a man who she feels is unworthy, Mrs. Yeobright is now appalled that her son should renounce his good fortune in Paris for a provincial philanthropy she finds entirely unconvincing. Middle class and struggling to keep her family upwardly mobile, Mrs. Yeobright is invariably correct in her assessment of Clym's and Thomasin's poor choices but fatally clumsy in her attempts to change their minds; every move she makes will be counterproductive. When Clym and Eustacia fall in love, so that the energies of him who is most determined to stay in Egdon and her who is most determined to leave now collide, the older woman's dismay knows no bounds.

To complete the odd picture there is the mysterious, quaintly named Diggory Venn. Originally a dairy farmer, Venn once dared to ask for Thomasin's hand in marriage and was rebuffed, because not of the right class. Since then he has become a reddleman, an itinerant tradesman selling red dye to sheep farmers, with the result that he himself is stained permanently red by the materials he works with. Still set on Thomasin, combining resilience, ubiquity, and benevolent cunning, Venn contrives to be at once frightening bogeyman and generous deus ex machina.

How on earth, you ask, could an experienced reader be deeply pained by the antics of such an unpromising dramatis personae? "Our sympathies [are] never . . . strongly enlisted in any of the three [major characters]," complained one contemporary reviewer of Eustacia, Clym, and Wildeve. Another felt the book's disregard for realism reached levels "repugnant to our sense of the probable." Its "people talk as no people ever talked before," complained yet another. "The story strikes us as intensely artificial." Indeed, key moments in the novel seem contrived beyond belief, not just a belief in the events, but in Hardy's having wanted to make his manipulation of them so evident; there are a dozen points where the plot turns on a character's overhearing precisely the part of a conversation that will give the wrong impression and lead to calamity. The tragedy is "arbitrary and accidental," wrote one reviewer, the sadness "unnecessary and uncalled for," "mournful and cruel," so that all in all for those "who have the weakness of liking to be pleasantly interested in a book it is also very disagreeable."

When critics quote early reviews of classic novels, it is usually to suggest the naïveté of the initial response, the superiority of our own understanding of fine literature and progressive thinking. Yet all these comments seem appropriate; all address those aspects of Hardy's fiction that are unique and demand a response, if only because, for all the mournfulness, cruelty, and disagreeableness, *The Return of the Native* is nevertheless riveting and actually *more* engaging and far more painful than the famously superior tragedies with, as they taught us at school, a great and noble character whose fatal flaws make his or her downfall inevitable. But why?

The most recent edition of Hardy's novel is published by Broadview and edited by the academic Simon Avery. Its appendixes include the reviews I have mentioned, Hardy's own prefaces to various editions, maps, excerpts from contemporary works of science and philosophy the author had read, a small selection of Hardy's poetry, pertinent passages from his essays, the complete script of a mummer's play that has a part in the plot, and the illustrations that accompanied the novel's first serialization in the magazine *Belgravia* in 1878. In addition to this welcome context, abundant footnotes elucidate the frequent archaic and dialect terms and wide-ranging references to myth, scripture, ancient history, local customs, nineteenth-century politics, and much else. At the beginning of the book a "brief chronology" of the author's life runs out at seven pages, while a textual note discusses amendments the author made to the book when coming back to it in later years.

So this is an edition for students, and Hardy's novel is presented very much as an object of study. However, if you assumed that Professor Avery's eighteen-page introduction would say something about the peculiar nature of the reading experience it offers, you'd be disappointed. The words "embody," "enact," "foreground," "configure," "transcend," "gender," "proto-modernist," and other exempla of the lit-crit lexicon abound, while a dozen or so Hardy experts are applauded for their "astute" or "highly significant" contributions. A cursory biography gives little sense of the author's urgent personal investment in the themes of his novels (in this regard the chronology contains the sublimely cryptic entry "1895—The Hardys' marriage becomes increasingly difficult"). We learn that Hardy had been "systematically moving toward this point of greater artistic integrity across the course of his life" and that in this regard Egdon Heath offered him the possibility of "unity of place" as well as being "as John

Bayley astutely suggests, nothing less than 'a microcosm of the dark indifferent universe in which human life has to be carried on.'" It thus "becomes the perfect setting for the social political, and intellectual upheavals of the age that the novel dissects and interrogates." In short: blah. Eustacia is "configured as nothing less than an image of Promethean defiance," a woman who "is shown to prioritize the individual need for physical and psychological freedom over conventional moral frameworks," this no doubt because of her "confrontation with the structures of discrimination and oppression embedded in the mid-Victorian patriarchal worldview." Clym's plans to run a school for the heath children "constitutes one of Hardy's earlier forays into consideration of the potential of education to change inherited systems of thought." All, as Avery would have it, is solemn and progressive and diligent and as far away as one could imagine from our impressions on actually reading the story. "Consequently," the professor concludes, "it is hardly surprising that the novel firmly established Hardy as one of Victorian Britain's major writers and socio-political commentators, and it still continues to speak to us in a variety of intriguing and compelling ways." About such intrigue and compulsion he has nothing to say.

As an antidote to this dull jargon, let's read a long passage from the book. At this point in the novel the ravishing Eustacia has renounced Wildeve, who marries Thomasin. Clym then marries Eustacia, taking her not to Paris but to a tiny cottage on the heath, where his long hours of study, preparatory to opening a school, have a disastrous effect on his eyesight. Reduced to near blindness, he is now fit for no better occupation than cutting furze for fuel, something that has to be done in a suit of protective clothing.

This man from Paris was now so disguised by his leather accoutrements, and by the goggles he was obliged to wear over his eyes, that his closest friend might have passed by without recognizing him. He was a brown spot in the midst of an expanse of olive-green gorse, and nothing more. Though frequently depressed in spirit when not actually at work, owing to thoughts of Eustacia's position and his mother's estrangement, when in the full swing of labour he was cheerfully disposed and calm.

His daily life was of a curious microscopic sort, his whole world being limited to a circuit of a few feet from his person. His familiars were creeping and winged things, and they seemed to enroll him in their band. Bees hummed around his ears with an intimate air, and tugged at the heath and furze-flowers at his side in such numbers as to weigh them down to the sod. The strange amber-coloured butterflies which Egdon produced, and which were never seen elsewhere, quivered in the breath of his lips, alighted upon his bowed back, and sported with the glittering point of his hook as he flourished it up and down. Tribes of emerald-green grasshoppers leaped over his feet, falling awkwardly on their backs, heads, or hips, like unskilful acrobats, as chance might rule; or engaged themselves in noisy flirtations under the fern-fronds with silent ones of homely hue. Huge flies, ignorant of larders and wire-netting, and quite in a savage state, buzzed about him without knowing that he was a man. In and out of the fern-dells snakes glided in their most brilliant blue and yellow guise, it being the season immediately following the shedding of their old skins, when their colours are brightest. Litters of young rabbits came out from their forms to sun themselves upon hillocks, the hot beams blazing through the delicate tissue of each thin-fleshed ear, and firing it to a blood-red transparency in which the veins could be seen. None of them feared him. The monotony of his occupation soothed him, and was in itself a pleasure. A forced limitation of effort offered a justification of homely courses to an unambitious man, whose conscience would hardly have allowed him to remain in such obscurity while his powers were unimpeded.

So much for "the microcosm of the dark indifferent universe." Freed from ambition by his eyesight problems, the "man from Paris" moves downward socially and submerges himself entirely in the natural world, putting himself beyond the recognition even of his closest friends. Hardy is loving it, conjuring the pleasures of flora and fauna with easy eloquence, giving us flesh, blood, and insect flirtation in a blaze of color. Freedom, it seems, lies in surrender to the present moment and untamed nature, not in the struggle for realization through career or love. One is reminded how frequently Hardy's characters wish to be out of the fray, even dead—of Tess Durbeyfield, for example, who looks forward to the moment when she will be "grassed down and forgotten." The question inevitably arises, how much do these people truly desire the goals they set themselves, the projects and ambitions that make them so unhappy? Are they really inhibited in the achievement of those goals by "the structures of discrimination and oppression," or are these social limitations, like Clym's partial loss of eyesight, rather excuses for renouncing a path that seems too hard, too strenuous, too frightening?

D. H. Lawrence thought so. Professor Avery mentions Lawrence's *Study of Thomas Hardy* and quotes his considerations on Clym, but doesn't tackle head-on the burden of Lawrence's criticism. Here is D. H. on Eustacia and Clym:

Eustacia, dark, wild, passionate . . . loves first the unstable Wildeve, who does not satisfy her, then casts him aside for the newly returned Clym. . . . What does she want? . . . Some form of self-realisation . . . to attain herself. But she does not know how . . . so romantic imagination says Paris and the beau monde. As if that would stay her unsatisfaction.

Clym has found out the vanity of Paris and the beau monde. What then does he want? . . . His imagination tells him he wants to serve the moral system . . . to teach little Egdon boys in school. There is as much vanity in this, easily, as in Eustacia's Paris. . . . What is Clym's altruism but a deep very subtle cowardice, that makes him shirk his own being whilst apparently acting nobly? . . . Thus both Eustacia and he side-track from themselves, and each leaves the other un-convinced, unsatisfied, unrealised."

All this strikes a chord. Even Lawrence's main criticism—that Hardy, by always allowing his more ambitious characters to be crushed by the forces of convention, is in fact encouraging the reader to remain inside the bounds of those conventions—makes good sense, and certainly fits with Hardy's own extremely cautious behav-ior throughout his life, rather as if the novels were written as warn-ings to himself of the dangers of overstepping the mark. But this still doesn't tell us why we engage with them so intensely, nor why the development of the narrative is so painful.

As *The Return of the Native* opens, Wildeve and Thomasin have gone to a neighboring town to marry, but failed to do so because the certificate Wildeve had procured isn't valid there. Thomasin isn't con-vinced that the problem is merely one of the certificate and wonders about Wildeve's commitment. Feeling compromised and slighted, she now questions her own commitment. We discover that a previous attempt to marry was blocked when Mrs. Yeobright intervened during the ceremony, claiming that she knew of an impediment to the union and thus humiliating both Wildeve and her niece. Initially she must have allowed the marriage to go ahead, then changed her mind to prevent it, then changed her mind again to allow it to go ahead. A situation has been created where, whatever ultimately happens, there will be bad feeling on all sides.

Rather than repeating the old complaint that Hardy's characters are not of the "great" variety necessary for "real" tragedy, it might be more useful to turn the proposition on its head and say that if we did have "great" characters, the Hardy kind of tragedy could not happen. Were Wildeve a more substantial figure, either he would know his mind on Thomasin and sweep her off her feet, or he would leave her alone altogether. Were Thomasin "great," she would hardly be thrown into confusion by a bureaucratic hitch. Nor would a more forceful guardian vacillate as Mrs. Yeobright does.

Eustacia and Clym are similarly uncertain. Eustacia has grown weary of Wildeve, but renews her interest when he turns to Thomasin; she then falls in love with the *idea* of Clym even before seeing him, simply because he has been living in Paris; later she falls in love with the real Clym, but without renouncing the idea that he can be persuaded to return to Paris. Clym falls in love with Eustacia's unconventional character and beauty but immediately and most improbably imagines her as a charity school teacher, then is rather too concerned about his mother's hostile reaction and the effect of this emotional upheaval on his philanthropic projects. First deciding to delay the marriage, he then allows himself to be hurried into it, because anxious that Eustacia is anxious that he will allow his anxious mother to change his mind. Curiously, even the landscape, with its tiny meandering pathways through thick vegetation over low hills under weird light effects, is accused of being a territory of indecision: "There was that in the condition of the heath itself which resembled protracted and halting dubiousness."

Uncertainty and vacillation prepare the way for unhappiness, misunderstanding, bitterness. Eustacia knows of Wildeve's attachment to Thomasin, Thomasin of his interest in her. Wildeve learns of Eustacia's interest in Clym, Clym of Eustacia's interest in Wildeve; Eustacia imagines Clym's possible interest in Thomasin and hers in him. Each is unsure of the other's affections and hence even more unwilling to commit to his or her own. One can see at once the opportunities for farce, and much of the novel, particularly the events surrounding Clym's mother's death, resembles farce, but with devastating consequences. "If you look beneath the surface of any farce you see a tragedy," Hardy tells us "and . . . if you blind yourself to the deeper issues of a tragedy you see a farce."

The root cause of this inability to make decisions and stick to them is fear. Just as it is a territory of "dubiousness," the heath can also "intensify the opacity of a moonless midnight to a cause of shaking and dread"; it is a place of fear. All Hardy's major novels are steeped in a vocabulary of fear to a quite extraordinary degree and all his main characters, rash or reckless though they may sometimes be, are fearful. Of what, exactly? To an extent, it is true, they are worried about social criticism should they break prevailing moral proprieties. But their main anxiety concerns the fatal, irreversible nature of experience itself, the fear of making a wrong decision that will change their lives forever. Sex is the most dangerous of these experiences and marriage the most determining of decisions. Indeed, it often seems that Hardy's characters are most afraid of the thing they most desire: a partner. Hardy himself showed the same trait; in 1868, writing of an attractive woman seen during a boat trip to Lulworth, he remarks: "Saw her for the last time standing on deck as the boat moved off. White feather in hat, brown dress, Dorset dialect, Classic features, short upper lip. A woman I wd have married offhand, with probably disastrous results."

One natural consequence of this fearful mindset is a growing desire to be spared experience and its tough decisions altogether. Here is Hardy in the biography he wrote with his second wife:

> If there is any way of getting a melancholy satisfaction out of life . . . it lies in dying, so to speak, before one is out of the flesh. . . . Hence even when I enter into a room to pay a simple morning call I have unconsciously the habit of regarding the scene as if I were a spectre not solid enough to influence my environment.

In *The Return of the Native* we hear of Clym:

> He had reached the stage in a young man's life when the grimness of the general human situation first becomes clear; and the realization of this causes ambition to halt awhile. In France it is not uncustomary to commit suicide at this stage; in England we do much better, or much worse, as the case may be.

While Hardy's immediate narrative, then, dramatizes the thrilling struggle toward love and self-realization, at a deeper level, the atmosphere of intense trepidation that surrounds the drama is such that both characters and reader begin to wish that everything would go wrong sooner rather than later, to get it over with. This is the modernity of

Hardy's narratives; his perception that the individual's felt need to become someone, or realize him- or herself in some way, presents itself as a truly onerous task. One is reminded of the narrator of *Notes from the Underground,* who in 1864 lamented that he had "never even managed to become anything: neither wicked nor good, neither a scoundrel nor an honest man, neither a hero nor an insect," indeed that "he has given up the struggle" and this because "modern consciousness" is simply incapable of deciding between this or that course of action, seeing and fearing too clearly the negative consequences of any choice, so that "with all his heightened consciousness" the modern person begins to regard himself "as a mouse and not a man." In Hardy as in Dostoevsky, a complete loss of self-esteem lies at the core of the characters' miseries. They trust neither their instincts nor their reasoning. "I ought never to have hunted you out," regrets Wildeve to Eustacia, "or having done it, I ought to have persisted in retaining you." "Should have" and "ought to have" are frequent laments.

Let's watch how this mentality plays out in the death of Clym's mother, how Hardy has the reader squirming, not out of a sense of pathos for the way Victorian society, or implacable fate, or bad weather, or just bad luck treats our characters, though they all do their worst, but out of a heightened awareness of how fatal words and action can be, and how the fear that springs from that awareness actually hastens the outcomes it fears; above all, how exhausting all this is.

"I love you to oppressiveness," Clym tells Eustacia before they marry. "Nothing can ensure the continuance of love," she replies. "It will evaporate like a spirit, and so I feel full of fears." She elaborates: "It will, I fear, end in this way: your mother will find out that you meet me, and she will influence you against me!" "The unknown," she says "always fills my mind with terrible possibilities." And again: "How terrible it would be if a time should come when I could not love you, my Clym!" And he: "Please don't say such reckless things. When we see such a time at hand we will say, 'I have outlived my faith and purpose,' and die."

In short, these two have already mapped out their catastrophe before it occurs. "I have feared my bliss. It has been too intense and consuming," says Eustacia. Well warned, the reader foolishly hopes disaster can be averted.

Clym's mother is furious and asks, "You give up your whole thought—you set your whole soul—to please a woman?" Clym answers, "I do. And that woman is you." This throws the reader completely. How can he say such a thing? Nobody seems able to maintain a steady state of mind. To assure Eustacia he is solid, Clym capriciously offers to marry at once. His mother refuses to come to the wedding, then relents and decides to hand over the hundred guineas left by her dead husband to be divided equally between Thomasin (now Mrs. Wildeve) and Clym. The manner in which this is done beggars belief, but the reader keeps reading because the psychology of what is happening between the family members is more than credible.

Mrs. Yeobright gives the money to dumb, fearful peasant Christian Cantle to carry across the heath in the dark. Christian has a drink too many and meets Wildeve, who gets wind that money is being passed to his wife behind his back. Wildeve proposes a little gambling and wins all the money. Unbeknown to either they are being watched (late at night) by Venn the reddleman, who, understanding, incorrectly, that all the money was meant for Thomasin, challenges Wildeve to gamble, wins it all back, then goes to hand it over to her in person. A situation is thus created (with what effort!) where Clym's money has gone to his cousin.

Hearing from Christian that Wildeve appropriated all the money, but hoping he was gentleman enough to hand over what belonged to her son, Mrs. Yeobright goes to see Eustacia. "Have you received a gift from Thomasin's husband?" she begins. Wildeve, that is. Having no information about the inheritance, Eustacia can only suppose she is being accused of maintaining a relationship with Wildeve despite her marriage, and a furious argument ensues. "You have caused a division which can never be healed!" Eustacia cries. "You stand on the edge of a precipice," Mrs. Yeobright rebuts. Neither of them is responsible for the original misunderstanding, but both seem all too eager to turn it into a tragedy.

Clym goes partially blind delaying his plans to move to Budmouth, where Eustacia might be happy. Eustacia is full of pity, but concerned how happy Clym suddenly is to be using up all his energies as a humble furze cutter. "It was bitterly plain to Eustacia that he did not care much about social failure." So much for the lady's being oppressed by Victorian discrimination. "Has your love for me all died, then," he needlessly provokes, "because my appearance is no longer that of a fine gentleman?" Again, neither of them is guilty of the predicament they are in, but everything they say makes it worse.

Bored to death, Eustacia goes to a country dance, where quite by chance she meets Wildeve and dances with him. The relationship is renewed, though Eustacia is in no way unfaithful. Hardy systematically does everything to complicate questions of intention and responsibility. Needless to say, Venn the reddleman sees the ex-lovers together and reports the incident to Thomasin, mindful of his ex-sweetheart's honor. When Wildeve goes to hang around Eustacia's cottage at night, Venn warns him off. So Wildeve goes by day, which will prove disastrous.

Now the core of the farce.

Concerned about his mother's estrangement, Clym decides to visit her to make up, but only after a day's work. He sets off to cut furze at 4 A.M. Meantime, Mrs. Yeobright decides to come to him, choosing the hottest day of the year for a walk of some miles across open heathland. Feeling ill, she gets lost, then follows her son's distant figure as he returns home in the early afternoon, but has to stop and rest a short distance from the house. This gives time for Clym to fall asleep and for Wildeve to turn up and knock at the door. Eustacia can admit him because her husband is in the house, though in bed. Now the mother clicks open the garden gate, Eustacia rushes to the window, and the two see each other. But the younger woman doesn't want to open the door with Wildeve there, fearing what the mother may imagine. He is taken to the back door. She hears Clym shout the word "mother!" and believes he has woken and is going to open for her. In fact, he is having a nightmare. When Eustacia returns, she finds her husband still asleep and the mother gone. Convinced that her son, who she knows is home, is refusing to see her, Mrs. Yeobright starts off into the blistering heat, where she unburdens her bitterness on a little boy who just happens to be around. Almost home, she is bitten by an adder and collapses.

The accumulation of coincidences here—at least a dozen—is extraordinary and deliberate. It's not that Hardy is such a poor author that he needs elements of chance to move his stories on; rather he tosses them in in mad abundance to create a situation where no one is responsible, but everyone can blame one another and themselves and the weather and destiny and witchcraft and Victorian bigotry and more or less anything you care to mention.

Clym wakes up, sets off on the planned visit of reconciliation, finds his mother already unconscious (no reconciliation possible), and has her carried to a deserted house, where, just before she dies, the little boy turns up to announce what Mrs. Yeobright told him: "She said . . . she was a broken-hearted woman and cast off by her son." Clym spends a month wishing he were dead and lamenting "an error which could never be rectified" before going to talk to the little boy again and discovering that his mother had actually been to his house, where another man had been admitted shortly before her. So now Clym believes that Eustacia deliberately kept his mother out because involved with a lover. As the irate husband heads home for a showdown, "his eyes, fixed steadfastly on blankness" and "vaguely lit by an icy shine," the narrator remarks:

> Instead of there being before him the pale face of Eustacia, and a masculine shape unknown, there was only the imperturbable countenance of the heath, which, having defied the cataclysmal onsets of centuries, reduced to insignificance by its seamed and antique features the wildest turmoil of a single man.

This is the essence of Hardy's vision: an intensely unhappy melodrama for which everybody and nobody is to blame is seen against the backdrop of a vast but rather beautiful indifference which now offers the promise—to characters, author, and readers alike—of quietude, closure, silence. Passionate yearning fizzes beside seraphic detachment, the latter ultimately preferable because the former is vulnerable to every kind of distress.

The final pages of the novel offer more of the same. "Having resolved on flight Eustacia at times seemed anxious that something should happen to thwart her own intention" is a typical chapter opening. The only curiosity is that having at last killed off Eustacia and Wildeve, again in circumstances as contrived as they are unclear, and having reduced Clym to a ghost of his former self, a man who feels that past torments now exempt him from any further engagement with

women, Hardy tags on a happy ending—Thomasin marries her old
flame Venn the reddleman—though he adds a note in later editions
that this was not his original intention, just a concession to the requirements of serialization in a popular magazine. "Readers can therefore
choose between the endings," he remarks. Professor Avery approves,
enthusiastically declaring the move "almost proto-modernist." In fact,
it aligns Hardy with his characters' unhappy habit of drawing back
from their original intentions, of compromising, of not quite knowing
their own minds.

The one person who does know his mind throughout the novel
remains the reddleman. Despite Thomasin's marrying Wildeve, Venn
continues to spend a great deal of energy looking after her from a respectful distance, and never dreaming of other women. His old-
fashioned steadfastness thus serves to set off everyone else's modern
inconsistency; an "isolated and weird character," Hardy calls him in
his note. The novel itself frequently warns us that reddlemen are a
dying breed.

Of Wildeve and Eustacia's corpses, laid out for burial, we
hear:

> Misfortune had struck them gracefully, cutting off their er-
> ratic histories with a catastrophic dash, instead of, as with
> many, attenuating each life to an uninteresting meagreness,
> through long years of wrinkles, neglect, and decay.

Was Hardy thinking of himself as one of those condemned to an
"uninteresting meagreness"? Turning to his biography, it is all too
evident how far he shares the mindset that leads his characters to
misery. Fearing the critics, he wrote precisely the kind of novels that
would provoke them, then suffered atrociously when they attacked

him. "Woke before it was light," he confided in his diary shortly after a negative review of *The Return of the Native*. "Felt that I had not enough staying power to hold my own in the world." A "pale gentle frightened little man," as Robert Louis Stevenson later remembered him, Hardy had abandoned an exciting London career in architecture to return to his country home and mother, then proceeded to marry against her wishes. His wife wanted to live in London, he in a village near home. Worrying that he hadn't made the right choice, he regularly sent his wife, through the novels, precisely the sort of messages guaranteed to make matters worse, but without ever acting decisively to bring an end to their mutual unhappiness, anxious as he always was in the face of Victorian censure. Indeed, thinking of Emma Hardy and her growing resentment over the way her husband's novels portrayed married life, it's fascinating to think that *The Return of the Native* is itself contributing to a domestic drama that will eventually be as unhappy as the one it recounts, and to a certain degree unhappy *because* of this recounting. Like his characters, Hardy sees marriage misery coming, and precisely in the foreseeing brings it on. It's a dangerous dynamic to be drawn into, and readers do well to resist. Rather than reflections on protomodernism, this wonderfully elaborate invitation to despair might be better accompanied by a health warning.

Anton Chekhov

Born in 1860, third of five brothers and one sister, in Taganrog, a port on the north eastern tip of the Sea of Azov, Anton Pavlovich Chekhov was left to fend for himself in 1876 when his father, a grocer, fled to Moscow to escape imprisonment for debt. Anton remained alone in Taganrog to complete his schooling, paying for room and board by giving private lessons and rejoining the family in 1879, when he found them living in poverty in a damp Moscow basement. From then until his early death from tuberculosis in 1904, Chekhov would never be away from them, particularly his mother and younger sister Maria, for so long. While his elder brothers, Alexander, a writer, and Nikolay, an artist, moved out and married, Anton stayed at home, rapidly becoming both breadwinner and darling of the family. The decision to seek an income writing short stories was part of that transformation: the money would tide the family over until he could complete his degree in medicine and practice a profession.

Chekhov's grandfather, a serf, had worked hard to buy the family's freedom from bonded labor; Chekhov's father, whose main interest was church choral music, had plunged it into poverty; now Chekhov would raise it to genteel society, eventually buying and building country houses where his parents and siblings could live together and paying for his sister to study to become a teacher. Maria kept a portrait of Anton in her bedroom and frequently worked as his secretary; he discouraged her from marrying. The youngest brother, Mikhail, was given the task of pestering publishers till they paid up Anton's royalties. In *Memories of Chekhov* (a compendium of first-hand accounts of meetings with the author), the future painter Zakhar Pichugin recounts a visit to the family when Anton was just 23:

> As I came in, I greeted the father of Anton Pavlovich, and heard in reply the words which he whispered in a mysterious tone,
>
>> "Hush, please don't make a noise, Anton is working!"
>>
>> "Yes, dear, our Anton is working," Evgenia Yakovlevna the mother added, making a gesture indicating the door of his room. I went further. Maria Pavlovna, his sister, told me in a subdued voice,
>>
>> "Anton is working now."
>
> In the next room, in a low voice, Nikolai Pavlovich told me,
>
>> "Hello, my dear friend. You know, Anton is working now," he whispered, trying not to be loud. Everyone was afraid to break the silence.

In 1886 Chekhov published a story, "Hush," in which a writer demands silence from his family but doesn't respect their need for sleep; Anton, it seems, used to wake his sister Maria to discuss his ideas. Aside from the fact that here the selfish protagonist is a mediocre journalist, the crucial difference between author and fictional character is that the latter's family is made up of a wife and small children who are portrayed as devoted and defenseless victims. Chekhov avoided such ties and usually described the relationship between father and children in negative terms, as if it were impossible to occupy a position of authority without abusing it; throughout his life he never stopped mentioning the fact that he had been beaten by his father.

Given the reverence that his first literary successes inspired in his family, together with his ease in producing and publishing stories (528 between 1880 and 1888), it was never likely that medicine would become Chekhov's main profession. But he did practice, first in provincial hospitals around Moscow and later, out of generosity, when he treated peasants living near the 575-acre estate he bought in his early thirties at Melikhovo, some forty miles south of Moscow. Chekhov would raise a flag to let people know he was at home, then find himself overwhelmed with requests for help. In *Anton Chekhov: A Brother's Memoir*, Mikhail recounts an anecdote which suggests the tension between involvement and withdrawal that characterized so much of Chekhov's life. It was 1884 and he was treating a mother and three daughters for typhoid:

Anton was a young and naïve doctor, willing to give up his life for someone's recovery. He spent hours and hours with those patients, exhausting himself. Despite his efforts, the women's condition worsened until one day the mother and one of the sisters died. In agony, the dying sister grabbed Anton's hand just before she passed away. Her cold handshake instilled such feelings of helplessness and guilt in Anton that he contemplated abandoning medicine altogether. And indeed, after this case he gradually switched the focus of his energies to literature.

Neither *Memories of Chekhov* nor Mikhail Chekhov's charming but brief memoir can replace the full-scale biographies of the author by Ronald Hingley and Donald Rayfield, but they do offer a strong sense of the milieu in which Chekhov lived and the curious way he positioned himself in relation to friends, family, and reading public. All those who met Chekhov spoke of his accessibility and charm, his willingness to read manuscripts by aspiring authors, or to hurry to the bedside of an acquaintance in need. Those who knew him well, however, noted a reserve behind the charm ("as if he was wearing iron armour," Pichugin wrote) and his habit of contributing to conversations only with rare wry remarks or alternatively a constant stream of jokes. Above all, there was his tendency to disappear without warning; reflecting that in reality "Chekhov did not have any friends at all," writer Ignaty Potapenko recalls that the author once aborted a business visit to Moscow immediately on arrival:

"Why are you leaving?" I asked Chekhov.
"I just met Mr. N. He came to me in the street, as I was getting out of my cab. He embraced me, greeted me, and asked me if I was going to stay at this hotel. He promised to come and spend the evening with me."

Chekhov was too polite to say no, Potapenko observes: "He didn't have the ability of hurting another person." Alexander Serebrov-Tikhonov, who went fishing with the author, remembers him explaining his love of the sport with the remark that while fishing, "you are not a danger to anyone."

If in company Chekhov often felt trapped, once alone boredom and feelings of exclusion became equally oppressive: "Despite its unquestionable loveliness, this place is my prison," he said of his house in Yalta. "Freedom, complete and absolute freedom," was the supreme value, something the author never tired of repeating, but where did it

lie? Not satisfied with oscillating between a hectic, hard-drinking social life in Moscow and periods of relative quiet in the country, Chekhov eventually looked for more idiosyncratic arrangements: in
Melikhovo he had a small study built away from the main house so
that he could invite as many guests as possible, then escape from them
as he liked; when he built a house in Yalta in 1898, he also purchased
a tiny secluded cottage on the coast nearby "so that I could have some
solitude." These solutions depended on the willingness of Chekhov's
family to entertain his friends while he was working: his mother and
Maria became famous for their abundant cooking; in his memoir,
brother Mikhail takes evident pleasure in naming the famous guests
he got to know while everyone waited for Anton to emerge from
his study. None of this careful social engineering, however, could re-
solve the question of what the author was to do about women and
marriage.

Placed mainly in small and far from prestigious newspapers and
reviews, initially published under a pseudonym so as not to compromise his medical career, Chekhov's early stories are light and very
short. In "A Blunder" two anxious parents eavesdrop on their daughter and a writing teacher; as soon as the young man makes an amorous move on the girl, they will rush in with an icon and bless the
couple, after which it will be impossible for the teacher to escape marriage. The couple flirt, the girl offers her hand to be kissed, the parents rush in and shout their blessing, the teacher is terrified that he
has been nailed. But in her haste the mother has picked up not the
icon but the portrait of an author. There are shouts and recriminations. Chekhov closes his story with the memorable line: "The writing master took advantage of the general confusion and slipped away."

In all these stories the decision to love, whether it be marriage or
an affair, is always an error and always leads to a prison from which

there is no safe escape; yet love is powerfully seductive and life a prison of boredom without it. In "A Misfortune" a principled wife resists the approaches of a passionate young lawyer and urges her husband to wake up to what is going on; but eventually she succumbs as, "like a boa-constrictor," desire "gripped her limbs and her soul." In "Champagne" a railway station master marooned in a loveless marriage in a remote corner of the vast steppe argues with his wife as they drink champagne on New Year's Eve. The wife predicts bad luck because he has dropped the champagne bottle, but rushing out of the house in a rage he reflects, "What further harm can be done to a fish after it has been caught, roasted, and served up with sauce at table?" Returning home, he finds the answer to his question; a train has brought his wife's very young aunt, who has just left her husband.

> A little woman with large black eyes was sitting at the table.
> ... The grey walls, the rough ottoman, everything down
> to the least grain of dust seemed to have become younger
> and gayer in the presence of this fresh young being, exhaling
> some strange perfume, beautiful and depraved.

The temptation is irresistible. A few lines and months later we discover that our narrator no longer has either wife, job, home, or lover.

At first glance extremely varied, Chekhov's stories always have at their core this superimposition of what is desired with what is most toxic or imprisoning. "Grisha" is written from the point of view of an excited two-year-old; taken out in the street by his nurse, he is left so "shattered by the impressions of new life" that he needs "a spoonful of castor oil from mamma." In "Agatha" the narrator goes fishing at night with Savka, a handsome young man who lives in complete idleness, relying on the gifts of the peasant women who are infatu-ated with him. The fishing is interrupted by the arrival of Agatha, a young wife risking her marriage to come and make love to Savka, who actually despises women but is unable to resist them, even at the cost of a beating from their husbands. While the two make love, the narrator, fascinated and appalled, falls asleep fishing.

As pressure for social and political reform intensified in Russia through the nineteenth century, the peasants became the focus for much debate. From a peasant background himself and with firsthand experience of peasant life from his medical practice, Chekhov was well placed to contribute, especially when, in 1888, his work broke into the more serious literary and political journals in St. Petersburg. But declaring himself "neither liberal or conservative," the author refused to be tied to any position, and in his stories peasant life is subsumed into the underlying tension that galvanizes all his narra-tive: vital, impulsive, and always ready for love and action, Chekhov's peasants can't fail to fascinate; at the same time they are ignorant, dirty, inaccessible, and dangerous. "The Robbers" shows Chekhov mixing questions of sex and class in typical fashion.

A doctor's assistant, Ergunov, loses his way in a snowstorm while bringing medical supplies to a hospital on his superior's best horse. Taking refuge in an inn of ill repute, he finds himself in the company of Liubka, the innkeeper's beautiful twenty-year-old daughter, Ka-lashnikov, "a notorious ruffian and horse thief," and Merik, a "dark peasant" with "hair, eyebrows, and eyes . . . black as coal." Fright-ened but assured of his social superiority, the doctor shows the men his gun. All the same he is sexually excited by Liubka and feels left out when the men won't let him join their bragging at dinner. After-ward, when Kalashnikov plays his balalaika and Merik and Liubka dance a Cossack dance, Ergunov "wished he were a peasant instead of a doctor." Hurrying out into the snowstorm when Kalashnikov leaves, to check that his horse hasn't been stolen, he finds that even nature is in tension between freedom and imprisonment:

> What a wind there was! The naked birches and cherry trees, unable to resist its rough caresses, bent to the ground and moaned. For what sins, O Lord, has thou fastened us to the earth, and why may we not fly away free?

Eventually, Liubka, who is evidently in a relationship with Merik, kisses the doctor while Merik steals his horse; later she punches him in the face when he tries to make love to her. The following morning, rather than feeling angry about the horse, Ergunov is enamored of the free life he imagines the peasants leading, to the point that he feels that if he were not "a thief and a ruffian . . . it was only because he did not know how to be one."

Published in 1890 and criticized for its amorality, "The Robbers" was written as Chekhov was facing a major life crisis. Throughout his twenties he had alternated winters in Moscow with summers in rented country houses, working hard all the time. His prose had been recognized at the highest level with the award of the Pushkin Prize in 1887, and his play *Ivanov* was well received in 1889. None of this brought contentment; on the contrary, Chekhov felt so exasperated with the literary world that he was again talking about abandoning writing for medicine. Then in spring 1889 his elder brother Nikolay died of tuberculosis. Chekhov himself had been spitting blood for some years, and though he refused to be examined by a doctor and never discussed his health with anyone, he must have known what it meant. In the months following this bereavement he wrote the unusually long and deeply pessimistic "A Dreary Story," in which an aging professor of medicine faces his forthcoming death in a mood of restlessness and irritation. His wife, once desired, is now ugly and pestering, his emotionally needy daughter provokes only a sense of helplessness, his beautiful young ward, Katya, a failed actress, both attracts and repels him; the doctor would like to feel one with family and friends but finds them inferior and demanding. Having refused to help Katya when she begs for advice, he suffers at the thought that she will not come to his funeral.

As he wrote this, the eminent and handsome Chekhov was surrounded by young women eager to make a life with him. Telling friends he was in a hurry to marry, he nevertheless withdrew from every flirtation and brief affair. For a while it seemed that the brilliant Lika Mizinov, ten years his junior ("Lika the Beautiful," Chekhov called her), might be the one. She was in love and his flirting was frenetic. Later she would write: "You once said you loved immoral women, so you can't have been bored with me."

Yet Chekhov's response to this combination of literary success, bereavement, and romantic possibility was to run: in spring 1890, out of the blue, he departed, alone, to visit the penal colony of Sakhalin Island, off the east coast of Siberia, a three-month journey over five thousand miles of difficult terrain with no railway and poor roads. On arrival he spent three months carrying out a census of the entire convict population of about ten thousand, interviewing more than 160 people a day, preparing a file card for each, and taking notes on forced labor, child prostitution, and floggings. The return journey was made by boat to Odessa via Sri Lanka, where the author had sex, so he boasted, with "a black-eyed Indian girl . . . in a coconut grove on a moonlit night." He also spoke of piles, headaches, and impotence. Back in Moscow he wrote: "I can say this: I've lived, I've done enough! I've been in the hell of Sakhalin and in the paradise of Ceylon." Ergo he was no longer obliged to worry about marrying.

Little is said about Sakhalin in the books by Pichugin and Mikhail Chekhov, and even the larger biographies limit themselves to documenting, as though in extended parenthesis, the awful conditions of the penal colony and Chekhov's bizarre and heroic one-man census. There is little comment on the book he eventually wrote about the colony, which does not appear to be available in English translation. Yet the trip to Sakhalin gives an insight into Chekhov's writing as well as marking a turning point in the way he would handle his personal dilemmas. Determined to stay free, he fled to contemplate those in the worst prison imaginable. Attracted and repulsed by life's teeming vulgarity, he tried to put order into the most degraded of communities. What were his six hundred plus stories if not, in their fashion, a census of unhappy prisoners, of people falling into traps of love, work, obsession? Above all, the trip to Sakhalin affirmed Chekhov's own position with regard to life's prisons: he was fascinated by them, but would not himself be locked up; he would not be bound to a political party or a woman or a single publisher or even a single profession. After Sakhalin, Chekhov's stories are fewer, longer and bleaker. One of the first, "Ward No. 6" (1892), tells the story of a lazy hospital doctor who becomes fascinated by a mental patient whose obsession that he would be arrested and imprisoned becomes self-fulfilling when he is certified as mad. The same fate befalls the doctor, whose interest in such a crazy patient is interpreted as insanity. The story includes such lines as: "Life is a vexatious trap; when a thinking man reaches maturity and attains to full consciousness he cannot help feeling that he is in a trap from which there is no escape."

Despite continued to-ing and fro-ing between Moscow and the country, the years from 1892 to 1898 were the most stable of Chekhov's life. He bought the estate in Melikhovo, put his family to work to rebuild and farm it, saw and avoided huge numbers of guests, and began a new activity as a philanthropist. Books were sent to Sakhalin Island to help the convicts climb out of their ignorance, and the author became involved in helping the local authorities organize famine relief and in sponsoring the building of schools for peasant children. To become less dangerous and ensnaring, life must be educated and organized. Many of the conversations in *Memories of Chekhov* have the author deeply pessimistic about the present but surprisingly optimistic about a wonderful future hundreds of years hence when man will use science to turn the world into a beautiful garden.

Chekhov's logical career move at this point would have been to write a novel. The most revered Russian authors were novelists. Publishers and critics expected it. Chekhov felt the pressure to perform and spoke of having a novel in preparation. It never materialized. It was part of his manner and message to create a complex, no-win situation, then bow out, leaving the reader with an acute sense of the distance between wishes and reality. The stories do not gain with greater length: the fascination and fear of life's unruliness come across in the way circumstances are rapidly but also tersely described, with appetite, but never excess. The novel, like marriage, would have been too great a commitment. Chekhov preferred flirtation and an atmosphere of fugitive brevity. Cut, cut, cut, was the advice he constantly gave the authors who sent him their manuscripts.

Instead, he began to concentrate on plays: *The Seagull* (1896), *Uncle Vanya* (1899), *The Three Sisters* (1901), and *The Cherry Orchard* (1904). More fragmented and elusive than the stories, they are hard to summarize; major speeches and rare moments of action are almost submerged in casual chatter and noises off. Nevertheless, the pattern is clear enough: over four acts, often separated by a considerable time, a dozen or so characters from a milieu which is now recognizably

Chekhov's dig themselves deeper and deeper into life's mire. In love in act 1, they are married and regretting it in act 2; longing to enter the workplace when we first find them, they are bored to death with paper pushing a few years on. Their own love unrequited, they marry someone who loves them, just to have something happen, and invariably end up hating their innocent spouse. All inadequate to the challenges of extended relationships, what talents they do have remain strictly peripheral to the action.

Chekhov called his plays farces; his main director, Konstantin Stanislavsky, saw them as lyrical tragedies. The two argued heatedly. But the genius of these dramas is to be right on the cusp. Speech by speech, it is impossible to know what seriousness to attribute to them, as indeed is the case with the numerous absurd and cryptic remarks Chekhov is remembered as passing in *Memories of Chekhov.* The plays make sense insofar as they challenge our habits of making sense; the uncertainty they arouse is heightened by the constant implication that life, as we have projected and expected it, doesn't happen.

The audience was important. In *The Seagull,* the writer Trigorin, who Chekhov admitted was an alter ego, speaks of seeking to seduce a public he imagines as "distrustful and unfriendly" and living in fear of audience reaction to his plays. So it was for Chekhov; the public was another manifestation of the life he sought to be part of and simultaneously despised. When the first performance of *The Seagull* was met with boos, Chekhov fled Moscow without a word to anyone. Later he was equally outraged when ecstatic audiences yelled "author, author," and demanded he take a bow. But with the actors, with whom he could be both one of the group and aloof from it, he was always happy. "We developed a good relationship with Anton Pavolovich," remarks Stanislavsky. "Along with him, we felt almost like one big family."

In 1897 a lung hemorrhage marked the beginning of the end. Chekhov sold Melikhovo and moved the family to Yalta for the better winter climate. No longer something he could deny, the disease exacerbated his old dilemma: with little time left him, it was even more important to live intensely; yet intensity fed the disease and shortened life expectancy. In 1899 Chekhov settled all his prose work, previously divided between numerous magazines, with one publisher. The time for hedging bets or worrying about freedom was over. "Suddenly in late May of 1901," writes Mikhail, "I read in the papers that Anton had gotten married. . . . I did not even know who the bride was." Mikhail's bitterness at his brother's decision was as nothing to the anguish of their sister Maria, who, having kept Anton and his girlfriends close company for so many years, felt deeply betrayed.

The bride, Olga Knipper, was the Moscow Art Theater's leading actress, a woman at the heart of life and society. Chekhov insisted they marry in secret; he feared hurting his family and being devoured by the public. "For him, this will be like committing suicide or being sent to prison," the writer Ivan Bunin remembers thinking when he saw them together. But since Olga was determined to go on working in Moscow and Chekhov condemned to living in Yalta, it was never likely that they would be spending much time together. A friend and doctor, Isaac Altschuller, recalls that on returning to Yalta from frequent trips to Moscow, Chekhov "would be suffering from serious throat bleeding, or coughing fits." At rehearsals of his plays he became so excited that the actors had to ask him to leave. The recriminations and reconciliations with Olga over their difficulties being together were interminable. Yet she was beside him at the end. Having spoken, in April 1904, of going to the Russian-Japanese war as a doctor, so as to get a close view of the action, Chekhov in fact went to Germany to seek treatment in the spa town of Badenweiler, where he died in his hotel room shortly after midnight on July 2.

Mikhail, in his account of the funeral, complains of the family's near exclusion as a huge crowd pushed "into the cemetery, crushing crosses, pushing monuments, breaking fences, and trampling flowers." Gorky, whose writing Chekhov had criticized for its excessive exuberance, understood the irony: Chekhov "fought his whole life against vulgarity," he remarked, yet his funeral was "a huge mess of noisy, crowded and vulgar men and women." Arguably, Chekhov, in his coffin, was well placed: he had always liked to be near crowds, but never quite among them.

James Joyce

What options are available to you if you yearn to belong to your community of origin, indeed to be one of its leading figures, yet simultaneously feel threatened and diminished by it? One answer might be to move far away while nevertheless constantly reminding people back home of your existence, your ambitions, your still being one of them.

How might you do that?

Perhaps you could write about the community critically, portraying it as a place of suffocating limitation, spiritual death even, the kind of place any sensitive intellectual would have to abandon, but write with an insistence, a passionate attention to detail, a capacity to transform the squalid into the lyrical such as to create an atmosphere of intense attachment and nostalgia. You might also portray all the people you knew in the community in an absolutely recognizable and for the most part negative fashion so that old friends and enemies remain constantly and anxiously attentive to what you write, even vulnerable in your regard.

Another idea might be to take with you into what you will call exile, since that word suggests grievance and unfinished business, a loyal companion or companions who represent all that is most accommodating and attractive to you in the community abandoned; this will perpetuate a sense of belonging in absence, but without threatening you; it may even allow you to become the center of a small community of your own; suitable candidates for such a role would be an admiring younger brother, or a young and loving wife whose humble social background and limited education guarantee that she will always be beholden to you, however you behave.

Such, conscious or unconscious, was James Joyce's long-term strategy with regard to home, to Dublin, to Ireland. From age twenty-two to fifty-eight he lived in the Austro-Hungarian Empire, Italy, Switzerland, and France, while all his creative attention remained focused on Ireland, and specifically on the Dublin community he grew up in, pre-1904. Though he spoke the languages of his adopted homes, he did not integrate in those countries, or write about them, or tie his destiny to them. In times of political upheaval he fled, though never toward home. What mattered was belonging, and not belonging, to Ireland.

Two questions arise: how was it that the young Joyce developed these conflicting needs, and what part did the consequent tension play in his special achievement as a writer? Gordon Bowker, in his five hundred–plus–page biography of Joyce, never frames these questions or discusses his intentions as a literary biographer. His account proceeds in linear fashion, most chapters covering a period of one or two years. Throughout the book, detail overwhelms reflection, while the connection between the author's life and work is reduced to a catalogue of correspondences, so that we know which real person gave which fictional character this or that physical attribute, or name, or occupation, or address. Readers familiar with Richard Ellmann's excitingly thoughtful biography of 1959 will be disappointed.

That said, the story as Bowker tells it offers abundant food for thought, and he does have fresh details to offer. Born in 1882, James

Augustine Aloysius Joyce was the first surviving child of John and May Joyce, whose recent marriage had been fiercely opposed by the parents of both partners. There was a previous baby, named after the father, who had died at barely two months. Hence the first healthy son was a crucial affirmation of the marriage and, despite thirteen further births producing nine other surviving children, James would always be his father's favorite and was always encouraged to believe he was destined for greatness. When, aged ten, he wrote a poem about the betrayal and downfall of the Irish leader Parnell, John Joyce, an avid supporter of republicanism and Parnell in particular, had dozens of copies made to circulate among friends.

To be singled out for glory will mean different things depending on the character and achievements of the person doing the singling out. By far the most important formative influence on James's life, John Joyce can best be described as a *spectacular* failure, a man whose descent into alcoholism and poverty during James's adolescence could not but command the appalled attention of all around him. They were many. A talented singer and raconteur, hard-drinking and gregarious, John spent countless hours in Dublin pubs squandering a considerable inheritance (the family had owned a number of properties in Cork) and neglecting the duties he had been assigned by the various government departments that hired and invariably fired him. He was well known, well loved, and beyond help. The impression one has of him from biographies and from Joyce's descriptions of Simon Dedalus, the character based on his father in *A Portrait of the Artist as a Young Man,* is of a patriarch who, while singing his son's praises, is himself such a dominating, magnetic, and boastful presence that it is hard to imagine anyone finding space beside him. It was thus not clear from the beginning what being a success in the vicinity of John Joyce and *for* John Joyce might entail.

James's infancy and adolescence were spent in two sharply contrasting environments: rigidly organized, hierarchical Catholic boarding schools and a turbulent, overcrowded family that was more and more frequently obliged to move house as John took pride in cheating landlords by decamping without paying rent. With ten children the logistics must have been complicated. But while the second son Stanislaus would eventually condemn his father and have nothing more to do with him, James never did, if only because he came to share many of John Joyce's habits: the overspending, drinking, and partying, the frequent moves at the expense of landlords, and, in general, the willful denial of what most of us see as the ordinary terms of reality. When John died in 1931, James would speak of him as "loyal to the end" but also "the silliest man I ever knew."

In this troubled, multitudinous family, these severe and regimented schools, what space or place was there for a boy destined for greatness? Written and rewritten through his twenties and early thirties, *A Portrait of the Artist as a Young Man* shows the author's alter ego forming around predicaments of positioning: where does he stand in relation to everything else? He is center stage in the story his father tells him in the opening lines of the book but then obliged to hide under the table as his mother and aunt demand apologies and conformity. Frightened at school, he keeps away from the action, lingering on "the fringe of his line" on the rugby field, keeping his head down in lessons, only feigning participation to avoid punishment. A constant sense of vulnerability resulting from physical frailty and weak eyesight leads him to cultivate a withdrawn mental space where he focuses on the language his companions use, at once feeding on them and detaching himself from them. But weakness and withdrawal invite enemies; a boy pushes him in a ditch, he catches a cold. Finally we find the one place at school where Stephen is happy:

the sick bay. Here he fantasizes his own death, the remorse of the enemies who hurt him, the regret of his parents. Now language embellishes and consoles:

How beautiful and sad that was! How beautiful the words were . . .

Later he identifies his own imagined death with Parnell's; he has been treacherously used and isolated, as was Parnell; like Parnell he will die and this will place him at the center of everybody's attention.

We hardly need to concern ourselves whether these events are strictly true: a behavior pattern is established that finds ample confirmation in the biography: vulnerability prompts detachment through a focus on the mechanics rather than content of language, after which a poetic manipulation of language brings consolation and a sense of belonging at a distance.

At school in his teens, Joyce found an easy way of belonging: religious devotion; but also a way of distinguishing himself, by pushing devotion to the limit, writing religious verse and toying with thoughts of the priesthood, something his mother would have appreciated. Much is made of the adolescent Joyce's swings between extremes of religious and profane behavior, moving from brothels and drunkenness to marathons with the rosary; however, there is nothing to suggest a deeply felt religious dilemma or a profound sense of guilt. "Agenbite of inwit" for Joyce seems to have involved no more than an anxiety that his sins might prevent him being thought well of, or thinking well of himself. It is rather, then, as if each type of involvement, religious or profane, allowed him to become part of a social group and master its language—something crucial to Joyce—pushing his behavior to the limit to gain distinction before moving on. After rejecting religion in his late teens and refusing in 1903 to take communion in obedience to his dying mother, he nevertheless continued to be a churchgoer who now made himself conspicuous precisely by forgoing the sacrament.

The trick of being simultaneously inside and outside the group is most evident with Joyce's singing. Sharing his father's talent, Joyce loved to perform wherever possible. Immersed in the music, he was as Irish as one can be, but in a way that required neither interaction nor submission. For preference he sang alone, insisted on singing better than others, and always thought of singing, and indeed writing, as competitive. Here, in the words of the diarist Joseph Holloway, is the twenty-two-year-old Joyce taking center stage to sing, before withdrawing to his own special space:

Mr J. Joyce, a (mysterious kind of) strangely aloof, silent youth, with weird, penetrating, large eyes, which he frequently shaded with his hand and with a half-bashful, faraway expression on his face, sang some dainty old world ballads most artistically and pleasingly, some to his own accompaniment. As he sings he sways his head from side to side to add to the soulfulness of his rendering. Later he sat in a corner and gazed at us all in turn in an uncomfortable way from under his brows and said little or nothing all evening.

That the teenage Joyce had absorbed his father's expectations and the praise of his Jesuit teachers is evident from the confident precociousness of his first literary productions. Written in 1900, at age eighteen, a first play, entitled *A Brilliant Career*, bears the dedication:

To
My own Soul I
Dedicate the first
true work of my
life.

In 1902, departing on a first trip to Paris, James told his brother and confidant Stanislaus that should he die during the trip, his poetry and prose "epiphanies" must be sent to all the great libraries of the world, including the Vatican.

Nor, as his parents fought and the family sank into poverty, did Joyce hesitate to contact major figures in the literary world: Ibsen, George Russell, W. B. Yeats, and Lady Augusta Gregory, among others. But even as he made these important contacts, the young man courted rejection; a long letter to Ibsen on his seventy-third birthday closes with the idea that the great playwright had "only opened the way" and that "higher and holier enlightenment lies—onward." It was implicit that Joyce himself would be the bearer of that enlightenment. Having arranged an interview with Yeats, he spent most of the conversation criticizing the older writer, remarking on leaving that "I have met you too late. You are too old." It was always Joyce's way to have others understand that he was the more important.

The habit of forcing himself into the limelight while simultaneously inviting exclusion is another facet that would emerge in his writing. None of Joyce's major publications—*Dubliners, A Portrait, Ulysses, Finnegans Wake*—was completed before being offered for publication. Each had first chapters, or sections, published at early stages of writing, and all these early publications ran into trouble with editors or censors, either for their avant-garde style or for supposedly obscene content. However, the effect on Joyce was never to back off as the book developed, but rather to raise the stakes and push the offense to the limit. For this integrity he has been much praised, yet the biographies suggest that this habit of exasperated provocation was standard in all Joyce's relationships, even those with his life partner, Nora, and his favorite brother, Stanislaus.

Did Joyce leave Ireland, as *A Portrait* and consequent legend would have it, because he needed to go abroad to develop his writing and escape the competing demands of Catholicism and republicanism? "Living in Ireland had lost all meaning for Joyce," Bowker tells us rather grandly, this at a moment when the young author had already completed a slim volume of poems, had published two of the stories that were to make up *Dubliners,* and was getting on with his novel *Stephen Hero* with the enthusiastic but attentive criticism of Stanislaus. He had also published reviews and was showing a rare talent for provoking ire and admiration with vicious satires of the Dublin literati. All this at age twenty-two. It's hard to imagine, then, that living in Ireland meant nothing to Joyce. Reading through the sequence of events before his departure, it is evident that Nora was crucial.

Joyce's mother had died in 1903, depriving the family of its main element of stability. The following June, James met Nora Barnacle. Up to this point his sexual experience had been mostly with prostitutes, who have the merit that they do not betray you, criticize your ideas, or make you wait long for satisfaction. However, in March 1904 a venereal infection had obliged him to become more wary. Now Joyce meets an attractive uneducated, sexually willing girl who has fled a severe father in Galway and is alone and unprotected, working as a chambermaid in Dublin. The story is love at first sight; nevertheless, Joyce is too ashamed of his scarcely literate beloved to introduce her to intellectual, middle-class friends or to a father who has quite other aspirations for him. To be with Nora in Ireland would mean a battle with his father and a drastic loss of image; but how long would a girl be faithful if her man continued to treat her as a mistress rather than a partner? Eloping just five months after they met, Joyce could enjoy an intensely erotic cohabitation with Nora while presenting himself back in Dublin, sincerely no doubt, as an intellectual who simply had to escape the "rabblement" that was the Irish literary world. On the day of departure, Nora, who had no experience of travel, was sent ahead to board the ferry alone, while Joyce enjoyed a proper sending off at the dockside from all his family and friends, who were to remain unaware of her presence. When his father found out, he was furious. Three years later he wrote:

> I need not tell you how your miserable mistake affected my already well crushed feelings, but then maturer thoughts took more the form of pity than anger, when I saw a life of promise crossed and a future that might have been brilliant blasted in one breath.

And Joyce was pitiable. Writing was not easier in Europe. From Paris to Zurich to Trieste and the remote Pola on the northern Adriatic, he struggled to find work as a language teacher, struggled to survive the boredom of language teaching, struggled to find rooms to rent, struggled to pay the rent, struggled to find people who would lend him money, struggled to keep Nora, who understood nothing, knew no one, and was soon pregnant, in good spirits. Communication with Ireland and publishers was slow and discouraging. Editors were willing to publish if he would compromise a little with the "obscenity" and disrespectful political opinions. He would not. The more depressed he became, the more he spent what cash remained on drink.

Conscientiously, Bowker records every disappointed request for work, every move from one drab flat to another. A first child was named George after James's younger brother who had died three years before. Such was the loyalty to home. Nora fell into depression. Bent on "the spiritual liberation of [his] country," Joyce wrote to his Aunt Josephine for advice and went to prostitutes again. Desperate for company, he invited Stanislaus to join them, then exploited him quite shamelessly, taking his help and language-school earnings for granted. On a whim he went to Rome, got a job in a bank, hated everything, then returned to Trieste and Stanislaus's charity. A second child, Lucia, was born. Only twenty-five, and already a patriarch, Joyce suffered declining health, his eyesight in particular. At this point it was clear that expatriation has slowed down his career.

In 1909 Joyce returned, twice, to Ireland, once alone, once with George, now usually called Giorgio, but not with Nora. On the first of these occasions he was told that Nora had betrayed him with a friend before their departure from Dublin and wrote her hysterical letters of accusation. Included in full by Ellmann, given only in snippets by Bowker, they show Joyce's readiness to feel betrayed and his intense fear of the loss of personal prestige he believed it involved. Later, persuaded that the story of Nora's unfaithfulness was a lie (hence an act of treachery by his enemies), he first wrote to her asking forgiveness for the earlier letters, then fantasizing a ferocious eroticism: "I wish to be lord of your body and soul," he announced. A situation had developed where life with Nora was essential, but only possible far away from Ireland, where she was unhappy and work difficult. To keep her company in the trap they had fallen into, Joyce brought back to Trieste two younger Joyce sisters from Dublin, first Eva, then Eileen. Later they would all be joined, at some expense for shipping, by the Joyce family portraits, as the author pursued his reconstruction of Dublin away from Dublin with himself as head of the community. It was at this point, in 1913, that Ezra Pound entered his life and everything changed.

Pound was seeking "markedly modern stuff" to publish in a small literary review, and Yeats had suggested that Joyce might provide it. This was a time when literature was becoming more and more an object of academic study; psychology was problematized, likewise narrative and representation; an aesthetic of difficulty and deep-coded meaning was coming into vogue. Joyce, with his extraordinary sensitivity to language, his belief that an appropriate use of words could somehow bridge the gap between belonging and not belonging, which was also the distance between Trieste and Dublin ("Joyce seemed to think that words were omnipotent," Huxley later remarked), was the right man at the right moment. His claim to be socialist and the fact that he wrote about the common people rather than the literary classes was welcome, while his habit of doing so in ways that were strenuously experimental was even more so: right-thinking intellectual readers found themselves simultaneously with the people and above them. On Joyce's birthday in 1914 *The Egoist* began serialization of *A Portrait,* later described by the Sunday Express as "the most infamously obscene book in ancient or modern literature." Three years later, the editor and patron of *The Egoist,* the wealthy, quiet, left-wing activist Harriet Weaver, made a first gift of money to Joyce. Over the next twenty years, she would spend, quite literally, a fortune on him, making it her mission to allow his genius to flower.

If you have an enduring image of yourself as "a stag at bay," which is also your image of the betrayed, humiliated Parnell, and perhaps too of your exhausted and drunken father, then success may be more disorientating than struggle. Perhaps the only thing to do with it will be to use it as a stepping-stone to greater calamity. Taking the family to neutral Zurich during the First World War, the thirty-one-year-old Joyce received financial support from the Royal Literary Fund and the British Treasury Fund. He did what he could to drink it away and spoiled his relationship with the British authorities by engaging in a futile argument over a small sum of money with a consulate employee, Henry Carr. Moving to Paris after the war, he spent the larger and larger incomes now settled on him by Harriet Weaver in extravagant accommodation, restaurant bills, magnanimous tips, and of course drink.

To meet the adult Joyce on the street in these years was to be asked to run an errand for him. To know him a little was to be asked for a loan. To be his friend was to be asked to read to him, type for him, and discuss his work at length. To be his publisher was to be pressed to bring out his work in an impossibly short time so as to coincide with his birthday or the anniversary of the day he met Nora. To be his partner was to be asked to satisfy his wildest erotic fantasies. If you ran a first errand, you would be asked to run a second, longer one. If you lent money you would be asked to lend more. If you survived the discussions of *Ulysses,* which were of course fascinating, then came the discussions of *Finnegans Wake.* If you agreed to publish his work on the given day, you were faced with hundreds of last-minute revisions. If you satisfied his erotic fantasies, he might then ask you to flirt with someone else; that too was exciting. To be Joyce's child, meantime, was to live absolutely in his shadow, to change home, school, country, language as was convenient for him. All this was acceptable because James Joyce was, as his father and Stanislaus and Pound and so many others had told him, a genius.

And he was.

In *The Dead* (written in 1907) he had depicted a young intellectual powerfully attached to a community that he feels he has no place in, a man who takes center stage at a Christmas party but gives a speech that he knows will irritate everyone. Returning home he seeks erotic consolation with his wife only to discover she is pining for a boyfriend who died long ago, a boy who had committed to her totally in a way he cannot. Abandoned, isolated, with no way forward, his static melancholy is transformed into a haunting vision of his whole country as a graveyard frozen to stillness under snow. The moment of greatest loneliness and loss of direction is the moment when the wholeness of the community is most beautifully and forlornly invoked.

In *A Portrait* (1907–14), a young man in a treacherous society that makes impossible demands on him saves himself by assuming the position that we have come to think of as the artist's: he who observes, but from outside. This move is presented as an affirmation of quasi-religious commitment to renewing the nation's conscience, an idea that will enchant young intellectuals throughout the twentieth century and that gains credence from the intensity of the book's lyrical evocations and the brilliance of its innovative narrative style.

Exiles (1915) never won Joyce acclaim yet marks a turning point in his development, a watershed between work that is entirely accessible and widely loved and writing that was much more adventurous and obscure. Austerely Ibsenite in construction, this unhappy play confronts head-on, without any of the lexical richness, stylistic experimentation, or sentimental evocation of Ireland so appreciated in his other writing, a love triangle, or rather rectangle. A couple, Richard and Bertha, blatantly based on James and Nora, return to Ireland with their eight-year-old son after nine years in Italy and promptly involve themselves again with Richard's best friend Robert, and Robert's refined cousin and ex-girlfriend, Beatrice. Robert has been trying to lure the uneducated Bertha into betraying Richard (whose avant-garde writing she can't understand) but though interested and playing along, she has been referring their meetings and even kisses to her husband, who, sexually excited by the situation, will not make it clear to her whether he really cares about an eventual betrayal or not. At the same time, Richard is pursuing a more literary and intellectual romance with the Dantesque Beatrice.

In scenes of tortuously self-regarding rhetoric, Richard insists on having everything out in the open; Robert is appalled by the fact that communications he thought had been secret were not; Bertha is upset that her duplicity with Robert has been revealed to him at her expense. Eventually all four characters reach a position of total impasse, in which they try saying everything and its opposite without avail. Robert and Beatrice are still eager to start their romances with Bertha and Richard but unable to force matters. Bertha seems ready to save her marriage but won't renounce the relationship with Robert if her husband won't assert his determination to keep her. Claiming he is just giving everyone else their freedom, Richard himself remains in a state of complete indecision, which curiously allows him to manipulate the other three. This is A Portrait of the Artist at a Rather Later State of Development. Bowker, like Ellmann, gives us details of the historical relationships it was based on, revealing once again Joyce's tendency to push those close to him toward the betrayal he seems to both fear and feed off.

Stalemate is a hard thing to dramatize, and *Exiles* is not a successful play; we have the narrative impasse typical of Joyce's fiction without the compensating lyricism or playfulness. Joyce, however, cared immensely about the play and constantly sought to have it produced. For Nora, who must have found it the most easily readable thing her husband had written, it was no doubt a shock; inviting the audience to construe this as the author's marriage, the play became a betrayal of trust in her regard of the very kind it sought to dramatize, and similarly impossible to condemn because justified by the ideal of honesty.

If impasse is accepted, how can one go on? This is the moment when Joyce's work shifts from solemn to comic, when Stephen Dedalus's ability, in *A Portrait,* to pick up on some odd word association in order to detach himself from domestic conflict blossoms into a vast encyclopedic evasion of the dramatic point, sometimes hilarious, sometimes whimsical and sentimental, sometimes verging on the obscene, sometimes incomprehensible. Jung would say at once of *Ulysses* (1922) that it displayed a schizophrenic use of language—discontinuities, coded messages, superimposition of different levels of discourse, every kind of imitation, pastiche, and distraction—such that the predicaments of the two Joycean alter egos at the core of the novel, Stephen's troubled relationship with his father, Bloom's difficulty responding to his wife's betrayal, are all but submerged under quantities of wordplay, extraneous information, and mythical parallel. Years later the anthropologist Gregory Bateson, one of the first to suggest that mental illness might arise from special problems of communication in the family, concluded that schizophrenics withdraw into coded, broken, often poetic language because they find themselves in a blocked and conflicted environment where any firm statement will lead to trouble. Writing the even more arcane and densely coded prose of *Finnegans Wake,* Joyce would refer to his style as the "J J Safety Pun Factory."

But Joyce's, as Jung pointed out, was a willed language, developed with the author's considerable creative powers and marshaling all his prodigious reading, not the helpless refuge of the patient. Indeed, it was the controlled use of such language, Jung thought, that had perhaps saved the author's sanity. Be that as it may, Joyce now began to accompany his texts with explanations and glossaries. He loved to set his many helpers puzzles and quizzes. Bowker reports Joyce reworking paragraphs because he feared they were too accessible. The secretive coding of the writing was becoming as important as what was encoded. And of course, the more intellectual and visibly *literary* the work, the more its erotic fantasies (another product of frustration) could be justified to the censor. Paralleled with the exploits of the mythical Nausicaa and described to the suggestive accompaniment of a firework display in the pastiched prose of popular magazines for young ladies, an adolescent girl's exposure of her knickers to the masturbating Bloom was not the same thing as a straightforward account of the same.

Written in Zurich and Paris, during and immediately after the First World War, while Nora and the children were asked to change language from Italian to German, then German to French, *Ulysses* was serialized in the New York–based *Little Review* but published in 1922 by the small Parisian bookstore Shakespeare & Company, this to avoid censorship problems. Remarkably, Joyce was granted a 45 percent royalty. Enthusiastically promoted, the book sold well by mail order. In addition to writing frequent begging letters to Harriet Weaver, Joyce could now send his children to Shakespeare & Company to ask for advances against royalties. Again Bowker reports the drunken evenings, expensive meals, expensive hotel rooms and apartments (usually kept in states of some disorder).

Joyce read reviews avidly. He rarely minded criticism or denunciations of scandal; what mattered was to be at the center of debate. Seeing that *Ulysses* had divided critics between those who praised it generously, using it to bolster their own agendas for experimental fiction, and those, including Stanislaus, who thought its obscurity and obscenity had gone way too far, in 1923 he settled down to put the loyalty of his supporters to the supreme test with a work whose title he wouldn't reveal until its publication sixteen years later and whose plot defies all summary but involves a father accused of sexual crimes, possibly incestuous, and a wife who asks her writer son (with weak eyesight) to write a letter defending the father. Neither accusations nor letter are ever clearly revealed, though the novel revolves constantly around them. While *Ulysses* had created its stylistic effects to a large degree through the curious order of words in the sentence ("perfume of embraces all him assailed"), here a high proportion of the words are portmanteaux, often made up with elements from various languages ("And thanacestross mound have swollup them all"). Almost at once the formula succeeded in eroding the support of both Pound, Joyce's main promoter, and Weaver, his main source of income, both of whom found it incomprehensible and unappealing. Depressed and inflamed by such treachery, Joyce made the book more complex.

One says Joyce lived in Paris in these years. In fact, he rarely stayed more than a few months in the same place, enjoying weeks at a time in luxury hotels in many parts of France, Belgium, and Switzerland, with frequent trips to England and even an attempt to set up home in London. Endless eyesight problems increased his already remarkable capacity to get people to do things for him. Despite frequent stomach pains—stress-related, he believed—he continued to drink heavily. His marriage was in stalemate, with Nora threatening to leave if he didn't change his ways, but staying despite his refusal to do so; in reality it was hard to imagine what life she could have built for herself away from Joyce at this point. Then, in 1932, her daughter Lucia showed everyone the only way to stop her father from doing exactly as he always wanted: as she and her parents prepared to board the boat train to London at Gare du Nord, she threw a fit so violent that Joyce was forced to abort the trip.

Those who subscribe to Gregory Bateson's ideas that mental illness may, at least in part, come out of certain kinds of impasse within
the family will read Bowker's account of Lucia's descent into schizo-
phrenia with interest. Both children had been encouraged to think of
themselves as artists, Giorgio a singer, Lucia a dancer. Bowker quotes
guests of the Joyce household describing the children and their father
performing for them after dinner parties. Between the two, however,
Joyce's preference was for Lucia. He had encouraged her to believe
she was a genius and was disappointed in 1929 when, aged twenty-
two, she abruptly gave up dancing despite being accepted at the
Elizabeth Duncan school in Darmstadt. When she then began to
study as an artist, he urged her to help him with an illustrated edition
of his poems. Bowker speaks of the adolescent Lucia as a possible
object of his father's sexual attentions, and certainly the young
woman now seemed to take a vindictive pleasure in letting her parents know all about a sudden spate of promiscuity. However, when
we hear Lucia herself speak, the bitterness is all for her father's monomania, his always occupying the center of attention, and his wasting
the money that might have been his children's inheritance. On one
visit to friends she threatens to leave if anyone so much as mentions
her father. On another we find her insisting to one of Joyce's admirers and helpers that "her father was a failure and a physical wreck
who could neither write nor sleep on account of a ruined constitu-
tion. What was more he was seriously broken down and his life was
now devoted to squandering her inheritance."

Such was the rivalry in the family for Joyce's attention that no
sooner had Lucia moved center stage than both Nora and above all
Giorgio (recently married to a wealthy American divorcée ten years
older than himself) were calling for her to be committed to a mental
hospital. At one point we see Joyce offering to buy Lucia a fur coat in

the hope that this will improve her self-esteem and solve the problem. In a family accustomed to exasperation, the stakes were quickly raised, with Lucia attacking her mother and twice setting fire to her room. Torn between his writing, where he was all powerful, and the appalled recognition that something real, terrible, and possibly irreversible was taking place, Joyce wavered, allowed Lucia to be committed, then fetched her back, then allowed her to be committed again, and so on. At this point, when he and Nora took their expensive holidays away from Paris, he arranged for postcards to be sent to Lucia from town as if he were still at home. He had understood the changes Lucia was demanding he make, but with her committed there was no need to make them.

In 1936 a Danish writer, Ole Vinding, met Joyce in Copenhagen and quoted him as admitting: "Since 1922 my book has become more real to me than reality. . . . All other things have been insurmountable difficulties." "He sucked energy from his surroundings," Vinding observed, and of the relationship with Nora remarked that Joyce "was like a spoiled boy with his quiet, eternally permissive mother."

One of the embarrassments of literary biography is that nobody seems sure how we should talk about the relationship between a writer's life and work, despite the fact that we are interested in the life, at least initially, only because of the work. A prevailing orthodoxy tells us that novels, poetry, and plays exist quite separately from their creators and can properly be discussed only in critical essays that ignore the artist's life; the critics themselves seem embarrassed by the idea that, however indirect, a piece of writing is always a form of communication between writer and reader.

On the other hand, when we see behavior patterns as constant as those in Joyce's life, it seems reasonable to imagine that the work would stand in relation to them in some way. We might think of a writer's novels over the years as a form of extended conversation between author and readership, in which the author naturally seeks to assume the position he is most comfortable with. To read Lawrence, for example, as Lawrence himself observed, is "to enter the fray." He was an argumentative man who liked to have intelligent combative opponents around him. The reader is urged to react, to fight back. Joyce, instead, was in the habit of collecting admiring helpers who ministered to him in all kinds of ways. He "will not serve," but wishes others to serve him. "He got people . . . to follow him wherever he wanted," remarked Stuart Gilbert, who himself helped Joyce in all kinds of ways, "to [cancel] their arrangements if he wanted their assistance for some trivial, easily postponed task."

Joyce's reader, particularly in the later works, is invited to become another such helper. How? By endlessly interpreting Joycean condundrums, running little semiotic errands between different sections of the text, perhaps participating at Bloomsday celebrations. "I've put in so many enigmas and puzzles," Joyce said of *Ulysses*, "it'll keep the professors busy for centuries." *Finnegans Wake*, with its cyclical structure, its broken first sentence that is the continuation of the last—"a history of the world" Joyce claimed—invites you to suppose that you are trapped in the book forever, drawn into a black hole of literary obsession that leaves no space for anything but awed admiration of its author. Wonderful in parts, but making such extraordinary demands upon our time and patience that only someone who could turn this labor into a career would settle down to understand the whole thing, *Finnegans Wake* contrives to be that phenomenon Joyce's life had always tended toward, a glorious failure, a monumental labor forever cited but rarely read.

In his perceptive introduction to Beckett's second volume of letters, Dan Gunn suggests that the Second World War changed

Beckett's hitherto Joycean style. He had seen so much turmoil and destruction that his own obsessions became less urgent. Where he had been contorted, exhibitionist, and self-regarding, he now becomes more straightforward and generous. In this sense, the war came too late for Joyce. Shortly after the invasion of Czechoslovakia we hear him objecting to a friend who is talking politics, "Let us leave the Czechs in peace, and occupy ourselves with *Finnegans Wake*." Months later, with the flow of money finally drying up, as he struggles to bring Nora and his grandson Stephen to the safety of Switzerland, we have the impression that Hitler's advance is indeed forcing him back toward reality—back, for example, to finding pleasure in walking a little boy to the shops to look for a toy. Some four weeks after crossing the border into Switzerland, however, Joyce was taken ill and died in a matter of days with a perforated bowel.

Samuel Beckett

At the turning point of the second volume of Samuel Beckett's letters, which is also the turning point of his professional life, the moment when, after so many years of "retyping . . . for rejection," his best work is finally to be published with enthusiasm by editors determined to let the world know what they have discovered, the author's partner, Suzanne Dechevaux-Dumesnil, writes to his publisher Jerome Lindon at Éditions de Minuit to advise that Beckett does not wish his novel to be entered for the prestigious Prix des Critiques. It is April 19, 1951, Beckett is forty-five, the novel in question is *Molloy;* Suzanne explains:

> What he dreads above all in the very unlikely event of his receiving a prize is the publicity which would then be directed, not only at his name and his work, but at the man himself. He judges, rightly or wrongly, that it is impossible for the prizewinner, without serious discourtesy, to refuse to go in for the posturings required by these occasions: warm words for his supporters, interviews, photos, etc., etc. And as he feels wholly incapable of this sort of behaviour, he prefers not to expose himself to the risk of being forced into it by entering the competition.

Thus is born the celebrated myth of a writer concerned purely with his art, oblivious to commercial concerns, and hence somehow superior to those writers who do attend such worldly events and will gladly stand before a microphone, check in hand. Ironically, it was a myth that would eventually play to Beckett's advantage, both critical and commercial. However, Suzanne's letter—and it is impossible not to hear Beckett's voice dictating it—makes no such claims. "Perhaps," she / he proceeds cautiously,

> he has an exaggerated view of a prizewinner's duties. But if, as prizewinner, he could without unacceptable rudeness stay out of it all, he would see no objection to being one. You see, it is not an aversion of principle, but simply the fear of the other side of the coin.

Like so many of the letters in this second volume, this was written in French. It was an excellent decision on the part of the editors to give us throughout both original and translation. Here the French reads:

> si, tout en étant primé, il pouvait sans goujaterie rester dans son coin, il ne verrait aucun inconvénient à l'être. Vous voyez, ce n'est pas une aversion de principe, mai simplement la crainte de la contrepartie.

"If he could stay in his corner . . . fear of the other side." Is this a boxing metaphor? Beckett had been a good boxer in his youth. What exactly is feared here, the opponent, or being in the position of the opponent? What would it mean, reading the English translation, to fear "the other side of the coin"? Does Beckett fear success? Five days later Suzanne / Beckett writes to Lindon again to announce that "Beckett will not hear of being interviewed, whether orally or in writing. I fear that on this he is not to be budged. He gives his work, his role stops there. He cannot talk about it."

There is no assumption of a high ground or aesthetic purity on Beckett's part: rather, he is setting out the rules of a relationship: "son rôle s'arrête là." Indeed, he "is really sorry for the extent to which this intransigence may be unhelpful and awkward for you as a publisher." The paragraph ends with a clarification that is also an imperative: "One must take him as he is."

This determination to establish rules for relationships emerges again and again in this second volume of letters as Beckett moves in a very short space of time from being a poverty-stricken Irish émigré in postwar Paris, living mainly off handouts from his family and his partner's work as a dressmaker, to finding himself at the center of international literary attention with a rapidly growing income that allows him to buy a piece of land in the country and build himself a modest cottage. But rigidly defined and often extravagantly asymmetrical relationships were nothing new to Beckett and had long been a staple of his narratives. In *Murphy* the eponymous unemployed hero lounges blindfolded on his rocking chair, philosophizing, while his girlfriend Celia is expected to pay for everything and obliged to prostitute herself to do so. Murphy is really sorry about this situation (as Beckett was genuinely sorry not to accommodate his publisher); he would like to find some other arrangement, but remunerative work is beyond him. It is not that Murphy needs to dedicate himself to any artistic endeavor. He just can't do it.

First Love, written in French in 1946, strips away realism to make the asymmetry grotesque. Sleeping in a park, the narrator is picked up by a woman who takes him to her flat. There is sex. The narrator, however, then barricades himself in a bedroom, insisting that his beloved bring him food, take away his chamber pot, and expect nothing else from him. Needless to say, such a one-sided situation is not sustainable, and eventually he is thrown out. In *Molloy,* begun in 1947, the equation is altered somewhat: old Molloy lies in what was his mother's room, has his food brought to him and his chamber pot removed, but once a week someone comes and takes away a few pages of writing as well and pays him for it. Throughout his life and frequently in these letters, Beckett refers to his writing as excretion. Never communication. Rather, it is an excretion which, becoming an economic commodity—though Molloy doesn't understand how this happens, since one hardly excretes for money—permits other non-communicative but necessary relationships to be sustained. What is fascinating in these six hundred pages of correspondence with friends, lovers, publishers, translators, aspiring writers, critics, and theater directors is the slow meshing in our minds of the Beckett narratives we know with the author's own peculiar manner of dealing with people and then with the aesthetic he sets out to define in pages of the most tortuous prose addressed to the art critic George Duthuis. The reader appreciates, that is, just how bound up with Beckett's personality the work is. This makes it doubly frustrating that the editors have been able to publish only letters overtly to do with Beckett's writing, leaving aside those considered merely private. In reality no such distinction can be made.

This second of four volumes, annotated with the most generous and attentive scholarship, covers the period 1941–56 and is markedly different in tone from the first, which included letters from 1929, when Beckett was twenty-three, to 1940. Those years were tormented by a dilemma that threatened the young man's mental health; Beckett's parents had wanted him to get involved in the family quantity surveying business. Instead, he studied languages and in 1928 went to Paris as a young academic. It seemed a sensible choice, at once sufficiently respectable for his parents to approve yet not so onerous as to prevent him pursuing a career as a writer. However, on return to Dublin and Trinity College in 1930, Beckett lectured for only one term before resigning his post—he simply couldn't face a classroom—thus declaring independence from all parental expectation while creating a situation in which he would remain financially dependent on those he had so disappointed. Like Murphy or the hero of *First Love,* Beckett needed to be his own man, but he also needed to be looked after.

A battle of wills ensued between mother and son, with Beckett frequently setting out from home for London, Paris, or various towns in Germany in an attempt to establish a life for himself, but remaining all the time economically dependent and afflicted by the anxiety that he was letting the family down. As the impasse intensified, he developed a number of physical symptoms—boils, anal cysts, pelvic pains, tachycardia, panic attacks (they feature prominently in the early letters)—and a tendency to oscillate between attributing an urgent conventional reality to his plight, at which moments he would feel desperate, and then denying or belittling it, as if from the lofty remove of some rarefied realm of aesthetics. So, guiltily abroad in London or Paris, the young Beckett of the first volume might repent and declare himself ready to return to Dublin and the humblest employment; but once back home, he writes to his friend Thomas MacGreevy dismissing the problem in tones of intellectual mockery with much self-conscious wordplay, before going on to reflect at length on poetry and painting. One of the high points of the first volume is an unusually candid letter to MacGreevy in 1935 in which Beckett, now under Jungian analysis in London, breaks through this habit and acknowledges a possible psychosomatic basis to his ailments:

For years I was unhappy, consciously & deliberately . . . so that I isolated myself more and more, undertook less & less & lent myself to a crescendo of disparagement of others & myself. . . . The misery & solitude & apathy & the sneers were the elements of an index of superiority & guaranteed the feeling of arrogant "otherness." . . . It was not until that way of living, or rather negation of living, developed such terrifying physical symptoms that it could no longer be pursued that I became aware of anything morbid in myself. In short, if the heart had not put the fear of death into me I would be still boozing & sneering & lounging around & feeling that I was too good for anything else.

There is little of this sort in the second volume of letters. Gone are the guilt and dilemma, gone the sometimes elaborately contorted prose that had previously served as much as a bolt hole as a means of saying anything. In his fine introduction Dan Gunn suggests that the war and Beckett's permanence in France from 1939 to 1945 must have worked the change. The extenuating back-and-forth between Dublin, Paris, and London, with each of the different personal destinies those cities implied, had been interrupted; Beckett had settled into France and French to the point that he had a life of his own; and he had seen so much turmoil and destruction, lost friends and known friends who had lost their loved ones, that his own personal problems must have seemed less urgent. This makes sense. Perhaps there were other factors too. In 1939 Beckett had offered to serve in the French army; he wasn't accepted, but he did then work for the Resistance. This capacity to commit himself and take risks on behalf of others may have attenuated the guilt he had felt at not being able to engage in a "respectable" life as his parents had wanted. But most of all there was Suzanne.

Already acquainted with Beckett, she had drawn close to him when he was at his most vulnerable, hospitalized in 1938 for stab wounds received in a mugging. Six years older than Beckett, Suzanne would allow him to depend on her economically while retaining his independence of action to a degree few partners would have granted. She would also provide a buffer between Beckett and the literary world, taking his manuscripts to publishers, writing to them for him, and later going to productions of his plays to check that all was being done as he wished. In short, while this is hardly the scenario of *First Love*— the man barricaded in his bedroom while the beloved provides— Beckett had found a remarkable facilitator. Yet we hear almost nothing about Suzanne from his correspondence: Suzanne sends her greetings, Beckett tells us at the close of many letters; she asks to be remembered; she thanks someone for chocolates. In one letter he mentions her "heroically spreading out her dressmaking," and in another that she has painted a wheelbarrow red. But nothing about their relationship or her opinions. What letters Beckett wrote to her and she to him have not survived; one can only assume this was deliberate. Toward the end of one letter to Georges Duthuis, written from Dublin in August 1948, Beckett comments, "Suzanne writes, letters that are more and more dismal. At bottom, she is inconsolable at living." And a few days later: "Suzanne's letters are becoming more and more desperate: do get in touch with her, even if it's not your turn." Both comments come in the middle of long paragraphs and are immediately preceded and followed by quite other considerations. The remark "even if it's not your turn" recalls Beckett's constant attention to the rules governing relationships and the question as to what things may reasonably be expected of us. Not, as it turned out, in Beckett's case, sexual faithfulness. What Suzanne knew about his affair with Pamela Mitchell, whom he met in 1953 and corresponded with regularly and affectionately over the coming years, we do not know. Spoken or un-spoken, there must have been an agreement between the two as to what Beckett's role was and where it stopped.

The opening years covered in the volume are ones of serious economic poverty and remarkable creative fertility. During the war, confined to a village in Vichy France, Beckett writes *Watt,* in some ways the most extraordinary of all his novels and the last to be written in English. In long central sections of the novel, we see Watt, who is telling his story to the narrator Sam, inverting the order of words in his sentences, of sentences in his paragraphs, of letters in his words, as if unsure whether he wants his story to be understood or not. As a result, the manuscript would be held by the English authorities, when Beckett returned to Ireland via London in 1945, as possibly containing coded messages. Why else would anyone write in such a way? One can only wonder what the military men made of it.

Then in the immediate postwar period Beckett switches to French—not a code or game of inversions now, but still a language not easily understood by Dublin literati or customs men, as if Beckett were not eager to be read back home—producing first a series of shorter pieces, including *First Love,* the novella *Mercier et Camier,* and the play *Eleutheria,* until, in 1947, his French apprenticeship over, he launches into *Molloy,* which he finishes in just six months, immediately begins *Malone Dies,* finished in 1948, takes a break from prose to write *Waiting for Godot* (in four months), then *The Unnameable,* which he completes in January 1950. In three years, and all in French, this man who "simply can't" do so many ordinary things had produced the work on which one of the greatest literary reputations of the twentieth century still stands.

Not surprisingly, many of the letters of these years are full of news about what he is doing and where he is up to. "Forgive all these details about my work," he tells his old friend Thomas MacGreevy in January 1948. "My life seems to be little else." And again, "Suzanne earns a little money with her dressmaking. That is what we are living on at present. . . . It's a quiet meagre life. With no friends. With only work to give it meaning." Rarely enlightening about the nature of that work and the huge leap forward he was making, these details that Beckett apologizes for mostly have to do with his difficulties getting published: "My play in French," he tells George Reavey of *Eleutheria*, "was almost taken by Hussenot-Grenier," or *Watt* "was nearly taken in London, I forget by whom" (a footnote informs us that Herbert Read at Routledge read the novel with "considerable bewilderment" and found it "wild and unintelligible"). Having been through the same interminable round of rejections with *Murphy* in the 1930s, Beckett seems resigned to disappointment and even claims to have forgotten what the novel was about. Perhaps he is buoyed up by the new work he is producing so rapidly: "I see a little clearly at last what my writing is about," he tells MacGreevy with unusual optimism, "and feel I have perhaps 10 years courage and energy to get the job done. The feeling of getting oneself in perspective is a strange one, after so many years of expression in blindness. Perhaps it is an illusion." Illusory or not, Beckett does not tell MacGreevy what it is he has seen and put in perspective.

For some account of this new understanding, we have to turn to his letters to Georges Duthuis, where the energy that produced *Godot* and *The Trilogy* spills over into the most complex prose in French to be found in this volume, a French that pushes George Craig, the translator, to the limit, and a prose that in both languages challenges the reader's powers of comprehension. Duthuis had asked Beckett to write something to promote the artist Bram van Velde, whose abstract paintings Beckett greatly admired. A debate ensues as to what van Velde's qualities are. The premise for both men is what Beckett calls "the avalanche of one's impossibility at every fragment of a moment": experience, that is, cannot be captured in art, hence mimetic art is always a failure, when not complacent and mendacious. The special nature of Bram van Velde's work, as Beckett sees it, is that he has had the courage to drop every attempt or pretense to make an art that is in relation to anything else, whether in the outside world or the mind (the "non-I" or the "I"), since, as Beckett remarks with an insight worthy of a Vedic *rishi* or a contemporary neurologist, "what are called outside and inside are one and the same," each bringing the other into cognitive existence. Such an approach shows

> respect for the impossible that we are, impossible living creatures, impossibly alive, of whom neither the time of the body, nor the investment by space are any more to be retained than the shades of evening or the beloved face, and painting quite simply a destiny, which is to paint, where there is nothing to paint, nothing to paint with, and without knowing how to paint, and without wanting to paint.

Very soon it is clear that Beckett is writing about his hopes for his own work. "I shall tend irresistibly to pull Bram's case toward my own," he confesses. And again, "Bear in mind that I who hardly ever talk about myself talk about little else." To talk about van Velde, then, insisting all the time on the impossibility of talking *about* anything, is actually to talk about himself, while in championing a form of expression free from all relation to the world Beckett is clearly getting into more and more intimate relation with Duthuis, to the point that the letters often have a confessional tone. Indeed, when Duthuis asks Beckett to set down his thoughts in an essay, he declares that he can pursue the argument only if stimulated by the dialogue; otherwise the ideas won't come, since, as he later explains, he has not yet reached the day "when I shall not need another hand to hold in my wrongness."

Alternatively, one might say that to talk about himself and his desire for an art independent of all relation, Beckett needs, ironically, the alibi of van Velde and the community of Duthuis. Eventually, so paradoxical is the aesthetic being offered, a form of expression that neither expresses anything in the world or the self, nor is about the impossibility of expression, but rather a "vomiting one's whole being," an expulsion or excretion free from any controlled relation, internal or external (but requiring a publisher!), that Beckett ties himself up in the most tortuous knots, before eventually declaring that the debate "is turning into a kind of madness into which no one has the right to drag anyone else."

Rather than any intellectual paradigm, what the reader brings away from this exchange, by far the most remarkable in the book, is Beckett's aspiration toward something he knows makes no sense, so that it comes as a clarification when he confesses, "I have this frantic urge to fix up for myself a situation that is literally impossible." His frequently stated loathing of his own writing—each work declared nauseating almost as soon as it is finished, whomever he is writing to and often apropos of nothing—is perhaps due, in part, to his awareness that try as he might to achieve this relation-free form of art, his writing is always very much about both the world and, above all, himself. "Shall I be incapable to the end," complains his narrator Malone, "of lying on any other subject?"

Always stressing incommensurability, difference, and distance, failure to connect, between species and species, mind and mind, mind and world, at one point in the correspondence with Duthuis, Beckett quotes some of his favorite passages from the Bible ("For my thoughts are not your thoughts, neither are your ways my ways, saith the Lord"), including one from "that bastard Paul (Corinthians 1.15)":

> All flesh is not the same flesh: but there is one kind of flesh of men, another flesh of beasts, and another of birds.

This brings us to a happy paradox: despite or perhaps because of this insistence on otherness, on the impossibility of evocation, these letters, including those to Duthuis, contain some of the most marvelous descriptions of birds, beasts, and their flesh that Beckett ever wrote. From 1949 on he and Suzanne had rented rooms near Ussy-sur-Marne, then bought a patch of land, then in 1953 built a small house on it. Beckett's pleasure at digging the ground to plant vegetables and trees, and his fascination for all forms of life, come across throughout the letters with a spontaneity and warmth as unaffected as it is unexpected:

> Never seen so many butterflies in such worm-state, this little central cylinder, the only flesh, is the worm. First flights of the young swallows, the parents who feed them on the wing.

Or again,

> Yesterday . . . we startled a huge woodpecker, green and yellow (of course). It dug its claws into the trunk, briskly put that between us and it, then ran up to the top branches, I suppose. An absurd joy welled up in me.

Typical here is Beckett's renunciation of meticulous description—"green and yellow (of course)"—his readiness not to understand—"ran up to the top branches, I suppose"—and above all his excitement that the bird is immediately putting distance between itself and him, running round the trunk, disappearing in the top branches. "Other" the bird may be, but it has the same instinct Beckett has when confronted with the press.

In other places empathy, irony, and practicality come together in wonderful glimpses of a Beckett who just can't get enough of mud and digging and planting.

I keep an eye on the love-life of the Colorado beetle and work against it, successfully but humanely, that is to say by throwing the parents into my neighbour's garden and burning the eggs. If only someone had done that for me!

I scratch the mud and observe the worms, an observation entirely devoid of scientific detachment. I try not to hurt them with the spade. All the while knowing that, cut in two, they at once fashion a new head, or a new tail, whichever is the case.

All my trees are down in the cold ground where I shudder to think what is happening to their roots.

It is nature's inarticulateness, its speechlessness, its making no demands of him, that seems to draw Beckett so strongly, and whenever he feels that it would be better to give up writing, disgusted as he is by his inability to achieve the goal he has set himself, it is never to embark on some other career but simply to sink into the soil of Ussy-sur-Marne. "I ask for nothing more," he writes to George Belmont in September 1951, "than to be able to bury myself in this beetroot-growing hole, scratch the earth and howl at the clouds."

Despite this propensity for retreat and sometimes quietism, the story that these letters tell, ironically and inescapably, is the banal old tale of the dream come true, of rags to riches, of long labors at last rewarded. And that is one reason why they make such good reading. Unexpectedly, there's a feel-good factor. In March 1950 a frustrated Beckett closes a letter to Duthuis: "Still do not understand in what way art can help us to wait patiently." But in December of the same year he is able to tell George Reavey, "I have signed a contract with Editions of Minuit for all work . . ." and "Pretty well certain now that the second play *En attendant Godot* will be put on by Blin at the Noctambules."

In truth, there would be another two years of frustration waiting for finance before *Godot* premiered on January 5, 1953. Anyone who has read these two volumes of letters will sense at once where the idea of the interminable wait for some life-changing encounter, ever announced, never materializing, perhaps feared as much as hoped, came from. Beckett was now forty-seven and had been waiting twenty years and more. "Godot himself," he will write in one letter, "is not of a different species from those he cannot or will not help. I myself know him less well than anyone, having never known even vaguely what I needed." A good publisher and a fine director with adequate financial support might be one superficial answer to that question.

Needless to say, Beckett did not go to see the play at once—he was too anxious—but sent Suzanne to give him the lowdown, and immediately we have this letter of January 9 to set the tone of his protective attitude to his work for years to come. It is addressed to the play's director, Robert Blin, who was also acting the part of Pozzo:

> There is one thing that bothers me: Estragon's trousers. Naturally I asked Suzanne if they fall down properly. She tells me

that he holds on to them half-way down. This he must not do—it's utterly inappropriate . . .

Beckett offers some halfhearted explanation: Estragon, he says, would hardly be worrying about holding his trousers when preparing to hang himself; then, the "spirit of the play" demands that tragedy be seen as grotesque. But then he adds:

> I have lots of other reasons for wanting this business not to be underplayed, but I'll spare you them. But please . . . let the trousers fall right down, round the ankles. It must seem silly to you, but to me it's vital.

What is all this about? What are the "lots of other reasons" why those trousers must fall down, reasons which we immediately intuit are the real reasons? In a letter to a radio journalist asking for elucidation about the play, Beckett seems almost rude at first:

> I have no ideas about theatre. I know nothing about it. I do not go to it. That is allowable ["admissible" in the French, with a possible pun].
>
> What is less so, no doubt, is first of all, in these conditions, writing a play, and then, having done so, having no ideas about it either.

If the letter were to end there, it would indeed be rude. But Beckett pushes on with such a generous list of things he doesn't know and cannot be expected to answer that by the end he has made it clear how he intends the play to be watched, as something excreted that the author has introduced into the public space, something that simply is what it is what it is.

As for wanting to find in all this a wider and loftier meaning to take away after the show, along with the programme and the choc-ice, I am unable to see the point of it. But it must be possible.

Along with the falling trousers, another thing Beckett would strenuously defend in the play, against the wishes of the English censor, were references to farting and erections. And only months after the premiere of *Godot,* in a serious falling out with Alexander Trocchi, editor of the literary review *Merlin,* what infuriates Beckett is the omission, from an extract taken from *The Unnameable,* of a few lines mentioning the penis, erection, and masturbation. "This affair concerns far more than just me," he writes with quite uncharacteristic pomposity to his publisher Lindon. On this occasion, unlike those where he refused to get involved in promotion, Beckett is willing to move into the public arena to defend his text and talks excitedly about legal action. "I'll have the bastard's hide, even if it means losing my own." A passage from *Molloy* helps to clear up why these issues, to risk a pun, matter so much to Beckett. The narrator is talking about how he keeps warm in winter.

And in winter under my greatcoat, I wrapped myself in swathes of newspaper, and did not shed them until the earth awoke, for good, in April. The Times Literary Supplement was admirably adapted to this purpose, of a never failing toughness and impermeability. Even farts made no impression on it. I can't help it, gas escapes my fundament on the least pretext, it's hard not to mention it now and then, however great my distaste.

My fundament! The fart is the inescapable emission that will never penetrate the pages of the *TLS,* a journal that until that moment had indeed been entirely impermeable to Beckett's effusions. To miss out the farts, along with the unnameable's penis or Estragon's nether parts at the end of *Godot,* is to miss out the uninterpretable fundament that the work is discharged from. "It is this dailiness and this materiality that need to be brought out," Beckett writes to Carlheinz Caspari, the first German director of *Godot;* and to Alan Schneider, director of the American premiere, who had been having difficulty understanding the part of Pozzo, he remarks:

> Pozzo's sudden changes of mood, behaviour, etc., may I suppose be related to what is going on about him, but their source is in the dark of his own inner upheavals and confusions. The temptation is to minimize an irresponsibility and discontinuity which should on the contrary be stressed.

Quite simply we have a character who comes out with things that may have nothing to do with what is going on around him. Like farts, they are private to him, but nevertheless heard and, as it were, smelled. Indecipherable. It sounds like a manifesto for the play itself.

The work achieved in French, there was the question of translation. Beckett writes frequently to a prewar friend, Marie Péron, who checked his French for possible errors and to Jacoba van Velde, Bram van Velde's younger sister, who translated his writing into Dutch. There is a pleasantness and ease in his letters to these women contemporaries that marks them out from the tenser missives to his male friends. But when it came to translating his French into English, Beckett was hesitant. If the work was expulsion, excretion, what sense was there in going back to it? "I am not particularly keen on seeing all this come out in English," he tells MacGreevy of *Molloy,* reminding us that one of the reasons for writing in French might have been to say things in a language that wasn't easily read back home. *Molloy* begins, we remember, with the narrator's obsessive search for his mother.

At first, in his distaste for returning to work he claimed to loathe, Beckett assigned the task of translating *Molloy* to Patrick Bowles, a young South African. The decision was extraordinary. In the late 1930s Beckett had, after an early attempt at collaboration, taken over the French translation of *Murphy* and done the job himself. It was an immense task to bring into a foreign language a work of such willful and arcane complexity. How much easier surely to translate the linguistically simpler *Molloy* into his own language. And if he was to give the work to another, why someone who had no distinguished track record in translation? Perhaps it was significant that Bowles was neither English nor Irish, as if the language he worked into was not that of home. In any event it was a decision Beckett would rue. Letter after letter has him sweating over Bowles's drafts, realizing he will have to do all the work himself. After which there was *Malone Dies,* then *The Unnameable,* then *Godot,* not to mention the need to bring *Watt* into French; "This will go on for years," he tells MacGreevy, lamenting that he can no longer write anything new: "An indigestion of old work with all the adventure gone." "Sick of this old vomit," he tells his American publisher, Barney Rosset, "and despair more than ever of being able to puke again."

Yet if ever translation was creative, equal to, or even more important than new work, it was Beckett's of *The Trilogy.* The French was to prove a stepping-stone to a new voice in English, one so much more beguiling than the voices of *Murphy* and *Watt,* however remarkable those novels remain. Answering a casual enquirer about the reasons why he wrote in French (and Beckett is always more generous when responding to the curious reader, rather than the predatory journalist or academic), he declines to give a straight answer but offers a tantalizing clue: since he falls, he says, into "the dismal category of those who, if they had to act in full awareness of what they were doing, would never act," in order to write he felt "the need to be ill equipped." The suggestion is that, because Beckett did not know French so well, writing in the language would encourage impulsiveness. Now, in translation, Beckett could bring that greater impulsiveness, the unknowingness and vulnerability of his French, into English, adding a sparkle of very knowing puns on the way. "In any case, this whole question of climate left me cold," Molloy concludes the discussion of the impermeable qualities of the *TLS*. "I could stomach any mess." Success brought new friends and correspondents.

Pamela Mitchell had come to Paris in 1953 to negotiate an option on an American premiere of *Godot;* the affair with her was thus consequent on a literary success facilitated by Suzanne. Then, as well as Barney Rosset, who contracted to publish all Beckett's work with Grove Press in New York, there were German and Spanish publishers and translators to write to, Irish theater directors, anxious actors of various nationalities, and critics whose positive reviews often brought gracious thank-you notes from Beckett. In 1954 he replied movingly to a German convict who had put on a performance of *Godot* in Luttringhausen prison. Responding to a BBC radio producer, he first declines to write a radio play, then accepts with unexpected enthusiasm. There follows a back-and-forth as to the use of real or simulated animal cries in the recording of *All That Fall,* with Beckett predictably insisting that real animal calls were preferable and the producer assuring him that this was not the case.

Throughout all these letters the one piece of information Beckett never fails to convey is how exhausted and weary he is: "Too tired and too sad to be able to write a proper letter," he tells theater director Roger Blin. It is as if, before he can engage with others, Beckett has to make it clear that they can expect very little of him. "I'm so tired," he tells Barney Rosset from Ireland in the autumn of 1954, all he wants to do is return to Ussy and "cower till the first cuckoo." "Translations on all sides," he tells Marie Péron, "people to see, I can't keep up." "Overwhelmed with silly requests and letters," he tells MacGreevy, "most of which I feel I have to answer." In particular, Beckett is always too tired to travel to premieres of *Godot*. Often he talks about his future self as of some unknowable creature whose actions he can only predict. "I am invited all expenses paid by the producer Myerburg [to see Godot on Broadway], but presume I won't go."

This attitude of weariness is particularly poignantly struck in letters to Pamela Mitchell, for whom he clearly felt a great affection. "Tired and stupid beyond belief," he tells her. "I'm as dull as ditchwater and can hardly hold the pen." Everything is done to send her the message that he cares for her but has nothing to offer.

> Whatever I do I do on impulse and suddenly, so what I feel now does not mean very much. I don't want you to forget me, but I think it would be the best thing for you. I'm over, as sure as if they were on their way to measure me for the box. I wish you were happy, you have all the equipment for happiness—it seems to me. All the mad things I wish—and the sad things I know.

But the constant refrain of melancholy and tiredness also sets up the Beckettian gesture of resilience, the "I'll go on" that follows the "I can't go on." One of the most attractive glimpses of his writing life comes as Beckett rediscovers his creativity and embarks on the play that would become *Endgame,* featuring yet another asymmetrical couple, the tyrant Hamm and his servant Clov. In February 1955, before the characters have been given their names, he writes to Pamela:

> The losing battle with my maniacs continues. I have A out of his armchair flat on his face on the stage at the moment and B trying to get him back. I know at least I'll go on to the end before using the waste-paper basket.

But from this amusing note, which Pamela was no doubt meant to find endearing, in the space of a few lines Beckett passes to this: "Bill Hayter [who was planning a show of illustrations of poems] asked me for a text and I gave him the following, written a couple of years ago":

> I would like my love to die
> And the rain to be raining on the graveyard
> And on me walking the streets
> Mourning her who thought she loved me

In the original letter the poem is in French—this translation is provided in a footnote—and of course Beckett had made it clear that it was not written for Pamela. But how could his lover not understand it as meant for her at this moment? And how was she to interpret his decision to include it in the letter with no further comment? A few lines on, having mentioned a poor Agatha Christie novel he is reading, Beckett concludes:

> Paris is lonely, and Montparnasse in particular, without you and I feel remorseful that I didn't give you a better time that

last fortnight? Make up for it some day. Je t'embrasse bien fort. Sam

What is the question mark after "fortnight" about? *Endgame,* we remember, like *Godot,* features a couple who are constantly talking about breaking up without quite managing to do so. Then there is a postscript: "Will you tell me if this letter is sufficiently stamped?" And the story is still not over, for a footnote tells us: "The envelope of this letter was marked 'insufficient postage.'"

Whether coded, or in a foreign language, on stage or in an envelope to a friend, Beckett, like Watt, who reversed the order of words in his sentences, never seems able to decide whether he really wants his pessimistic conviction that communication is impossible to reach us. Or is he perhaps afraid that it might reach us, in which case he would be proved wrong. Insufficiently stamped as it was, this letter of February 17, 1955, did make it from Ussy-sur-Marne to New York, and indeed, still intensely alive with its freight of comedy and pain, into the pages of this wonderful book. One can only hope it didn't upset Pamela too much.

Georges Simenon

In 1974, aged seventy-one, having announced the end of a writing career that had produced literally hundreds of novels, and having retreated from a huge mansion with eleven servants to a small house in Lausanne, where he lived with his second wife's ex-maid, Georges Simenon dictated a "Letter to My Mother," Henriette Simenon née Brüll, who had died in 1970. He wants, he says, to understand her at last. To accomplish this he returns to the week he spent with her in hospital before her death. We are given the drama of mother and son watching each other intently day by day, barely speaking, as she approaches the end and he reconstructs her life from the beginning: the poverty of her childhood, the opportunist marriage to middle-class Désiré Simenon, her bitterness over her husband's failure to earn a decent living, her introduction of lodgers into the family against his wishes, including, during the 1914–18 occupation of Liège, German soldiers, her hysterical fury whenever she didn't get her way, her suspicion of her eldest son, Georges, and proud refusal to accept any money from him, her preference for her second son, Christian, and finally her second marriage to a railway worker with a house and a safe pension. The whole life is considered as a dogged struggle to achieve the one goal of economic security that "you set yourself at five years old." "You outwitted them all," Simenon concludes.

GEORGES SIMENON

Just as the two marriages were battles ("You were both afraid the other would poison you," he says of Henriette and her second husband), so is the relationship between mother and son, this long week in the hospital room being the final showdown. "Why have you come, Georges?" the mother gets in the first blow. She is dominant. "You know everything now," her son admits; "that's why you're superior." But over the week Georges will catch up, piecing together all he knows about her and deducing what he doesn't. And his is to be a different kind of victory. Simenon had long gone beyond his mother financially (the letter has frequent allusions to his wealth). Now, understanding her, finally recognizing that she did no more than "follow her destiny," he will go beyond conflict, so that ultimately he can say, "Don't imagine, Mother, that I bear you any grudge, or that I judge you. I don't judge anyone. If men have always fought each other since time began, it is out of their failure to understand their neighbours." Whether this overcoming of conflict is real or just a more complete expression of victory over an antagonist who can no longer answer back is something readers must decide for themselves.

Letter to My Mother suggests three kinds of winners, three kinds of losers: the mother who begins life with nothing, achieves the security she longed for, but was always tormented and hysterical, "always suffered life, never lived it"; the middle-class father who appeared such a failure to his wife, but in fact was always serene and happy within himself ("My father lacked nothing, my mother lacked everything," Simenon wrote elsewhere); and Georges himself, the most widely read and financially successful writer of his time and a man who had lived life to the full—"I have had sex with 10,000 women," he would declare in an interview in 1977—but who had not won the Nobel, as he had predicted and hoped. His own two marriages had both collapsed. His beloved daughter Marie-Jo was in and out of a mental hospital; in 1978 she would commit suicide. Afterward, Simenon dictated a memoir in which he blamed the girl's mother, his second wife, Denyse. She fought back in the courts. The battle went on.

This unhappy vision of life as conflict and the consequent dream of overcoming conflict through understanding is also at the heart of one of Simenon's finest *romans durs* (meaning a literary rather than genre novel), *Dirty Snow*. The book was written in the United States in 1948 after Simenon had left France, where he had been accused of collaborating with the German occupation; he had allowed a Nazi-run film company to adapt his novels, turning one into anti-Semitic propaganda. Meantime, his younger brother, Christian, had been condemned to death for collaboration in Belgium. Simenon had helped him to escape to Vietnam with the French Foreign Legion, where he was killed in 1947. Certainly there was plenty of conflict around.

As with *Letter to My Mother,* in *Dirty Snow* both conflict and the search for understanding are dramatized by having a protagonist who constantly puts himself in the presence of his antagonist without necessarily speaking or making their quarrel explicit. In an unnamed town in an occupied country, eighteen-year-old Frank Friedmaier seeks initiation into adult life through murder. Illegitimate, having never known his father's name, son of a prostitute who has turned her flat into a brothel, Frank grows up spying on prostitutes and their clients through a hole in the wall. But although money, power, and self-gratification seem the only values in the world he lives in, the surly Frank is nevertheless fascinated by the entirely wholesome ménage in the flat beneath his own, where a widower, Holst, lives with his fifteen-year-old daughter, Sissy. When Frank lies in wait to commit his first, entirely gratuitous, murder, he deliberately allows Holst to see him; indeed, that contact with the respectable older man becomes the only point of the murder, and when Sissy falls in love with him, it is the opportunity to attract Holst's attention that persuades Frank to court her. Eventually, having lured the girl to his flat to make love, he slips out from the dark bedroom at the crucial moment to allow his crony, the loathsome Kramer, to replace him and have the girl.

It is a disgraceful trick and one that almost costs Sissy her life. But again Frank seems most interested in Holst's response and deliberately hangs around the man's place of work as if demanding a reaction. Eventually, Frank is arrested by the Germans and interrogated for weeks without knowing why. Once more we have the proximity of two people engaged in a battle to understand each other, as Frank and his interrogator sit together hour after hour, often in silence, Frank desperately seeking to delay his inevitable execution by pretending to know things he does not. The reader too is drawn into the interrogation process since we are constantly in the company of Frank, constantly trying to understand the mystery of his self-destructive behavior. Eventually Frank achieves the victory we now realize he always wanted: Holst and Sissy come to visit him. Holst explains that he had a son who committed suicide after being caught stealing. He understands Frank. He forgives him. Overwhelmed, Frank wishes he were Holst's son. "It would have relieved him of such a burden—to say 'Father!'" The logic behind his provocation of Holst is at last clear. From this point on Frank makes no further attempt to delay his execution.

Almost all Simenon's serious novels would follow the pattern of transforming elements of his biography into nightmare scenarios of the most disturbing kind. Sometimes the protagonists would manage to step back from the brink of disaster. Such is the case in *Three Beds in Manhattan,* which dramatizes Simenon's 1945 meeting with his second wife, Denyse, and his violent jealousy of her sexual past. Eventually the battling couple find a way forward when she forgives him an infidelity and he gives her the power to make the major decisions in their relationship. However, when the same story is rerun in *Letter to My Judge*, Simenon's alter ego strangles the woman who has drawn him to leave his "cold" first wife. Spared the death sentence for what is considered a crime of passion, he kills himself in prison. It's worth noting that both these novels were written within a year of Simenon's meeting Denyse on arriving in the United States and while the two were living together with his first wife and child in a ménage à trois. Simenon was mapping out futures, more or less tormented, for the three of them. As Patrick Marnham remarks in his excellent biography, "The account of the experience became part of the experience." Neither woman headed for the door. Simenon by this time was a multimillionaire.

How does Inspector Jules Maigret fit into all this? For if Simenon is being drawn to our attention twenty-five years after his death, it is not for the forty-four novels he thought should win him the Nobel, most of which are out of print, but for the seventy-five "Maigrets" that Penguin is reissuing at the rate of one a month and with the expensive luxury of new translations by some of the profession's best-known practitioners.

Simenon published the first Maigrets in 1930 and 31. He was twenty-eight. Like most of his writing up to that point, the books were part of a project of self-affirmation as implacable and dogged as his mother's search for financial security. Having left school in Liège at fifteen, he had become a prolific journalist in his late teens, correcting a reckless, dissolute private life by marrying, age twenty, an artist three years older than himself, something that never prevented him visiting prostitutes and having sex with anyone who attracted him, however momentarily. A typical sentence from Marnham's biography reads: "In the Hotel Bertha he quickly discovered that one of the chambermaids was the niece of a novelist who had won the Prix Goncourt, and, hoping to launch his literary career, he had her in the hotel corridor one morning while she was kneeling down cleaning the shoes." Having moved to Paris in 1922, Simenon supported his wife's painting by writing scores of short popular novels under the pseudonym Georges Sim. Meantime a young maid had been acquired, who quickly became Simenon's lover and would remain so for more than thirty years, something his wife would discover, or admit to having discovered, only in 1944. Amid these precarious domestic arrangements, Simenon's financial success was extravagantly flaunted in endless parties and drinking bouts, until once again in 1928 the writer sought to protect himself from his own appetites, this time taking wife and maid to live for a year on a boat traveling through the waterways of France and Northern Europe. From then on the oscillation between indulgence and withdrawal would be a constant.

It was during these travels that Simenon began to plan the Maigret books, and in fact the first ten Maigrets were all published between 1930 and 1931. In a sense we might say that the burly, imperturbable detective was conceived as the kind of providential figure who might pick up the pieces and offer a generous version of events when the tensions in lives like Simenon's own finally blew apart.

Each Maigret novel is presented as a struggle, a battle, or a number of battles. There is the concealed battle that has led to the mysterious death with which each story opens, the battle between Maigret and any other detectives, magistrates, or politicians involved in the case (all obtuse, obstructive, or endearingly incompetent), then, principally, the battle of wits between Maigret and the murderer him- or herself. While all this is going on the inspector will quite likely have to struggle against the most appalling weather conditions, cycling tens of miles along muddy canal paths in pouring rain, fighting wind or snow, or laboring under suffocating heat. He will be endlessly tempted by strong drink. Women will seek to seduce him. Men will try to buy him off. Even geese attack him. He will be deprived of sleep, punched, and shot at. He moves through crowds as though "fighting against a strong current." Often it looks as though "everything [is] joining forces to unsettle him." But Maigret hangs on, grimly determined, his bull-like physique sustained by beer, sandwiches, pipe tobacco, the warm stove at police headquarters, and the knowledge that at home his chaste wife is patiently preparing the kind of dish that will not spoil however long it is kept waiting. Then there is his genius . . .

It does not show. On the contrary, Maigret's greatest stroke of genius is never to reveal his genius. There is no brilliant conversation. For the most part the inspector appears boorish, disinterested, disgruntled, absolutely resistant to theory, suspicious of advanced forensics, "devoid of subtlety." When asked what he is thinking, he invariably replies that he does not think. Asked about ideas, he tells us he has no ideas. Presenting himself as impenetrable—a "lifeless bulk" with eyes "dull as a cow's," "burly as a market porter," "a pachyderm plodding inexorably toward its goal"—he becomes more of a mystery than the mystery itself. The only intelligence that is occasionally allowed to cross his face is a mocking irony. Precisely this quality will be fatal to the murderer who is drawn into a battle of wills he can only lose.

Like Simenon himself in *Letter to My Mother*, or Frank Friedmaier in *Dirty Snow*, Maigret proceeds by enforced proximity. He goes to the scene of the crime, which usually takes place in a small, well-defined community, at the center of which there is probably a seedy hotel where Maigret will book a room. All is rapidly, effectively, evocatively described. He hangs around bars with the suspects, visits their homes alone and uninvited, eats with them, walks and talks with them. He establishes who is an insider and who an outsider, who is sexually satisfied and who isn't, which women are attractive and which plain or plain ugly, whose ambitions are thwarted, who has delusions of grandeur and power. If there is a pretty maid, he may ask her bluntly whose mistress she is. When he thinks he has his man, he sticks to him like a limpet, waiting for the other to break down.

In *A Man's Head,* convinced that a young Czech immigrant is the guilty party, but without any evidence to nail him, Maigret follows him everywhere, openly, ostentatiously, drinking in the same bars, catching taxis to follow his taxi, climbing on the same trains, encouraging an atmosphere of mute challenge. The real nature of police investigation hardly comes into it, nor, for all the claims made for these books, does Simenon show an acute penetration of "the criminal mind," whatever that may be. Essentially, the same dynamic that surrounded the author's private life is projected onto group after group of characters in seemingly endless and always fascinating permutations. The one character who has no parallel in Simenon's real life is Maigret himself, a fantasy fusion of extreme willfulness with benevolent understanding, a man who drinks enormously without ever getting drunk, who has an eye for the ladies and never falls for them, who always wins and never does any harm. Who would not love him?

A Crime in Holland, the seventh in the series, is typical. Improbably, Maigret is sent to the small port of Delfzijl in northern Holland, a place Simenon knew from his boat travels, where a French professor, expert in criminology, is suspected of shooting Conrad Popinga, an ex–sea captain turned teacher at a naval college. On arrival and already in possession of a list of other suspects provided by the professor, Maigret ignores the Dutch police and heads off alone to find the one young woman of the group, the eighteen-year-old farmer's daughter Beetje. In a very short time the two are delivering a calf together. Afterward, having tea in her bedroom, he understands from the quality of her French, the "silk dress that moulded her generous curves," and the books on her shelves that Beetje has quite other ambitions from farming. As she generously gives him a detailed account of the evening preceding the crime—the French professor's lecture and the party afterward at Popinga's home—Maigret quickly intimates that she had a relationship with the victim and perhaps wouldn't mind having one with him. His intuitions in this regard are never wrong. Despite the murders, every Maigret is also a comedy.

On Maigret's meeting the French criminologist conveniently staying with the family of the victim, "a tussle" at once begins, Maigret deliberately playing dumb as the other pompously expounds his theories. The Dutch police, when they turn up, are equally eager to impress their Parisian colleague. Maigret isn't impressed. Maigret is never impressed. As always, complications abound. The tricky geography of canals and quays and intermittent lighthouse beams, together with the awkward logistics of connecting bedrooms and bullet trajectories shot from this or that window, are a challenge to even the most attentive reader. At one point Maigret will cross a canal by stepping on floating logs to prove how one character could have moved from A to B more quickly than otherwise seems possible. Suspects include Beetje herself, her severe father, her panicky would-be fiancé, the victim's puritan wife, her sour, flat-chested, academic sister, and, for color, a local black-market wheeler-dealer whose sea cap just happens to have turned up at the scene of the crime.

Fearing that Maigret is homing in on a truth that would cause a local scandal, the Dutch police in league with the criminologist treat Maigret to an extremely heavy lunch, washed down with bottle after bottle of wine, during which they claim to have evidence the murder was committed by a sailor passing through town who had an old score to settle. Our inspector outeats and outdrinks them but does not take the bait. Though we have no more idea than anyone else what he might be thinking and hence are challenged ourselves, we are always invited to take pleasure in his victories, to feel that we are on the winning side, that we can trust him to sort things out.

Eventually, a familiar play of forces emerges. Popinga, the victim, loved life, loved music, loved dancing, and above all loved women, "all women," but was surrounded by repressive forces, by people who believed in respectability and preferred academic theories to living. He drank heavily, spent time with local black marketeers, made passes at his maid under his wife's nose, and was even conducting an affair with the wife's crabby sister. But the latter's love turned to hatred when she became aware of competition from Beetje, with "her two splendid ... eighteen-year-old breasts." Passion spurned, there remains "only the desire to conquer." At the end the real conqueror is Maigret, as he has Dutch police, French professor, and local lowlife slavishly obeying his orders while they perform a reconstruction of the crime, during which the inspector shows all his sympathy for the dead man's appetite for life and his weariness with the representatives of respectability, officialdom, and academe. But intuition and understanding do not bring happiness. Hearing much later that the sour sister-in-law killed herself on the day of her trial, Maigret "contrived excuses to shout at all his inspectors." The victory of comprehending the world comes at the cost of realizing just how awful it is.

One figure who turns up constantly in these Maigrets is the suspect who panics, has attacks of hysteria, cannot face the truth. In *A Crime in Holland* it is the young man Cornelius, who has courted Beetje, was jealous of Popinga, and breaks down in tears every time he is questioned. Faced with this behavior, Maigret is sometimes understanding, sometimes contemptuous, always impatient. He knows an attempt is being made to distract him. On reading biographies of Simenon, one discovers that such hysterics were as much a trait of the author's as the womanizing and the will to win. Simenon would often have panic attacks at crucial moments—when his first wife was giving birth, when his daughter was taken to hospital. The effect was to draw all the attention to himself when others were in danger. In 1940 he came back from a medical examination convinced he had been told he had a fatal heart condition and did not have long to live, a situation that had been his father's fate. Soon enough his wife discovered from the doctor that on the contrary her husband had nothing wrong with him at all. One can imagine the pleasure, then, for Simenon, of conjuring up a figure like Maigret, so utterly immune to panic of any kind, and likewise of describing those bold criminals who oppose him so ingeniously, then acknowledge their defeat with dignity, aware that they have been outdone by a real master. "You've won," says the beautiful Else toward the end of *Night at the Crossroads*, "but admit it: I put on quite a show." The difference between Simenon and the criminals, remarked his second wife, is that Georges "lacked the courage to be a criminal." To read the breadth of Simenon's work is to be made aware of the unbridgeable gulf between genre fiction and serious fiction.

The Maigret novels are immensely attractive. Simenon always creates a fine sense of place, simultaneously real and quaint; the characters are rapidly and effectively drawn, reassuringly recognizable, neatly arranged in relation to each other. Maigret's habits, his pipe, his beers, his brusque ways, his refusal to kowtow to authority, and his generosity with the humbler classes are always comforting. It is impossible not to like him, impossible not to enjoy his no-nonsense victories over human complexity as he puts everyone in their place and tells us exactly what happened and why. Even his willingness not to pursue a murderer when the criminal is more sinned against than sinning is heartening.

But after reading five, six, seven Maigrets, one grows weary. Nothing new can happen in these books, however intriguingly the old pack is reshuffled. It doesn't matter what country we are in, what town, what milieu, the same dynamics will prevail. Characters of the same kind interact in the same way. Maigret sits patiently beside them and understands. Yet despite our flagging interest we pick up the next one anyway. And the next. It's an addiction. The carefully circumscribed melodrama and the triumphant wisdom of Maigret with all the charm of a France gone by, made more charming still by the faint atmosphere of incongruity that hangs over translated dialogue, is as irresistible as sugar. Here is Maigret in *The Yellow Dog,* interviewing a barmaid. As usual, the people he talks to are generous with biographical details.

"How old are you?"
"Twenty four."
There was an exaggerated humility about her. Her cowed eyes, her way of gliding noiselessly about without bumping into things, of quivering nervously at the slightest word, were the very image of a scullery maid accustomed to hardship. And yet he sensed, beneath that image, glints of pride held firmly in check.

She was anaemic. Her flat chest was not formed to rouse desire. Nevertheless she was strangely appealing, perhaps because she seemed troubled, despondent, sickly.

"What did you do before you came to work here?"

"I'm an orphan. My father and brother were lost at sea, on the ketch *Three Kings*. My mother'd died long before. . . . I used to be a salesgirl at the stationery shop near the post office."

What was she watching for, with her restless glance?

"Do you have a lover?"

She turned away without answering. Maigret watched her face steadily, puffed on his pipe slowly and took a swallow of beer. "There must be customers who make a play for you! . . . Those men who were here earlier—they're regulars, they come every evening, and they like good-looking girls. . . . Come! Which one?"

Her pale face twisted wearily as she said, "The doctor, mainly."

No doubt Simenon was chuckling as he wrote, and it is all so easy to swallow. But when we do manage to break away to read *Dirty Snow* or *The Man Who Watched Trains Go By*, we sense at once that each of these novels alone is worth a dozen Maigrets. Without the reassuring inspector, there is a real danger in Simenon's writing; anything can happen and much appears to be at stake for the author himself. With their genuine exploration of how people push relationships to extremes, they offer a far more arduous and exciting level of engagement. One can understand why the French call them *romans durs*.

Why, then, did Simenon write so many Maigrets? Why did he go on writing them when he was already fabulously wealthy? In the final page of *Letter to My Mother*, the author has a revelation: along with her implacable struggle for security, his mother had always felt the need to be good, or to believe herself good. There was no point in winning and believing oneself bad. This was why she always had time for the humblest passerby, while largely ignoring her own children. Maigret, one might say, was the nearest Simenon came to being good, or rather to giving us a figure who is as good as one can be in the ferocious conflict life is. "The artist," Simenon remarked, "is above all else a sick person, in any case an unstable one—Why see in that some form of superiority? I would do better to ask for people's forgiveness." Unlike his creator, Maigret is triumphantly healthy, genuinely superior, and always ready to forgive those who love life.

Muriel Spark

Muriel Spark converted to Catholicism in 1954 and published her first novel to critical acclaim three years later. She was thirty-nine. Strange as it may seem, she always insisted that the publication could not have occurred without the conversion. Catholicism had enabled her to write. I cannot imagine another novelist, however devout, making this claim. So what is going on here, and what does it tell us about one of the most eccentric yet consistent bodies of postwar fiction by any British writer?

In *The Bachelors* (1960) the Catholic Matthew has invited Elsie to dinner with amorous intentions, but the idea of falling into a state of sin makes it hard for him to follow through with his project. Cutting up an onion for the meal, he decides that if he eats it raw the girl will be so put off by his breath there will be no danger of sinning. Then he is cheered, or tempted, by the thought that this is his last onion, hence absolutely necessary for the meal, a circumstance that seems to legitimize his opening himself to sin. But is it *really* the last onion? If there is another "miraculous onion" in the vegetable box, this will be a sign that he should eat it to stay pure.

As it turns out there is "a small shrivelled onion nestled in the earthy corner among the remaining potatoes." Surely not "big enough" for the supper, Matthew reflects. He considers eating the small onion, but fears it will not be sufficient to put a girl off, then "thinking lustfully of Elsie," eats the large onion instead. As it turns out Elsie's previous boyfriend was a great eater of raw onions. She is not put off at all and the two end up in bed.

Described like this the episode seems a tongue-in-cheek comedy of moral conscience. But beneath the competition between sin and purity another struggle is being played out. Matthew seems less concerned by any real wrong he might be doing by seducing his dinner guest than by the idea that his sexual inclinations are a sign of "weakness." In making love to a woman he will lose that absolute control over his life that all the bachelors of *The Bachelors* seek. In this regard a large onion is "a mighty fortress," a source of strength, while, comparing the two onions, readers will find it hard not to feel that the shriveled specimen nestling between potatoes suggests an impotent organ. Matthew "seizes" the bigger "peeled onion" and eats it "like a man," in order *not* to have sex. Virility lies in controlling one's own urges, in the victory over oneself.

From beginning to end Spark's work is shot through with these tensions. Whether it is a matter of controlling one's weight, being disciplined about work, ending a relationship, resisting a con man, or simply persuading others rather than being persuaded by them, the question of control and loss of control, or more simply winning and losing, is always at the fore. Her novels are full of ingenious frauds and manipulators on the one hand and ingenuous victims ever ready to succumb to them on the other. In *The Bachelors* a spiritualist medium is taking everybody for a ride. In *The Ballad of Peckham Rye* (1960) a man employed as a consultant on absenteeism ruthlessly manipulates both employers and staff of the two companies he works for. In *Loitering with Intent* (1981) an aristocrat and publisher is seeking to control the lives of prominent men and women by inviting them to publish confessional autobiographies, then blackmailing them.

But aside from the larger trajectory of the plot, almost every encounter, every relationship is a struggle to assert power, something that often leads the more sensitive characters toward mental breakdown. In Spark's first novel, *The Comforters* (1957), Caroline imagines that her whole life is being manipulated by hidden observers who are writing a novel about her. She hears voices, the sound of a typewriter. This paranoid delusion (based on hallucinations Spark herself had suffered while taking the slimming drug Dexedrine), though apparently a weakness, provides her with a weapon for manipulating her boyfriend, Laurence: she will not do as he wishes when to do so would satisfy predictions announced by the novel-writing voices. But Caroline's newly found Catholicism is also a tool of manipulation. Having accepted a higher value than romantic love, she can now deny Laurence sex without ending the relationship. She can call all the shots and still present herself as "good." "I love God better than you," she tells him.

To dominate with success, then, one must be able to believe one is not morally in the wrong, since this might cause anxiety and attract opposition. Likewise, it is good to have rules that prevent your behaving *too* ruthlessly, since if you start destroying the people around you—and Spark's characters are often disturbingly willing to cause another's death—society will ultimately exclude and imprison you; at the very least you will lose the antagonist whose weakness guarantees the dominance you enjoy. In this regard Catholicism offers both a tool and a brake in the struggle for power. Competing with others one *nevertheless* (Spark claims she became a Catholic on this "nevertheless principle") bows down to a strict moral code and a religious practice that cannot be questioned. One also acknowledges the triviality of earthly aspirations beside the all-important truth of our mortality and afterlife in an unknowable eternity beyond. Again and again Spark's characters find their scheming unsettled by reminders of death. In *Memento Mori* (1959) the plot revolves around a series of anonymous phone calls inviting the novel's geriatric but always embattled characters to "Remember you must die." In general, Spark makes ample use of prolepsis in her novels, with frequent flashes forward to the deaths of her characters that give a sense of the futility of their various machinations. The author's total control of her material is thus emphasized, often with great irony and comedy, but at the same time contained and legitimized in a project of Catholic admonition. Of her decision to start writing novels, Spark remarks, "Before I could square it with my literary conscience . . . I had to work out the novel-writing process peculiar to myself, and moreover, perform this act within the very novel I proposed to write."

The Driver's Seat (1970) performs that process and brings all these elements together in a schematic tour de force. Lise, who terrorizes others at the office where she works, whose straight-lipped mouth "could cancel them all out completely," takes a rare holiday. From the opening pages we learn that she will be killed the first night. Capricious and excitable during her flight and on arrival in Italy, she offends and bewilders everyone she meets, rejecting all attempts to seduce and control her, alternately playing the victim, the flirt, or the generous companion to break down and dominate everyone who crosses her path. Apparently on the lookout for a man, she eventually finds a reformed sex offender and persuades him, against his will, to kill her. Handing him a knife and telling him exactly how to cut her throat, Lise thus controls the one event that is normally understood to lie beyond control. Beside a story like this the decision to set limits for oneself by recognizing the authority of the Catholic Church seems a rather benign, if always "conflicted," solution.

Where did this unhappy vision of life come from? Born in Edinburgh in 1918, Muriel Camberg was the first child of a working-class

Jewish father and Presbyterian mother. Her Catholicism, then, would be very much a matter of setting herself apart, of joining a cultural elite that included Graham Greene and Evelyn Waugh. In *The Informed Air,* a posthumous collection of essays, she remarks of her humble Edinburgh origins: "The influence of a place varies according to the individual. I imbibed, through no particular mentor, but just by breathing the informed air of the place, its haughty and remote anarchism."

This hardly tells us much, and in general, in both her autobiography *Curriculum Vitae* and the essays in *The Informed Air* that touch on her life, Spark tells us little about her early or intimate relationships, as if to do so might be to place a weapon in our hands. *Curriculum Vitae* opens with lavishly detailed accounts of Edinburgh, what was eaten, how it was prepared, shops, prices, children's games, and so on. Observation is always a cause of pride and an instrument of control in Spark's novels. (Of Laurence in *The Comforters* we hear that "he is so observant it's terrifying.") However, in a rare moment of unguardedness Spark does admit: "We often laughed at others in our house, and I picked up the craft of being polite while people were present and laughing later if there was anything to laugh about, or criticizing later if there was anything to deplore." Mockery is in fact a constant for Spark's characters, who are forever putting one another down and, arguably, are themselves collectively put down by the writer with the amused connivance of the reader. Here in *The Comforters* is the "psychological thug" Mrs. Hogg exchanging words with Laurence's charming and ambiguous grandmother.

> "I learn," said Mrs Hogg, "that you call me a poisonous woman."
>
> "One is always learning," Louisa said . . .

"Do you not think it is time for you," said Mrs Hogg, "to take a reckoning of your sins and prepare for your death?"

"You spoke like that to my husband," said Louisa. "His death was a misery to him through your interference."

Of his grandmother's improbable relationship with a group of jewel smugglers, Laurence remarks, "We don't know who's in who's hands really." This question of who is manipulating, or just mocking, whom provides the dramatic core of all Spark's narrative. Speaking in her biography of her childhood encounter with the charismatic schoolteacher Christina Kaye, she remarks: "I fell into Miss Kaye's hands at the age of eleven. It might well be said that she fell into my hands." Thirty-three years later, in fact, Christina Kaye would be transformed into Jean Brodie in *The Prime of Miss Jean Brodie* (1962), the novel that made Spark's name and fortune. At this point Christina was very much in Muriel's hands, as indeed is the reader.

A word needs to be said here about the trajectory of Spark's writing career. A precocious poet at school, her talent recognized among others by Christina Kaye, at nineteen Muriel Camberg married the thirty-two-year-old math teacher Sydney Spark, who took her to Zimbabwe, then Rhodesia. Perhaps "he had a hypnotic effect on people," she says in *Curriculum Vitae,* unable or unwilling to account for this decision. Certainly there is no mention of love. Perhaps Sydney's offer of a household with servants and the leisure to write was persuasive. However, by the time she gave birth to a son a year later, her husband was behaving in an unhinged and domineering fashion, and all too soon she would be demanding a divorce. "If my husband had not been an object of pity," she remarks, "I would have been much tougher." Compassion in Spark's narratives almost always emerges as a weakness and certainly little is shown to the characters in her novels, whether the compulsive manipulators or their all too willing victims. One must look after oneself. An essay in *The Informed Air* argues against arousing compassion in novels since this allows readers to "feel that their moral responsibilities are sufficiently fulfilled by the emotions they have been induced to feel." Satire and ridicule are more effective tools of correction, she suggests, though reading Spark's stories it never seems that she requires a moral purpose to engage in mockery. It comes naturally enough.

Returning to England in 1944, Spark left her son first with nuns in Rhodesia and later with her parents in Edinburgh. She would never again marry; future lovers would soon be transformed from friends to foes. It is on the next thirteen years of her early maturity up to the publication of her first novel in 1957 that most of *Curriculum Vitae* and the autobiographical essays focus. This was a period when she held minor posts in various publishing houses and was briefly head of the Poetry Society, a role in which she rapidly accumulated enemies. The theme is always the same: Spark's struggle to emerge, the depth of her poverty and strength of her commitment, the resistance of the obtuse English upper classes, the eventual triumph of her brilliance, and, above all, the universal recognition it brought her. In an essay, "The Writing Life," she tells us,

> The majority of those one-time [rejected manuscripts] have become a part of my oeuvre, studied in universities. . . . I was really hungry and undernourished in those days. . . . Graham Greene, who admired my stories, heard of my difficulties through my ex-companion; he voluntarily sent me a monthly cheque with some bottles of wine for two years to enable me to write without economic stress. . . . I was now, also, Evelyn Waugh's favourite author, since *The Comforters*

touched on a subject, hallucinations, which he was working on in his novel, *The Ordeal of Gilbert Pinfold;* he was generous enough to write a review of my novel in the *Spectator* in which he said that I had handled the subject better than he had done.

Curriculum Vitae records personal praise from T. S. Eliot and various other famous names as well as including ferocious attacks on those people Spark felt stood in her way, all invariably dismissed as contemptible and misogynist. In short, even in essays written as late as 2001, Spark constantly feels the need to insist on her achievements, her winner's status, and though this is hardly attractive, it does help us understand the complex relation between form and content in her creative work. However grim the picture of human relations that emerges from her stories, the manner of their telling is always sparkling, terse, formally brilliant, determinedly *cheerful.* Spark as author will never appear downcast or deny us her wit and entertainment. We will not come away depressed. Our intellect will be wonderfully stimulated with complex metafictional games that constantly alert us to the writer's manipulative powers. Again we have "the nevertheless principle": society is a grim free-for-all, life chaotic and dangerous; nevertheless, I am on top of it and laughing. *Loitering with Intent,* an autobiographical fantasy in which a young woman outwits a ruthless manipulator to publish a successful first novel, which itself manipulates the stories of those seeking to control her, ends with the sentence: "And so, having entered the fullness of my years, from there by the grace of God I go on my way rejoicing."

Never is this surface brilliance and cheerfulness more evident than in her sixth novel, *The Prime of Miss Jean Brodie.* In the Edinburgh of Spark's 1930s adolescence the charismatic schoolmistress

Jean Brodie uses unconventional teaching methods and immense energy to take over the lives of a group of girls, the Brodie set, simultaneously befriending and bullying them, dazzling with wonderfully peremptory precepts—"Where there is no vision the people perish"—intriguing them with details of her love life, and seducing them with the notion that they are becoming a superior "crème de la crème" amid the sour milk of other envious students and teachers. In particular, having stepped back from a relationship with the school's married art teacher, whom she supposedly loves, Brodie has an ongoing affair with the younger music teacher, to whom, however, she will not commit herself entirely. She will not marry him. That would be a weakness. At the same time she seeks to have one of the girls become the art teacher's lover in her place. Needless to say, for all her brilliance and the immense energy of her "prime," events finally overwhelm and destroy her. One of her girls will betray her, suggesting to a hostile headmistress that Brodie could be dismissed from the school on the grounds of her enthusiasm for Mussolini and Fascism; once she has lost her position and with it her power, Miss Brodie's decline and eventual death, all foreseen early on, will be rapid.

Of the Brodie set, the girl who betrays, Sandy, is the one most enthralled by her teacher, the most intelligent, and for that reason the most in need of freeing herself. Almost at once she begins writing imagined love letters between Brodie and her old boyfriend to savor and take over, at least in her head, the life that has taken over her own. Writing is a tool of resistance and affirmation. Years later Sandy is appalled by the realization that Miss Brodie "thinks she is Providence. . . . She thinks she is the God of Calvin, she sees the beginning and the end." Hence her decision to "[put] a stop to Miss Brodie," as she tells the headmistress. After which, having vanquished her mentor and antagonist, Sandy retreats to a convent, becoming a cloistered nun and writing a book of psychology that makes her famous. Visited by old school friends and new admirers of her writing, she clutches the bars of the grille through which they speak to her, still entirely torn between the earthly ambition she learned from Miss Brodie and the ambition to curb that ambition she has learned from Catholicism. It is the same conflict that had Matthew choosing between onion eating and sex in *The Bachelors.*

Following *The Prime of Miss Jean Brodie*'s enormous success, Spark also withdrew from the scene of her earlier struggles, not to a convent, but first to New York, then to Rome, where she enjoyed life among the rich and famous, even buying a racehorse from the queen in caricature confirmation of her concern with competition and victory. But the highpoint of her career was already behind her. Success seemed to take the edge off her talent, perhaps because it was the visibility she had been fighting for, not the work in itself, and when the later writing does convince it is always via a return to the London of her earlier poverty, as in *Loitering with Intent* and *A Far Cry from Kensington* (1988), the latter galvanized by the revenge Spark is taking on her old boyfriend Derek Stanford, who had published what she felt was an unflattering and largely incorrect biography of her. In this case the plot turns on the moment when the kindly and overweight young widow, Mrs. Hawkins, can suddenly put up with the pushy would-be writer Hector Bartlett (Stanford's stand-in) no more and denounces him as a "*pisseur de copie,*" thus beginning a battle that will lead to her taking control of her weight, changing jobs, refusing to play dogsbody, finding herself a boyfriend, and generally becoming a winner rather than a loser.

More ambitious still, *The Only Problem* (1984) has a scholar contemplating a book on the sufferings of Job, something Spark herself had considered in the bad old days of her own sufferings. In

Curriculum Vitae she quotes fellow novelist Tony Strachan as telling her, "No one has ever been as poor as you were in those days. I mean someone of education, culture and background." *The Informed Air* also has essays on Job, with Spark characteristically concentrating on the contest of wills between Job and his "comforters," who insist that his suffering must be a punishment for sin.

Turning from the novels to the essays, one is struck by a continuity of tone. Spark is always emphatic, peremptory, authoritative. "I wouldn't touch the Bible if it wasn't interesting in historical, literary, and other ways besides its content," she tells us. Sometimes the voice is alarmingly close to Jean Brodie's: "Art and religion first; lastly science. That is the order of the great subjects of life." Or indeed Mrs. Hawkins's in *A Far Cry from Kensington:* "It is my advice to any woman getting married to start, not as you mean to go on, but worse, tougher." Her many put-downs are always splendid: "of course" *Gone with the Wind* "is bad art," she tells us, "but you cannot say fairer than that it is, like our Albert Memorial, impressive." Or again: "Mrs Gaskell possessed an interesting minor talent. She wrote badly most of the time. In spite of her social zeal it is impossible to take her altogether seriously."

Ranging from 1950 to 2003 the essays of *The Informed Air* are organized, not chronologically, but according to subject, an arrangement made possible by the fact that Spark's voice and opinions show no change over the years. However, while the essays about writing are embarrassingly but always energetically focused on her own success, a number of travel pieces seem limp and mechanical by comparison, as if the author were doing little more than fulfilling a commission. Only the appraisals of other writers really hold the attention. Mary Shelley, Spark tells us, writes about a man whose fabulous ambition creates a monster that reduces him to "a weak vacillating figure."

Spark clearly sees the affinity with her own themes. "Was Mary Shelley's life a failure, then?" she asks, reflecting on how little she produced and few friends she had. It is hard to imagine other critics putting this question. "She would have denied this," Spark immediately reassures herself.

An essay on the Brontës reverses the normal sympathetic portrayal of them as geniuses condemned to wasting their talents teaching the dull children of the rich, imagining instead what hell it must have been to be tutored by the likes of Charlotte. "Genius," Spark concludes, "if thwarted, resolves itself in an infinite capacity for inflicting trouble." Heathcliff is an example: a "moral hypnotist . . . able to manouevre his victims." Again we are in Sparkian territory.

But she saves her greatest enthusiasm for Georges Simenon. His extraordinarily prolific output, his frank admission that he wrote for money, his complete control over his art and "formidable" self-discipline all attract Spark's approval; even the fact that he dominated a love triangle for many years and that his daughter, "trapped by her hopeless love for her father," committed suicide seem part of her admiration. Simenon was "phenomenal." "He had a Catholic education," she tells us.

Philip Roth

In the 1980s I had the fortune to translate the late novels and stories of the elderly but still prolific Alberto Moravia. Abandoning observation of society for personal concerns with aging and sex, these books did not get a good press and have since disappeared from the shelves, while Moravia's earlier work will be a staple of any Italian education for decades to come. Translating, I was struck by the combination of a ruthless narrative dispatch and an almost cavalier perfunctoriness, the weightiest of themes being tossed off with an insouciance that bordered on slapstick. Thirty years later, reading Philip Roth's late short novels, one has something of the same impression. Above all, the author's chronicling of modern American history is now little more than alibi: the draft and the Korean War in *Indignation,* the 9/11 aftermath and Bush reelection in *Exit Ghost,* and the 1944 polio epidemic in *Nemesis* interest him only insofar as they induce an atmosphere of collective fear.

Death is everywhere in these novels. The words "dread," "terrified," "frightened," "scared" "horror," "jeopardize," "imperil," "vulnerable," "panic" abound. Only pages into *The Humbling* we hear that celebrity actor Simon Axler is "awash with terror and fear." In each story a close acquaintance of the central character unexpectedly dies in a way quite unconnected with the main events. Ask not, of course, for whom the bell tolls. Roth's question rather is: how to get one's living done given the precariousness of the human condition where "the tiniest misstep can have tragic consequences." Again and again, as one protagonist after another is denied happiness, the reader is reminded of the intensely phobic atmosphere in Thomas Hardy's novels, or of D. H. Lawrence's obsession with the need to confront and overcome fear at whatever cost. "Everything gruesome must be squarely faced," says Axler.

Roth is unashamedly didactic, and every aspect of plot development is bent to his theme. Death breeds fear, and fear spawns religion and social convention, reducing us to an oppressed half-life from which we break out at our peril. Under parental protection, childhood may be relatively happy, offering, as the young narrator Marcus tells us in *Indignation,* "unimperiled, unchanging days when everybody felt safe and settled in his place," but no sooner has the sex instinct kicked in than protectiveness is transformed into restriction. As Marcus ventures away from home, his hitherto stalwart father is suddenly and inexplicably terrified that any small act of misbehavior on his son's part will lead to disaster. The family, as with almost all Roth's families, is Newark Jewish and of only modest resources, circumstances that increase the protagonist's sense of vulnerability. Comically, Marcus is so infected by his father's apprehensions that, when excited by a girl in the university library, he decides not to masturbate in the bathroom there in case eventual discovery should lead to expulsion from college and consequently the draft, Korea, death. It is not American foreign policy that threatens him but his erotic drive.

Determined to overcome fear and become adult, Marcus unwittingly brings about exactly the outcome his father foresaw in a sequence of events that reads like an extended exemplum from psychologist Paul Watzlawick's classic work *The Situation Is Hopeless, But Not Serious: The Pursuit of Unhappiness.* Questioned, for example, by the dean about his difficulty with roommates, Marcus is so disgusted by his own fearful response that he launches into a blustering counterattack quoting Bertrand Russell's condemnation of religion and social convention at such great and vehement length that the dean is bound to single him out for punishment. Later Marcus will realize that even the apparent innocence of childhood depended on the constant slaughter that was his father's butcher's shop. The shop, of course, is there for the symbolism, not because the author is interested in cuts of meat.

Since *The Dying Animal* in 2001 Roth has alternated in these short novels between protagonists of his own age (*The Dying Animal, Everyman, Exit Ghost, The Humbling*) and young men on the brink of adulthood (*Indignation, Nemesis*). All were born around the same time as Roth, so that the novels of old age are set in our contemporary world and the novels of youth in the forties and fifties. Each story offers a new take on what is essentially the same plot: a sudden transformation, internal or external to the main character, induces a state of fear (in *The Humbling* Simon Axel has inexplicably lost his acting talent; in *Nemesis* we have a polio epidemic); fear heightens the desire to live and in particular the erotic drive: "I was determined to have intercourse before I died," says Marcus in *Indignation.* Eros and Thanatos are never allowed to lose sight of each other and will eventually be brought into abrupt juxtaposition as the story closes in catastrophe; having dreamed of a connubial happiness that might reconcile him to lost artistic powers, Axler is abandoned by his new woman and promptly kills himself.

At no point is any character allowed to challenge Roth's scheme. In the exhilarating opening pages of *The Dying Animal,* an exuberant sixty-two-year-old David Kepesh, ever "vulnerable to female beauty," has evaded retribution for abandoning his wife and child years ago and, largely thanks to the genius that won him a professorship and regular appearances on radio and TV, has been able to enjoy a life of sexual freedom. Society does allow some people to live full lives; but they must be brilliant and they must be artists, sportsmen, entertainers.

Even for Kepesh, however, there are rules. For fear of censure he no longer seduces his pretty students until *after* they have completed his course and taken their exams. With great gusto and clearly immense pleasure on Roth's part (his work, like Thomas Hardy's, has been accused of voyeurism), we hear how Kepesh seduces the extravagantly well-endowed, indeed "devastating," Consuela Castillo, "a creature so gorgeous everybody is afraid to sit next to her." All Roth's young women are objects of intense yearning, for it is the urgency of erotic attraction that creates a sense of vulnerability. Sure enough, no sooner does the professor get his girl than he moves into the realm of dread, afraid he will lose her, afraid she will devour him. To maintain some mental stability, he continues an old affair with a more experienced woman who he is now also afraid will leave him should the truth out about Consuela.

While Kepesh's determination to live intensely doesn't bring happiness, Roth won't allow a conventional way of life to seem more attractive: the professor's son is brought into the book to show how things can be even worse when one tries to suppress instincts behind a facade of probity. Determined never to perpetrate his father's crime by leaving his own children, the forty-year-old Kenny is nevertheless subject to the same erotic longings, eventually takes a mistress, and, with maudlin earnestness, commits to her as well as to his wife, establishing a second and even more suffocating prison for himself. The conversation in which the son with pious complacency describes his decision to meet and reassure his mistress's parents while Kepesh responds with scathing incredulity is one of the funniest in the book, but also an example of the author's refusal to allow anyone into the story who might challenge its assumptions. "One either imposes one's ideas or is imposed on," Kepesh tells us, acknowledging the fear that underlies didacticism. All Roth's voices, whether in dialogue or narration, are energized by an urgent, sometimes seductive, sometimes hectoring need to persuade. Internal monologue is rare. All is assertion and insistence, between the characters themselves and between narrator and reader.

If fear and the counter drive to overcome it are central, guilt and innocence, good and evil, at least until *Nemesis,* are rarely an issue. Kenny Kepesh's "good" behavior is governed by the fear of losing his self-image as a good person: "He lives in fear of a woman telling him he's not [admirable]." In *Indignation* Marcus is never morally concerned with "wrongdoing," only with getting caught. Guilt and good behavior are a polite mask for the codes erected by collective fear. *The Humbling* is one of the few books that give us "a horrible transgression": Axler meets a woman in a mental hospital who tells how "having lived so long in the constraints of caution," she went mad on seeing her "rich and powerful second husband" abusing her eight-year-old daughter. The story then focuses on her fear in confronting the problem. Axler's only advice is that she must "get strong." All the books are constantly concerned with the need to be strong in the face of danger. Of Roth's characters one does not ask what their moral flaw was, but where they made their fatal mistake.

Much of *Exit Ghost* revolves around what is supposedly a terrible transgression but which the reader is never able to conceive as such. Returning unadvisedly to New York after eleven years' seclusion in the forests of New England, the aging Nathan Zuckerman, another of Roth's established alter egos, is appalled that a young biographer is planning to reveal how a largely forgotten writer and mentor of

Zuckerman's, E. I. Lonoff, had an incestuous relationship with his half-sister in adolescence. Convinced that the revelation will destroy Lonoff's reputation, Zuckerman vows to block the book's publication. Unimpressed by the supposed crime (who actually cares whether a writer had a relationship with his half-sister in adolescence?), the reader soon intuits that Zuckerman's real concern is that his own transgressions may become the object of biographical scrutiny. Since Roth rarely risks leaving us without proper explanation, the matter is made explicit in the final pages. "Once I was dead, who could protect the story of my life?" Zuckerman asks. The fear that is the prime mover of all these plots now extends to events after death.

Of these recent novels, those focusing on older men gain from the alignment of the protagonists' predicament with Roth's. In these, quite schematically, we are given one protagonist who still just about has his charisma (Kepesh in *The Dying Animal*), one who is losing it (Zuckerman in *Exit Ghost*), one who has lost it, and with it, he senses, his freedom (Axler in *The Humbling*), and one who may have had talent but chose not to use it, the protagonist in *Everyman*. The closer the character is to Roth's own position the more energy the book has.

As a result, the novels of youth start at a disadvantage, though by setting them in Newark where he himself grew up, Roth does inject a note of fond nostalgia. Marcus in *Indignation* has talent and drive, and it is the young man's manic oscillation between self-assertion and fearful withdrawal into the safety of convention (he destroys a roommate's LP but then immediately buys him a replacement) that give the book its nervous edge. Eugene Cantor in *Nemesis*, however, is a different matter. The challenge in Roth's final novel is to explore the fate of a young man who is no more (no less) than worthy.

One figure who frequently recurs in Roth's novels is the solid if unimaginative father who provides his family with protection (a key

PHILIP ROTH

word for Roth). Indeed, insofar as the novels are interested in "good" and "bad" at all, it is the willingness, in a perilous world, to provide protection for the young and the weak that is the most prized of moral qualities, while failure to do so, or worse still, abuse of the role of protector to enforce constraint and mete out punishment (the dean's position in *Indignation*), is the worst possible crime. Deprived of parental protection by the death of his mother in childbirth and the imprisonment of his father, Eugene Cantor has been brought up by his grandfather, who "saw to the boy's masculine development, always on the alert to eradicate any weakness," eventually raising him to be a "fearless battler" and nicknaming him Bucky for the courage he displayed when killing a rat in the family's grocery shop.

A boy with no special intellectual powers, Bucky devotes all his energies to becoming the strong, positive, protective figure his parents were not. Rather than fighting society like a Kepesh or a Zuckerman, he aims to achieve self-realization by placing himself at the conventional heart of it. When America enters the Second World War, Bucky, unlike Marcus in *Indignation,* yearns to join the fight, to make his destiny one with that of his country. Alas, he is too nearsighted to enroll. Ashamed, he falls back on his sporting abilities and becomes a gym teacher. He will train boys to be strong, confident, fearless Americans.

For most of the narrative Bucky is referred to as Mr. Cantor, a curious anomaly until we discover, in the closing pages of the book, that the story is being told, not by an omniscient narrator but by one of the boys under Bucky's protection when, in the sweltering summer of 1944, he took charge of a Newark City playground providing activities for the town's youth during the vacation. The repeated formality, "Mr. Cantor," stresses Bucky's aspiration to the conventional role of teacher and protector.

Organizing games for the children, making sure they have enough to drink and don't get too much sunshine, the twenty-three-year-old Bucky is a positive, generous, confident figure who would surely have been equal to the task were it not for the outbreak of polio and the consequent welling of collective fear and ethnic tension as the Italian and Jewish communities accuse each other of causing the epidemic. When a band of Italian kids turns up, threatening to infect the weakling Jewish boys by spitting at them, Bucky faces the enemy down to the admiration of his charges. He is their hero fighting their war as surely as if he were on the Normandy beaches. The analogy is frequently drawn.

But polio is not an enemy Bucky can see or repulse. In 1944 the disease remained a mystery. All that was understood was that it was an infection passed on by poor hygiene and exacerbated by heat and humidity. As the first of his playground children fall ill and remain paralyzed or die, Bucky finds himself in the role of protector without possessing the means to protect. He visits stricken families, attends funerals, places himself as a pillar at the heart of society, but can't help but be aware of his impotence. When mourners sing God's praises, he rebels. Why praise the divinity who rather than protecting his people is a "cold-blooded murderer of children"? Thus does Roth use the experience of the epidemic to draw his conventional young man over to the anticonventional position of a Kepesh or a Marcus. It would be better, Bucky now feels, to worship the sun than this killer God with his "lunatic cruelty." "Better for one's dignity, for one's humanity, for one's worth altogether, not to mention for one's everyday idea of whatever the hell is going on here."

At the moment of Bucky's maximum disorientation, enter Eros to ruin him. Mr. Cantor has a fiancée. The girl is from a richer, intellectual family, something that intensifies her attractions and his sense of inadequacy and vulnerability. But Marcia loves Bucky, the couple plan to marry, and her father, a doctor and a protective figure par excellence, treats the young man as an equal. "Fostering less fear," he tells him, "that's your job and mine."

Marcia is a counselor at a summer camp for better-off children situated on a lakeside in the hills of Pennsylvania. Concerned for Bucky's welfare, praying to God, "Please protect Bucky," she finds a job for him there as a swimming instructor when another counselor is drafted. Bucky's whole identity is invested in his role as heroic protector of poor city children. On the other hand, Marcia has promised evenings of lovemaking on a secluded lake island.

Roth is not much interested in the vacillating mind. Dilemmas in these novels are short-lived. Despite misgivings, the will to pleasure, sanctioned by the anxious invitation of a socially superior girlfriend, quickly prevails. Bucky initially tells Marcia no, but only the following evening changes his mind, reneges on his contract, deserts his city post, and heads for the camp haven, where he hopes to reestablish himself as mentor and role model to another group of children who "could actually be shielded from mishap by an adult's vigilant attention."

Marcia has a "slender elfin" body, "vulnerable as a child's," something that enormously excites protective Bucky, but the couple's lovemaking on the island is spoiled when he expresses his rage against God. Marcia is a conventional girl and unwilling to listen to his provocations; if Bucky wants conventional happiness he must toe the line. "So, just in time, before he began to ruin things, Bucky reined himself in." Actually, he has already ruined things. For now he is tormented by the conviction that he should have stayed in the city protecting the charges God has abandoned.

If he could not fight in Europe or the Pacific, he could at least have remained in Newark, fighting their fear of polio alongside his endangered boys. Instead he was here in this haven devoid of danger. . . . Rashly he had yielded to fear and under the spell of fear he had betrayed his boys and betrayed himself.

An exasperated literariness pervades these novels, with their sudden revelations of unusual narrative points of view (in *Indignation* Marcus tells us that he believes he is dead and writing from beyond the grave), their frequent references to other works of literature, their elaborate extended analogies, symbolism, melodramatic overtones. So at this point of Bucky's story the rapidly sketched comic interlude of the summer camp's "Indian Night," when the children pretend to be squaws and braves, is charged with portentous implications and foreshadowings. As always, fear is the key. A boy in a fur coat plays the marauding bear that "ravages [the tribe's] borders": "I am fearless Mishi-Mokwa . . . the mighty mountain grizzly." The "braves" track him down: "Ho Mishi-Mokwa . . . if you do not come before I count to a hundred, I will brand you a coward wherever I go." The bear, who, like Bucky, cannot seem to be afraid, comes out from hiding and is clubbed to death, at which the campers cheer, their "delight enormous at finding themselves encompassed by murder and death."

As it turns out, the person who has "ravaged" the camp is Bucky. Six days later one of the younger counselors and his closest friend at the camp comes down with polio. Other victims follow, including one of Marcia's younger sisters. Bucky rushes to have himself tested and is found to be a healthy carrier. Entrusted to protect, he has brought destruction. As Bucky and Marcia talk together on their island rendezvous we have the predictable superimposition of Eros and death: "The birch trees encircling them looked in the moonlight like a myriad of deformed silhouettes—their lovers' island haunted suddenly with the ghosts of polio victims."

Such is Bucky's reward for having abandoned his playground post for the luxury of his girlfriend's body. Days later he himself shows symptoms of the disease and has to be hospitalized.

In the haste with which all these short novels are wrapped up, our narrator Arnold Mesnikov now introduces himself and explains how, twenty-seven years after that summer in which he also contracted polio, he recognized his old teacher Mr. Cantor in the street and heard his story. Wheelchair bound, limbs disfigured, Bucky rejected Marcia's desire that the couple marry anyway, isolating himself in a prison of guilt, remorse, and anger, living alone, seeing no one, growing unhealthy and overweight, laboring at a modest post office desk job. In terms of Roth's positioning of his characters, he thus enjoys neither the cautious pleasures of the conventional man nor the riskier satisfactions of the charismatic intellectual, Kepesh or Zuckerman; accusing God, yet paradoxically taking responsibility for events beyond his control, Bucky has got the worst of both worlds; seeking to recuperate lost honor by sparing his girlfriend life with a cripple, he has scarcely lived at all. "Nobody's less salvageable than a ruined good boy," remarks the now caustic narrator, onetime admirer of the athletic and inspiring Mr. Cantor.

Over the whole book hangs the title *Nemesis,* inviting the reader to interpret events in the light of Greek tragedy and in particular with reference to the grim goddess who made sure that nobody would challenge the authority of the gods. In case the reader misses the point, Arnold undertakes the discussion for us, criticizing Bucky for the "stupid hubris" that leads him to imagine he was "an invisible arrow" shot by an "evil being" to bring disease. Improbably, however,

Arnold then winds up his reflections, wondering whether after all "maybe Bucky wasn't mistaken. Maybe he wasn't deluded by self-mistrust. Maybe his assertions weren't exaggerated and he hadn't drawn the wrong conclusion. Maybe he was the invisible arrow."

The introduction of Arnold as a narrator allows Roth to remind us how the Greeks saw as divine intervention what modern man thinks of as the merest bad luck, while at the same time distancing himself from the debate and leaving his own position unclear. So brazenly, however, are we thrust toward this textbook enigma, prompted, as it were, to perform our own lit crit (with Arnie's help) on the neat story Roth has invented, that readers may find themselves more intrigued by the author's loyalty to tired literary stratagem than interested in the fate of characters who were never much more than pieces on a chessboard.

Exit Ghost contains much bitter criticism of the crude literalism of a biographical approach to a writer's oeuvre. All the same, these novels, each a little disappointing if taken singly, become interesting precisely if we are willing to think of them as an extended conversation the author has been conducting with himself about his own negotiations with social convention. *The Dying Animal, The Humbling,* and *Exit Ghost* all revel in the prospect of a return in old age to an active, wayward sex life, insisting on its legitimacy in the teeth of moral nicety, yet their unhappy denouements carry the stern and conservative warning (for whom if not for the charismatic writer himself?) that such a path can only lead to disaster. Stepping back from that immediate subject, *Indignation* and now *Nemesis* remind us of the intensities and delights of youth (in the memory-drenched territory of Roth's childhood Newark), but also of all its fatal pitfalls, inseparable as ever from Eros: Marcus dies young and Bucky, who never had the charisma required to be a successful moral rebel, lives as the ghost of himself. At least Kepesh and Zuckerman, however frustrated in old age, have had long and fruitful lives.

The construction of the novels shares many of the traits Roth repeatedly describes in his characters: the same catastrophic vision and consequent need to keep tight control on everything; the same desire to shock, to be free of convention's shackles, but simultaneously to seek society's approval (through that traditional literariness, for example, or through evident self-caricature in abject alter egos); the same yearning to be at the heart of life—hence the long lingering descriptions of female beauty—and the same fear of being destroyed by life—hence the sudden distancing tactics in these dissatisfactory endings where melodrama is hurriedly wrapped up in a flurry of literary allusion that drains reality from the story.

When the gorgeous, devastating Consuela abandons him, Kepesh, who likes to rhyme "aestheticizing" with "anesthetizing," seeks refuge in masturbation and music. "I played Beethoven and I masturbated. I played Mozart and I masturbated." These lonely pleasures allow him to partake safely, as it were *in memoriam,* of a little of life's intensity. Later, in *Exit Ghost,* he is reduced to sketching out a screenplay of an erotic encounter that will occur between himself and a woman forty years his junior. Literature as a form of protection from life, perhaps, a strategy for evoking and then overcoming fear, as the Indians called up the bear and killed it? Certainly, it is insofar as this body of work draws our attention to Roth himself and the endgame he is doggedly playing out that they begin to exercise some power over the imagination.

J. M. Coetzee

Following *Boyhood* (1997) and *Youth* (2002), *Summertime* concludes John Coetzee's autobiographical trilogy. It is a teasing and surprisingly funny book, at once as elaborately elusive and determinedly confessional as ever autobiography could be. If *Boyhood* and *Youth* were remarkable for Coetzee's use of the third person, the author declining to identify with his younger self, and the present tense, a narrative device more commonly associated with fiction than memoir, *Summertime* takes both distancing and novelizing a step further: despite our seeing Coetzee's name on the cover and hence assuming the author alive and well, we are soon asked to believe that he is now dead, the book being made up of five interviews conducted by an anonymous biographer who is speaking to people he presumes were important to the writer during the years 1972–75. Coetzee's reflections on his younger self are thus articulated through his imaginings of what people might remember of him and choose to disclose to an unauthorized biographer who is increasingly anxious that the material he is gathering will disappoint. It is at once clear that any attempt to establish the truth status of *Summertime,* or indeed the trilogy as a whole, is unlikely to yield satisfying results.

All three books bear the subtitle *Scenes from Provincial Life,* suggesting an attempt to shift the focus away from biography and to remind us that "no man is an island, entire unto himself"; each of us must be understood in relation to those we live among. The irony here is that in *Youth* the young Coetzee is determined to prove "that each man *is* an island" (my emphasis), while in *Summertime* an ex-lover remembers Coetzee as having an "autistic quality," not "constructed to fit into or be fitted into. Like a sphere. Like a glass ball. There was no way to connect with him." If personality is to be understood through one's negotiations with others, the burden of this trilogy is that for Coetzee such negotiations have always been arduous.

Boyhood tells of a child trying to find a position he can be comfortable with, first inside a family, then a larger community. But in the South Africa of the 1940s, in a family of Afrikaans origin that has chosen to speak English, in a stridently Christian community where his parents are agnostic, with a father who never hits his children but allows a black servant boy to be whipped, this is far from easy. The young John wants his mother to be always "in the house, waiting for him when he comes home to her," but at the same time resents her possessive love and is secretive in response. He does not speak about his problems with violence, his revulsion from it—whether it be the castration of farm animals, canings at school, or the whipping of black boys—yet fascination with it.

It is over the issue of violence that John first feels isolated. Other boys in the class have been caned, he has not. He fears the cane, the humiliation of punishment, but feels he must undergo this initiation to take his place in the world. However, initiation is understood as a test that might expose his inadequacy. John behaves scrupulously to avoid arousing his teachers' ire and works hard to be top of the class, hoping this achievement will substitute for initiation, though in fact it only emphasizes his isolation.

The question of religion provides another comedy of positioning. Leaving Cape Town for provincial Worcester, on arrival at his new school John is asked whether he is Christian, Catholic, or Jewish. Since his family is "nothing," he says Catholic at random, unaware that as a consequence he will be excluded from the morning assemblies of the Christian majority, mocked as Jewish by other boys, and harassed by the school's few real Catholics, who realize at once that he has never been to catechism. The predicament would be hilarious if the boy didn't suffer so much. He now wishes to declare himself Christian and join the majority, but fears that if he does so his shameful ignorance will be exposed and he will be "disgraced." "Disgrace" is an important word for Coetzee; it marks the point where a test is failed, shame is made public, and the guilty party ostracized.

In a world divided into blacks and whites, Afrikaans and English, Christians and Jews, the boy tries to line up the various sides and decide where he stands. The Afrikaans are surly and violent, the English gentlemanly and nonviolent, except that then it is a nice English friend of his father's who whips the black boy. Confused, John looks to his mother for guidance, but "she says so many different things at different times that he does not know what she really thinks." Exasperated, he nevertheless sympathizes with his mother when his father's relatives are less than warm to her on their huge farm in the Karoo. However, this Afrikaans farm is the only place where John feels at home. "The secret and sacred word that binds him to the farm is *belong* . . . : *I belong on the farm.* What he really believes but does not utter, what he keeps to himself for fear that the spell will end, is a different form of the word: *I belong to the farm.*" It is a fatal attraction, for, as John will later appreciate, the farm, the Karoo, Africa itself, does not belong to him or his forebears. It was stolen. There is no honorable place for John in the Karoo he loves.

Boyhood ends with the disgrace of John's father. Expelled from legal practice for shady dealings, he lies on his bed tossing cigarette stubs into the urine in his chamber pot while his wife works all hours to save the family from ruin. John cannot bear the thought that his mother's self-sacrifice will demand a lifetime's gratitude in return. Yet he fears her judgment of his mean-spiritedness. "He would rather be blind and deaf than know what she thinks of him. He would rather live like a tortoise inside its shell." It is the closest the boy gets to imagining a position for himself.

Youth picks up the story as Coetzee, in his late teens, seeks an escape from his dilemmas in literature, "For he will be an artist, that has long been settled." Yet at Cape Town University he is studying mathematics, and in London he will work as a computer programmer, hiding his vocation for fear of being exposed as a fool. While in *Boyhood* John looked for his place among religions and ethnic groupings, now he measures himself against great minds past and present. Rousseau and Plato would approve of his simple diet. Pound and Eliot warn him to be ready to suffer, Picasso and Henry Miller invite him to initiation through passion. Sexual passion is a sign of election in an artist. So John allows himself to be seduced by the neurotic, older Jacqueline, who moves in with him and makes his life a misery for six months. Again, and always with Coetzee's characteristic precision and restraint, the book allows comedy and misery to vibrate together, never quite inviting us to laugh or weep out loud, but constantly forcing the smile on the wince, the wince on the smile.

There have been other memoirs written in third person. In *The Education of Henry Adams* (1907) the author passes disparaging remarks about himself with polished irony, preempting more aggressive biographers while eliding uncomfortable sections of his private life, in particular his marriage and his wife's suicide. Thomas Hardy wrote a guarded autobiography in third person, arranging for posthumous publication under his second wife's name. Anxious about exposure of any kind, Hardy destroyed the letters and notebooks he worked from, forcing biographers to use his own version of his life as their principal source. But while Coetzee has always been an extremely private man and his trilogy offers only a very incomplete account of his life, it would be hard to claim that he is guarding against exposure. Unflinchingly, he describes a younger self whose inadequacy when faced with a girlfriend's unwanted pregnancy, or the bloody sheets of a lost virginity, or simply a stranger's generosity, comes across as cowardly and caddish. Perhaps, having worried constantly in his youth about being shamed, the older Coetzee is determined to be so "ruthlessly honest" that no future biographer can outdo him. Alternatively, one might say that in the absence of the corporal punishment he still feels he deserves, he is obliged to run the whole show on his own—transgression, trial, judgment, *and* punishment—the third person he uses suggesting the divided self that such a solipsistic project entails.

Where *Youth* differs from *Boyhood* is in its obsessive use of questions, the young man's thinking being made up of one uncertainty after another. So when Jacqueline makes a scene after discovering what John has written about her in his diary, we have:

> If he is to censor himself from expressing ignoble emotions—resentment at having his flat invaded, or shame at his own failures as a lover—how will those emotions ever be transfigured and turned into poetry? And if poetry is not to be the agency of his transfiguration from ignoble to noble, why bother with poetry at all? Besides, who is to say that the feelings he writes in his diary are his true feelings? Who is to say that at each moment while the pen moves he is truly himself. At one moment he might truly be himself, at

another he might simply be making things up. How can he know for sure? Why should he even want to know for sure?

Having no clear position in the world goes together with an uncertainty as to who one is. In *Summertime* one ex-lover will pronounce John such a "radically incomplete man" that it was impossible to fall in love with him. Yet toward the end of *Youth* there is a growing sense that precisely this incompleteness, his failure to become a South African, or a Londoner, or a passionate lover, his feeling that he hasn't really lived, will be his subject. In the British Museum he discovers the chronicles of early travelers in South Africa. Aware that this is "the country of his heart he is reading about," John is "dizzied" by the realization that these men "really lived, their travels were real travels," and it occurs to him that he might, in prose, construct a tale that, though fiction, would have the same "aura of truth" as these old travel books. It will be the "purely literary" project of one who didn't experience these things but whose concentration is such that the account will seem more "alive" than that of men who were there. This achievement will enable him to "lodge" his book in this "library that defines all libraries." Unable to find a home or to place himself in an intense relationship, Coetzee will be a lodger in the house of literature, writing fiction that seems truer than truth.

"How to escape the filth?" *Summertime* opens with a would-be biographer reading from Coetzee's notebooks of 1972–75 to a woman who was his lover at the time. The "filth" is the South African government's brutal repression of the antiapartheid movement as reported in the newspapers and denied by the politicians. Refused residency in the United States, John, aged thirty-two, is back in Cape Town and living with his widowed, apathetic father. Once again, positioning is important. Barely a half mile from their gloomy home with its rotting mudbrick foundations is Pollsmore prison, "the South African gulag." Most of the middle-class community live in denial, but John feels shame and frustration. In indirect response, he labors at putting a "concrete apron" of a thousand square feet around the crumbling house, doing "what people like him should have been doing ever since 1652, namely, his own dirty work"—as if this refusal to resort to black labor could make up for the shame of apartheid and earn John an honorable place in South Africa. What does Julia, the ex-lover, think about all this, the biographer asks.

There follows a sixty-five-page interview in which Julia, now a psychotherapist in Canada, speaks as much about herself as about Coetzee. John, she says, was actually "a minor character" in a drama played out between herself and her husband. While the latter was traveling, the lovers enjoyed an "erotic entanglement" in the marital bed. Yet John was peripheral to her life; at the one moment when she was ready to leave her husband and he could have become a major player, he "took fright" and sneaked out of the motel where she was sleeping.

Julia, or rather, of course, Coetzee, who is writing Julia's part, puts this behavior in relation to his fiction. *Dusklands,* she says of the novel published during their affair, is largely about cruelty, but the source of that cruelty "seems to me [to lie] within the author himself." Not that Coetzee was cruel to her. On the contrary, "His life project was to be gentle." He had "announced to me he was becoming a vegetarian. . . . He had decided he was going to block cruel and violent impulses in every arena of his life . . . and channel them into his writing." As a result, John was "the only man I knew who would let me beat him in an honest argument. . . . And I always beat him," since "pragmatism always beat principles. . . . Principles are the stuff of comedy. Comedy is what you get when principles bump into reality." Certainly there's comedy to be had in the description of this willfully unassertive man partnering a woman who sees sex "as a contest, a variety of wrestling in which you do your best to subject your opponent to your erotic will." "He was not in my league," Julia complains. When John tries to persuade her to moderate her lovemaking to fit the slow movement of a Schubert string quintet, the better to "re-experience" the sexual feelings of a bygone age, Julia shows him the door. "The man who mistook his mistress for a violin," she comments.

The humor intensifies in the next interview. This time the biographer has already written up the taped transcript as a colorful narrative and is reading it back to Coetzee's cousin, Margot, who frequently objects that "your version doesn't sound like what I told you." So we are constantly reminded that *Summertime* is a most indirect account of the author's life, Coetzee taking the same resourcefully guarded approach to the reader that his novelized self assumes in his relationships.

Margot tells how John brought his father to the family farm for Christmas, spending much of his time repairing his pickup truck because determined not to resort to black labor. As a result the vehicle breaks down while they are driving across the desolate Karoo and the two are forced to spend a shivering night leaning against each other across the gearstick. John, "whose body manages to be both scrawny and soft at the same time"—not a good fit for Margot— withdraws at once into twitching sleep while Margot berates him as a "failed runaway, failed car mechanic too, for whose failure she is at this moment having to suffer."

John's enemy on the farm is another cousin, Carol, who feels John is "affected and supercilious." Married to a successful German engineer and planning to escape to the States before South Africa collapses, Carol is a "hard" woman who is nevertheless "soft" when it comes to the suffering around her. "She is the one who . . . blocks her ears when the slaughter-lamb bleats in fear." In short, Carol, like the middle-class whites round Pollsmore prison, lives in denial. In his wry, roundabout fashion, Coetzee is giving us clues here to the political side to his work. When Margot asks John whether he remembers how as a boy he once pulled the leg off a locust, he tells her: "I remember it every day of my life. . . . Every day I ask the poor thing's forgiveness." Later, when Margot can't see the point of his studying the now dead Hottentot language—who can he speak to in Hottentot?—John replies: "The dead . . . who otherwise are cast out into everlasting silence."

Uneasy about his position in a violent world, experiencing every forceful action of his own as crime, Coetzee steps aside and in an expiatory gesture writes against the denial of the majority who are at ease, giving voice to the suffering that people like Carol are determined to shut out. Coetzee's insistence on evoking the world's unloveliness is part of this assault on the deniers, while his constant reminders that his text is made up prevent us from rushing to verify it or disprove it—he will no more confront us than he will Carol. Rather, we are forced back on our own experience to decide what truth there is here.

One sufferer unlikely to have had her story told if she hadn't crossed Coetzee's path is the subject of the third interview. Adriana, a Brazilian dancer, had gone to Angola with her husband in the sixties. Expelled, they came to Cape Town, where the husband was brutally assaulted. While he languishes in a coma, Adriana teaches dancing and raises her two daughters, paying for the youngest to take extra English lessons. But hearing that the teacher has an Afrikaans name, she fears he is not a native speaker. Worse still, the teenage Maria Regina has a crush on him. "Mr Coetzee is not an Afrikaaner," the girl protests. "He has a beard. He writes poetry." Indeed! Determined to investigate, Adriana invites Coetzee to their home.

What follows is high comedy. Coetzee tries to explain his Platonic "philosophy of teaching" to this no-nonsense mother. "*What a strange vain man,*" she thinks. And weak. And frightened. And ignorant. He invites the family to a hopelessly organized picnic. Convinced that he is after her daughter, Adriana withdraws the girl from his classes, only to find Coetzee writing love letters (about Schubert!) to *her* and embarrassing her by attending her dance classes. In *Youth* the young Coetzee had seen "no reason why people need to dance." Now his incompetence provokes Adriana's contempt. "*The Wooden Man,*" she dubs him. "Disembodied." "*He could not dance to save his life.*" Nowhere else does Coetzee have so much fun at his own expense, while simultaneously pushing toward the core of his uneasiness: he is not even at home in his own body.

The remaining two interviews, with university colleagues, confirm the bundle of character traits that over the trilogy we have been persuaded to recognize as Coetzee's. Nobody who actually knew him, the author would have us believe, found him convincing. "He had no feeling for black South Africans," Professor Sophie Denoël, a colleague and ex-lover, reflects; he romanticized them as "guardians of the truer, deeper, more primitive being of humankind." It was "politically unhelpful." Then *Summertime* ends as it opened, with fragments from Coetzee's notebooks. His father has cancer of the larynx and is operated on. John realizes he is being called on to nurse a dying man. The book's closing words are: "He is going to have to abandon some of his personal projects and be a nurse. Alternatively . . . he must announce to his father: *I cannot face the prospect of ministering to you day and night. I am going to abandon you. Goodbye.* One or the other: there is no third way." It is the last of a long series of tests. How John fared we do not know.

Nor is it clear how the reader is to respond to the fact—available for all to read at www.nobelprize.org—that in 1972 John Coetzee was married with two children. Presumably his family remained in the United States when he returned to South Africa. That he might never have mentioned this to lovers and friends is possible; that they, at the time of these interviews, would not have commented on the fact seems unlikely. So is *Summertime* an autobiographical novel that simply elides one part of Coetzee's life but is otherwise more or less accurate? Or does it excite the prospect of biography only to offer something mostly fictional? Or is the omission of the author's marriage and children at once the most discreet statement of his uneasiness and the loudest proclamation that we must leave aside categories and genres and make of the book what we will? Whatever the case, *Summertime*'s shifty position between biography and fiction becomes a powerful analogy for Coetzee's difficulties positioning himself in the world; it is as we struggle to get to grips with its mixture of disclosure and secretiveness that we come closest to him. And precisely as we fail to pin him down, we feel sure that this trilogy has earned its place at the heart of contemporary literature.

Julian Barnes

There are those who wish to have their cake and eat it too, and those who have learned to settle for one or the other. But there are also rare cases of people determined neither to have their cake nor to eat it. Such is Julian Barnes in his book on death, *Nothing to Be Frightened Of.*

Describing his "grown-up fear of just not existing," his nighttime panic attacks, and his inability to find consolation for the eventual extinction of his personality, he goes on to reason that, bereft of a reassuring metaphysics and given the findings of science, life this side of the grave is anyway irretrievably devalued, and individual personality doesn't in fact exist: we imagine ourselves "creatures of pure free will," but biologists have demonstrated that we are "mere micromoments of biochemical activity." *Nothing to Be Frightened Of* thus elaborates the author's fear for the loss of something he is already, paradoxically, grieving over: himself.

Yet Barnes remains very much the amusing author we know, entirely in character, writing a prose his admirers and critics would recognize even if his name were not on the cover. There is the same mix of intellectual dazzle and wayward flippancy, the same range of cultural reference (mostly nineteenth-century French), the same gift for witty and poignant anecdote, the same self-deprecating self-regard. Looking back at his earlier work, and in particular *Metroland,*

Flaubert's Parrot, and *A History of the World in 10½ Chapters*, all exuberantly spoilsport in denying the reader the satisfactions of traditional narrative, one appreciates that the doomed search for meaning and the willful self-entrapment in paradox are constants throughout his writing. The more the argument against character and personality is pursued in *Nothing to Be Frightened Of*, the more the reader recognizes Barnes's personality and character.

"I don't believe in God, but I miss him," the book opens. Barnes's older brother Jonathan, a philosophy professor, finds the statement soppy. This derogatory adjective from an adolescent lexicon appears on numerous occasions. Like his young alter ego in *Metroland*, Barnes is anxious throughout not to be soppy. To do that, he must accept brutal truths: that there is no meaning in death and no afterlife, that behavior is biologically determined, that the stories we tell ourselves to give structure to our experience are false and self-serving, that the immortality of the writer is a joke since his works will soon disappear, that in the eons to come "Bach, Shakespeare and Einstein will seem as distant as mere bacteria and amoebas."

Barnes accepts these propositions as facts but can't feel at home with them. He wants meaning. He feels "we long for the comfort, and the truth, of being fully seen." ("I had a dream of being judged," says one character in *A History of the World in 10½ Chapters*, "some kind of summing up.") Religion, Barnes insists, "gave human life a sense of context and thus of seriousness." It offered a "supreme fiction," not the deconstructed kind he tends to write. "Religions were the first great inventions of fiction writers," he writes. They allowed us to experience life and above all art more intensely:

Missing God is focused for me by missing the underlying sense of purpose and belief when confronted with religious

art. . . . Imagine looking on a Donatello as the actual face of
the suffering Christ or the weeping Magdalene. It would—
to put it mildly—add a bit of extra oomph, wouldn't it?

The Christian story is beautiful, Barnes feels, or rather: "If it were
true, it would be beautiful; and because it was beautiful, it would be
the more true; and the more true, the more beautiful; and so on."
That flippant "a bit of extra oomph" can be read as indicating the
author's determination not to come over as soppy.

But does it make any sense to talk of religions being invented by
fiction writers? And is a narrative that condemns to eternal damna-
tion those who don't believe in it really so beautiful? Hasn't it frequently been argued (often by church authorities) that the Renaissance
artists' increasingly realistic representation of human figures in biblical stories marked a shift of attention away from religious experience
and toward the profane? Do we really long to be fully seen and
judged? (I count myself out. I have no desire for such scrutiny.)

Objections of this kind spring up with great frequency as one
reads *Nothing to Be Frightened Of.* "Is there anything sadder than an
unvisited grave?" Barnes asks rhetorically at one point. Any number
of things, is my immediate response. But let's put these perplexities
aside and ask: Is there room for movement in the no-win trap Barnes
creates for himself: on the one hand, the "truth" of a mechanistic,
meaningless world that he finds psychologically devastating; on the
other, the yearning for a divinity who will assess his life and pronounce him fit for heaven, a reassuring idea, but, alas, as his brother
insists, "NOT TRUE YOU IDIOT"?

No sooner has he introduced the question of religion than
Barnes starts telling us his family history. Immediately there is high
comedy:

Grandpa, in his male armchair, deaf aid occasionally whis-
tling and pipe making a hubble-bubble noise as he sucked
on it, would shake his head over the *Daily Express,* which
described to him a world where truth and justice were constantly imperilled by the Communist Threat. In her softer,
female armchair—in the red corner—Grandma would tut-
tut away over the *Daily Worker,* which described to her a
world where truth and justice, in their updated versions,
were constantly imperilled by Capitalism and Imperialism.

At once we have a situation where characters (and newspapers)
define themselves in relation to each other. The absolute truths that
the author pursues are not on offer, but the milieu is convincing and,
as narrative, attractive. When communist Grandma subscribes to a
magazine that is mailed directly from revolutionary China, little
Julian gets the pretty postage stamps. His elder brother didn't object
because he

had decided to specialise in the British Empire. I, to assert
my difference, announced that I would therefore specialise
in a category which I named, with what seemed like logic to
me, Rest of the World. It was defined solely in terms of what
my brother didn't collect.

This, we recognize with a smile, is exactly how siblings become
different from each other and set out on different paths, their
characters and areas of interest at once distinct and complementary.
Julian's parents, too, fit together in an age-old behavioral double
act: the mother bossy, the father bossed. This disturbs the young
Barnes:

His clothes, the house they lived in, the car they drove: such decisions were hers. When I was an unforgiving adolescent, I judged him weak. Later, I thought him compliant. Later still, autonomous in his views but disinclined to argue for them.

Very soon, through a series of deftly evocative fragments, we have a picture of a family where emotion and affection must never be expressed, not even on one's deathbed, where the mother hides all larger issues behind her concern for her fingernails and the etiquette of setting the table, where the father (a teacher of French) comes to the fore only on the annual summer holiday in France, when his linguistic ability puts his wife in the shade, where the couple's early love letters are pragmatically torn up to provide the stuffing for a leather pouf. Barnes recalls only one occasion in his adulthood when he and his father were alone and free from the suffocating presence of his mother. "In all my remembered life, he never told me that he loved me." Later, speaking of his longing for judgment, Barnes describes it as a function of love; he who loves you knows you profoundly and judges you (positively): an almighty father.

"This is not, by the way, an autobiography," Barnes breaks off to warn us at about page 30, unwilling as so often to let us settle in a narrative. His parents have now died and, as part of the book's proposed discussion on death, he is "trying to work out how dead they are." This will involve, it seems, an assessment of how far their genes live on in their children (the brothers have inherited their father's partial deafness) and in memory. That the brothers' recollections of their parents prove not to coincide and sometimes to clash with documentary records will lead into the attack on traditional assumptions about character and memory, the first being a fiction and the second falsifying and unreliable. This in turn opens the way to an endorsement of biological determinism.

> There is the angle I sit at a table, the hang of my jaw, the incipient baldness pattern, and a particular kind of polite laugh I emit when not really amused: these . . . are genetic replicas and definitely not expressions of free will.

Barnes concludes the argument with a dismissal of our fictional view of ourselves:

> We live as if nature and nurture were equal parents when the evidence suggests that nature has both the whip hand and the whip.

This is astonishing. Only determined masochism could provoke such careless thinking in such a brilliant man. The patterning of a man's baldness is no doubt genetically determined, but it's hardly likely that if the infant Barnes had been taken from his family and transported to a radically different culture, he would have developed that polite laugh. This is learned behavior. Nurture. Indeed, as the reader discovers more about Barnes's parents, it becomes evident that, beyond genes and memories, one way they live on is in their younger son's continued resistance to open, flippancy-free expression of emotion and his simultaneous anxiety that he is missing something. This is a state of mind he was brought up to. The declared dichotomy, of creature of pure free will versus bundle of genetically determined impulses, is thus understood to be needlessly reductive. The way our natures tangle with those around us, those we grew up with, is far more interesting and complex than Barnes would have us believe.

Buttoned-up as his parents were and encouraged him "by moral osmosis" to become, it's no surprise to find that Barnes's "worst imaginings involve enclosure." He imagines entrapment in an overturned ferry, in the trunk of a car, even in a crocodile's lair (in *The World in 10½ Chapters* he defends the possibility that Jonah could indeed have been trapped in a whale). Suspicious of those who put dreams in books (too soppy, too revealing?), he nevertheless tells us of his dreams of burial, dreams of being underground "in some narrowing pipe or tube." In a short story written after his father's death he imagines a figure in a stuffy marriage like his parents' having an affair. "I was retrospectively . . . giving [my father] a bit of fun, of extra life, of air." Elsewhere, mortality is described as a box from which "the mind still seeks an escape." Even with his parents dead, Barnes is still bound by them and to them, still has to fight the need for their approval: "behind most writing," he announces, lies "a vestigial desire to please your parents."

Again, I must beg to differ.

Aside from affairs, or imagined affairs, one way of avoiding entrapment is to travel, abroad, or into the past, or into another language. So in his discussion of his fear of death, Barnes repeatedly takes time out from family history to draw on his lifelong engagement with France and French literature. He recounts the deaths and views on death of Montaigne, Flaubert, Zola, and, above all, the less-well-known (hence more privately possessed) Jules Renard. "Such artists," he claims (in the teeth now of biological determinism), "are my daily companions, but also my ancestors. They are my true bloodline."

Though Barnes's artistic heroes provide many pithy quotations and intriguing anecdotes, this strand of the book (amounting to perhaps one-third of its content) adds little to the overall interest except insofar as we are constantly reminded that French was the domain of

Barnes's father, the parent to whom he felt closer, potentially the more sentimental and certainly the more oppressed of the couple. Never simply an escape into learned cultural reference, the immersion in French literature can thus be understood as a piece of side-taking in Barnes's still lively engagement with his dead parents, a tussle that lies at the center of the book and is possibly bound up with his panic attacks.

In an article in *The Guardian* in March 2005, Barnes explained the structure of his most famous novel, *Flaubert's Parrot,* thus: "Geoffrey Braithwaite is about to tell you a load of stuff about Flaubert because he is unable to tell you the real story he is loaded down by. It will be a novel about emotional blockage, about grief." Certainly there is a load of stuff about Jules Renard in this book.

Readers coming to *Nothing to Be Frightened Of* for enlightenment on death and dying will be disappointed. As the young Beckett remarked in his essay on Proust: "Whatever opinion we may be pleased to hold on the subject of death, we may be sure that it is meaningless and valueless." Should we insist, then, that "Whereof one cannot speak, thereof one must be silent"? No. There may be nothing here we didn't know about death, but there's an enormous amount about Barnes and the conflicts out of which his work comes. In particular, we are allowed to glimpse the source of those antithetical energies that prompt him to create fictions with all their attendant emotions and simultaneously to disparage them, deconstruct them, avoid any illusion or soppiness.

The book may also help us to understand Barnes's relationship with the traditional thrillers he writes under the pseudonym Dick Kavanagh, novels where character and identity are still comfortingly possible and there is no danger of the self disintegrating. He allows himself this escape, but won't tie his name to it.

But above all, *Nothing to Be Frightened Of* offers the great pleasure, rare in nonfiction, of reading between the lines. When, summing up his life, Barnes talks of his decision not to have children as "an act of free will in the face of biological determinism," the reader cannot help remembering that twelve pages before he quoted his mother telling him, "If I had my time again, I'd paddle my own canoe": that is, avoid marriage and children. The "act of free will" begins to look like a response to a suggestion from the member of the family Barnes least likes, but whose apparently emotionless stoicism in the face of death he deeply admires.

Colm Tóibín

Here, in *The Empty Family,* are nine stories, one set in London, five in Ireland, three in Spain, three focusing on women, six on men, one set in the nineteenth century, the rest more or less in the present, all but two ending in a stoically endured unhappiness expressed with Colm Tóibín's now familiar quiet and rhythmical delicacy. So dominant is the unhappiness, so exquisite the prose that the reader cannot but wonder about the relationship between suffering and style.

"Silence," the opening story, is prefaced with an anecdote that Henry James recorded in a notebook as possible material for fiction. Discovering, only hours after his wedding, that his wife had previously been passionately in love with another man, an "eminent clergyman" refuses to consummate the marriage but nevertheless spends the rest of his life with the woman. The cruelty and sadness of this situation work the more powerfully on the reader's imagination for being left unstated.

We then pass to the story's main character, Lady Gregory, a historical figure who, like Henry James, has been the object of Tóibín's admiring attention in the past. Not as pretty as her older sisters, she married a man thirty-five years older than herself, achieving respectability but not happiness.

In the night . . . as she tried to move towards him to embrace him fully, to offer herself to his dried up spirit, she found that he was happier obsessively fondling certain parts of her body in the dark as though he were trying to find something he had mislaid.

Later, after the birth of a son, Lady Gregory had an affair with the highly politicized poet Wilfrid Scawen Blunt, a man whose "talents as a poet," in Tóibín's version of events,

> were minor compared to his skills as an adulterer. Not only could he please her in ways that were daring and astonishing but he could ensure that they would not be discovered.

This genius for deception is not entirely an advantage. Tóibín is convincing as he evokes the growing dismay of the person whose most intense and intimate relationship can never be acknowledged to others:

> The fact that it was not known and publicly understood that she was with him hurt her profoundly, made her experience what existed between them as a kind of emptiness or absence,

so that

> when the affair ended, she felt at times as if it had not happened.

This is what interests Tóibín, not just in this story, but throughout *The Empty Family:* how to respond to a painful sense of absence at the core of life, where family and belonging should be, how to avoid the feeling that there is no difference between "life now and the years stretching to eternity . . . in the grave."

Lady Gregory was resourceful. She wrote a cycle of love sonnets and convinced Blunt to publish it under his name, relishing the thought that people could read her story without knowing its source. When this subterfuge is not solace enough, she takes advantage of a moment at a dinner party to talk to Henry James. She cannot risk telling him the truth, but urgently needs to convey her unhappiness. So she invents, with the hope that he will rework it in a novel, the anecdote of the clergyman that we read at the opening of the story. It is not her life, but the aridity and sadness are hers.

That it was Lady Gregory who told James this anecdote is fact. That she was using it to refer indirectly to her own experience is perhaps Tóibín's intuition. In any event the implication is that fiction can offer a vehicle for expressing what cannot easily be made public. To an extent it respects society's rules even as it seeks to find consolation for the pain they have caused. Indeed its creativity in finding "a new background . . . a new scenario" (James's words) that make expression possible is actually stimulated by those rules. The reader is invited to wonder, then, whether Tóibín's story isn't itself a reformulation of circumstances and emotions its author may not wish to disclose, or whether the story has been placed at the opening of the collection to have us speculate that all the stories here may have this function, since, as we saw with Lady Gregory, one reformulation is not enough; the need to express remains. We may even ask whether the satisfaction of achieving an aestheticized expression of personal suffering does not preserve the pain by making it functional to the life of the sufferer turned artist.

The second story bears the book's title, "The Empty Family," and brings Tóibín closer to home and a possible alter ego. An unnamed, middle-aged male narrator addresses himself to an ex-lover, also male. He has returned from life in California to his erstwhile home on the Irish coast and after running into the ex-lover's brother and his wife is excited by the thought that "you must know that I am back here," though it seems there is no prospect of the two men renewing their relationship.

Tóibín is a master of literary tropes and very consciously seeks out images that deepen his themes and offer analogies of the way he works. The lover's brother enthuses over a telescope he has bought, and the narrator visits his coastal home to try it out. Here he focuses the telescope on the waves out at sea, which were "like people battling out there, full of consciousness and will and destiny and an abiding sense of their own beauty." He follows a single wave that

> had an elemental hold; it was something coming towards us as though to save us but it did nothing instead, it withdrew in a shrugging irony, as if to suggest that this is what the world is, and our time in it, all lifted possibility, all complexity and rushing fervor, to end in nothing on a small strand, and go back out to rejoin the empty family from whom he had set out alone with such a burst of brave unknowing energy.

Like the narrator and his telescope, fiction sees life in close detail, but from a safe distance, and everywhere transforms the particular into the universal. On meeting the son of the ex-lover's brother, the narrator remarks:

> He could have been you, or you when I knew you first, the same hair, the same height and frame and the same charm

that must have been there in your grandmother or grandfather or even before, the sweet smile the concentrated gaze.

In California the narrator had frequently visited lonely coastal landscapes, the better to miss his Irish home, which is not only the empty house but also the graveyard where he himself will "eventually lie in darkness as long as time lasts." In the meantime, "I will, if I have the courage, spend my time watching the sea, noting its changes and the sounds it makes." Like Lady Gregory, that is, who could hardly see any difference between her loveless life and eventual death, he will spend his time seeking out images that express his condition. He "will not fly even in my deepest dreams too close to the sun or too close to the sea. The chance for all that has passed." Thus the artistic impulse might seem to substitute for any return to life.

Is this satisfactory? The story ends with the narrator dreaming of purchasing a telescope "to focus on a curling line of water, a piece of the world indifferent to the fact that there is language, that there are names to describe things, and grammar and verbs." He is "desperate to evade, erase, forget . . . to know at last that the words for the colours, the blue-grey-green of the sea, the whiteness of the waves, will not work against the fullness of watching the rich chaos they yield and carry." Now the sufferer seeks an escape from both the intensity of experience and its inadequate expression. Paradoxically, we feel sure that he will want to write about this.

Having given us, in these two melancholy tales, a key to understanding his approach, Tóibín now offers seven rather richer stories, all variations on his theme, all calling to one another, reinforcing or undermining one another, like so many waves riding toward the shore, alike and individual. These are stories that need to be read together.

In "Two Women," Frances, a specialist in preparing film sets, returns in middle age from New York to her native Dublin to work on a film. Her cantankerous, overpurposeful manner is soon understood to be a strategy for surviving a life without intimacy. The actor who was her one great love, though never more than a lover, has been dead ten years and in any event had tired of her long before that, marrying a woman willing to focus on him rather than her work. Without close relationships of her own, Frances has installed a family from Guatemala, whom she employs to drive and clean, in a small cottage on her property, enjoying with them a relationship of mutual respect and affection, but where she has total control. In Ireland, which irks her because it recalls an idea of belonging that she feels neither here nor in the States (a common predicament for Tóibín's characters), she persuades the director whose film she is to work on to use colors more intense than those found in Ireland, thus creating an artificial, more beautiful world. In particular she is anxious about using the cluttered interior of a real pub for one scene. A studio mock-up would be so much easier to control and integrate with the rest. But the director insists; he wants the real thing. Stripping the pub bare in an attempt to make it manageable for the shoot, Frances is furious with two customers who will not leave, until she discovers that one of them is her ex-lover's widow.

If Tóibín himself sometimes seems a little too tightly in control of his material, a little too intent on pointing up colors and creating beautiful "literature," nevertheless it is a wonderful touch when he has Frances go to her car to put on makeup before confronting the woman who married the man she lost. She needs the protection of artifice.

Three of the remaining six stories are particularly effective in coming at the book's themes of loss and dislocation from new angles.

"The Pearl Fishers" has at its center a case of sexual abuse by Catholic priests, something Tóibín has written about elsewhere, explaining how, as a schoolboy, he knew and enjoyed the company of priests later accused of abuse. Here, an unnamed narrator, author of popular thrillers and violent film scripts, reluctantly accepts a dinner invitation from two old friends, Donnacha and Gráinne, once his school debating partners. It was after a school debate that he and Donnacha had begun a homosexual liaison that lasted many years. But Donnacha was "very much part of the culture that produced him," a man with a "deep laziness and contentment" that allowed him to "tolerate" and "enjoy" his homosexual lover "until something more normal and simple moved into his orbit," which is to say Gráinne, his ambitious and forceful wife. The narrator's hard-boiled fiction, like Frances's belligerence in the earlier story, would appear to be a defense mechanism in response to lost affection. "You're actually a big softie," Gráinne will remark over dinner.

About the time the adolescent affair with Donnacha began, the narrator went through a religious phase that saw him sitting in the study of priest and theologian Patrick Moorehouse, who encouraged him to read John Donne and Simon Weil, though, as the narrator acknowledges, "my fascination" was "entirely sexual." Often Gráinne would also come to these discussions, and now, decades later, in the Dublin restaurant she explains that she has written a book denouncing Moorehouse for having abused her sexually. She has invited the narrator to dinner to ask for his corroboration.

Here, then, is another occasion where one who has suffered seeks expression. But the narrator, who was not abused, suspects that Gráinne is cashing in on the interest in priestly pedophilia and that her anger is a function of prima-donna ambitions. Meantime, he has promised Donnacha that he will never reveal to Gráinne that they were lovers, a reticence he finds painful. The ensuing clash between a brash, self-serving political correctness and a wounded, defensively cynical sensitivity is excitingly dramatized, while at the structural level a story that may be imagined as a creative reformulation of real experiences balances one character who out of loyalty suppresses truth against another who exploits and magnifies her victimhood. Ironically, the lesson Moorehouse sought to teach both of them was to find words to "match their feelings," "working our doubts and fears into sentences."

"The New Spain" is another story of expatriation, return, and alienation from a family of origin. Pursued for her communist activism, Carme fled Franco's Spain and spent eight years in London, living on handouts from her grandmother and idealizing her Barcelona childhood. She returns not immediately on Franco's demise but only after the death of her grandmother, who has bequeathed her considerable property on Carme and her sister, not their parents. Hence when Carme finds mother, father, and sister in their holiday home in Minorca, she is no longer the deplored rebel but the powerful owner.

Tóibín is skilled at turning clichés on their heads. Nostalgic and sentimental, Carme is upset that her father and mother have "spoiled" the old family home, developing cheap bungalows on the surrounding coastland, replacing olive trees with a swimming pool, selling off the grandmother's antique furniture. On the other hand, her brusque response, repurchasing the furniture and threatening to reverse all the changes, is a declaration of war that will destroy all family feeling. She wants the house and its traditional Spanish charms, "but emptied of the people who might be in them." She wants to enjoy the all-night village festivities to celebrate San Juan, the folklore and the color, but when she picks up a man there and brings him home in the early hours, the intention is clearly to let her mother know that she does what she wants and will respect no one.

Again Tóibín invites us to distinguish between an action and the deeper sentiment that motivates it. However courageous and politically appropriate at the time, Carme's communism, we now suspect, was, like Gráinne's crusade for the truth, largely to do with a penchant for contrariness and grabbing the limelight. That said, the achievement of this story, which stands out as the most accomplished in the book, is that we can't help feeling a certain attraction to the feisty and destructive Carme. Perhaps the absence of a stoic sufferer of lost love demanding all our sympathy leaves us free to contemplate the story's intriguing complexities.

If Tóibín is ambitious in "The New Spain," offering in English a story with only Spanish characters, who converse, one presumes, in Catalan, in "The Street" he is even more so, portraying the lives of Pakistani immigrants in Barcelona. Tóibín knows Barcelona and Catalan, but it's hard to imagine he speaks Punjabi or Urdu. This, then, is the most radical formulation of "a new background . . . a new scenario," suggesting that the sentiment it deals with will be the most intense, the one that most needs to be held at a distance.

Newly arrived in Barcelona, Malik shares a room with seven other Pakistanis and is uneducated, unloved, and without prospects. In this he resembles Eilis in *Brooklyn,* Tóibín's novel about a young Irish woman immigrating to the States in the 1950s. Albeit on a smaller scale, we have the same savoring of a simple, vulnerable life, and the same affectionately meticulous reconstruction of this person's world, his or her humiliations, slow accumulation of knowledge, and eventual coming of age. Under the brutal control of his minder Baldy, Malik graduates from sweeping the floor of a barber's shop to selling phone cards and eventually mobile phones. Above all he discovers love.

Tóibín likes to describe men being gentle with each other, and his prose is at its best when he does so. Here is Henry James in *The Master*, caring for his sick brother Wilky:

> He went down to the hallway and sat close to Wilky, who was groaning softly. He moved closer to him . . . and held Wilky's hand for a moment, but since this seemed to cause him pain he withdrew it. He wished that his brother could smile as he had always smiled, but his drawn face now appeared as though it would never smile again.

And here is Malik taking care of Abdul, one of the older men in the room who has fallen ill:

> He knelt and gently opened the top of Abdul's pyjamas and whispered to him that he was going to sponge him with cold water. Abdul nodded slightly and lay quietly as Malik began to sponge his chest; then, having made him sit up, Malik took off the pyjama top and sponged Abdul's shoulders and back. Abdul looked as though what was happening caused him mild pain.

Unlike *The Master*, this is a love story. Abdul is aroused. Tóibín spends fifteen patient pages inching the men closer together until their first lovemaking is interrupted by a homophobic Baldy, who beats them ferociously. Malik will spend a period in the hospital and some time alone before the lovers are allowed a brief idyll sharing the same suffocating attic. Here, despite the younger man's evident involvement, Abdul is always a little distant and uneasy; when his cousin Ali arrives from Pakistan to share the room with them, we discover why: Ali has a photograph of Abdul with his wife and children.

Malik now seems set for that loss of love that has shaped the lives of Tóibín's other protagonists. But Abdul at last affirms his affection and insists that Malik return to Pakistan and live with him together with his wife, three children, and an extended family of brothers and cousins, some of whom have "friends who stay." Malik, who is never stupid, enquires:

"Friends like me?"

"No. But no one will think it strange that you are staying."

"But your real family is your wife and your children?"

Abdul looked away and was silent for a while. Then he whispered something that Malik could not catch.

"What did you say?"

"I said that my real family is you."

Here at last is a moment of optimism, not an empty family but a full one. Yet though the story closes with a tender account of the couple's day off together, the reader can't help but wonder whether this family won't be rather too full. Is Tóibín really inviting us to imagine that Malik will be happy with Abdul and his wife in Pakistan? Is he suggesting, or simply wishing, that the extended family of an older culture might allow for a more satisfying emotional life? Or is Malik heading for the distress Lady Gregory felt when her love could never be acknowledged, or more likely the misery that will follow when the relationship is discovered? One of the pleasures of reading Tóibín is our awareness of a disciplined and arduous balancing act between sentiment and intelligence, feeling and form. Nowhere is the balance more precarious or intriguing than at this, the collection's culminating moment.

Geoff Dyer

On a hot summer evening in 1999 in the Italian town of Reggio Emilia, the English writer Geoff Dyer told a crowd how much he preferred Italy to England: the Italians were vibrant, free, warm, loved life; the English were dull, conformist, surly, glum. One development, however, offered hope: the invention of the rave and the discovery of Ecstasy meant many Englishpeople were opening up and becoming more Italian, they were learning to love life. The crowd applauded.

Beside Dyer on the stage, I foolishly took issue. In Italy all my adult life, I know how the country suffocates in its Catholic conformity. Nor was the English vocation for bingeing new. On any Saturday midnight in the early nineteenth century about half the population of Manchester was drunk. There had been surveys.

A graciously grinning Dyer didn't trouble to rebut. Only later did I realize I'd misunderstood. Alien to anthropological analysis, he was simply setting up a polarity—carefree creativity against plodding conformity—and making his own allegiance clear. He was also being flippant. This was part of his war on dullness. He was seducing the crowd. We were having a good evening. It was difficult for an old literalist like me to know how to respond.

At the beginning of *Jeff in Venice,* the first part of Dyer's most ambitious novel to date, the author's alter ego goes into a newsstand

and is served by an Indian girl who gives him "a bright smile, unusual in her line of work." Immediately Jeff compares the teenager with "her surly father who, though he spoke little English, had so thoroughly adjusted to British life that he looked every bit as pissed off as someone whose ancestors had come over with the Normans." This vitality/killjoy contrast is at the heart of Dyer's work. In *Death in Varanasi,* the second part of the book, the narrator remembers how his own anxious English father "hated spending money to the point that holidays were a torture." As if in belated reaction and fearing, as anybody in Varanasi must, that death may be imminent, the narrator decides that "since this life was the only one you got, the only real crime was not to make the most of it."

So, carpe diem. But how exactly? Raves? Ecstasy? Is "to make the most of life" sufficient prescription? Jeff goes into the newsstand to buy chewing gum to disguise his obsessive habit of talking to himself in the street but comes out of the shop with a chocolate bar. He doesn't know what he wants. Reflecting anxiously on a book he should have written but didn't, he seems unable to weigh immediate gratification against the pleasures of achievement through labor. Briefly he wonders what kind of underwear the charming Indian girl might be wearing but is not so unwise as to try to make the most of the smiles they have exchanged. On impulse, he goes into a classy hairdresser and has his graying hair dyed, something he has never consciously wanted but which actually cheers him up immensely. He can now convince himself that time is not running out for making the most of life, whatever that might entail.

Unlike the traditional novelist who builds up characters by establishing their relation to one another in the tension of developing drama, Dyer has a trick of setting up entire books in insouciant relation to other books, thus placing himself in relation to other writers (invariably great writers). Hence the drama, in a sense, lies in the writing of the work itself, rather than the story it tells. The nonfiction *Out of Sheer Rage* (1997), for example, has Dyer struggling (hilariously) to write a biography of D. H. Lawrence and declaring such a powerful affinity with a man who would never have had the patience to research a biography that we know at once that the scholarly work will never be written. What is written, however, gives us a wonderful insight into Lawrence, or one side of him—his restlessness, impatience, vocation for irritation—and a fascinating picture of Dyer as someone anxious to feel he has the same restlessness, the same genius, anxious to avoid the dullness of the mere scholar, the person who hasn't lived. As if that were not enough, there are frequent references to Thomas Bernhard (who wrote more than one book about failing to write a book), and an astute awareness that the rhetoric of the impotent rant (usually directed against the world's dullness) was common to both Bernhard and Lawrence, and to Dyer.

One of the rants that Dyer's fans (they seem to number everyone who has ever struggled to sit still at a keyboard) always mention is his attack on literary academe in *Out of Sheer Rage*. Dyer has just been lent the Longman Critical Reader on Lawrence, edited by Peter Widdowson.

> I could feel myself getting angry and then I flicked through the introductory essay on "Radical Indeterminacy: a postmodern Lawrence" and became angrier still. How could it have happened? How could these people with no feeling for literature have ended up teaching it, writing about it? I should have stopped there, should have avoided looking at any more, but I didn't because telling myself to stop always has the effect of urging me on. Instead I kept looking at this group

of wankers huddled in a circle, backs turned to the world so that no one would see them pulling each other off. Oh, it was too much, it was too stupid. I threw the book across the room and I tried to tear it up but it was too resilient. By now I was blazing mad. I thought about getting Widdowson's phone number and making threatening calls. Then I looked around for the means to destroy his vile, filthy book. In the end it took a whole box of matches and some risk of personal injury before I succeeded in deconstructing it.

If Dyer objects to dull academics forever shut up in universities pretending to understand vibrant people like Lawrence, it nevertheless has to be said that "radical indeterminacy" would not be a bad description of the state of mind of someone who never knows whether he wants chewing gum or chocolate, to write a book or to go out for a drink, and "Radical Indeterminacy: A Postmodern Lawrence" might not be a bad title for an essay on Geoff Dyer, whose works are at once so densely and deliciously literary and so determined to avoid genre pigeonholing as to invite exactly the sort of analysis he loathes, or rather enjoys entertaining us with loathing. Dyer is aware of all this and suspicious of his performance, which itself is a source of comedy. He thrives on paradox, especially when it seems to come at his own expense. One notes in passing that he doesn't tell us how the friend who lent him the book reacted to its destruction.

So *Jeff in Venice, Death in Varanasi* plays cheekily with the Jeff/death assonance to give us a title that recalls Thomas Mann's Aschenbach, who, in *Death in Venice* also dyes his hair in a less successful attempt to look younger. But the very invitation to draw parallels establishes a defining difference: Thomas Mann, like D. H. Lawrence or Thomas Bernhard, would never have set up his work in teasing relation to another's. Such writers would never have invited us to question their towering seriousness, their vatic superiority. Always ready to fall into flippancy, even inanity ("the opportunity to say something serious resulted only in the impulse to say something glib," we hear at one point), Dyer appears to question the very possibility, or at least the nature of seriousness, thus obliging us to pay him serious attention.

Jeff is a hack journalist divorcee in his mid-forties, known to friends as Junket Jeff (hence quite the opposite of the hardworking, overachieving Aschenbach). His improbable surname is Atman. Again, in the gap between Grub Street sleaze and the Sanskrit for "soul" we have Dyer's characteristic provocation. The junket that Jeff is on this time is an expenses-paid trip to the Venice Biennale, where his problem of never knowing what he wants will be exacerbated by the sheer abundance of artworks to see, parties to attend, wines to drink, drugs to do.

> Jeff studied the invitation, noting the sponsor's logo—Moët, nice—and the time. Shit, it clashed exactly with the Australia party which, in turn overlapped with a dinner he'd cancelled as soon as the Australia invite turned up. That was also part of the Biennale experience: not getting invited to things was a source of torment; getting invited to them added to the logistical difficulties of wanting to go to far more things than you had any desire to go to.

When it comes to describing freeloading and parties, Dyer is second to none, and Jeff's three bellini-swilling, dope-smoking, coke-snorting days and nights in the Serenissima include comic descriptions that vie in inebriated disorientation with Henry Green's *Party Going* and Antony Powell's *Afternoon Men* (once again reaffirming the glorious tradition of the English binge). There are also some fine descriptions of the kind of installations that appear in the Biennale, mostly "puerile" but always betraying the artist's "ravenous" "hunger to succeed." Ominously, Jeff is attracted to

> a simple wooden boat . . . adrift in a frozen sea of broken, multi-coloured Murano glass . . . gradually filling up with water dripping from the ceiling. Every now and again—so infrequently Jeff wondered if he was imagining it—the boat rocked slightly. He was transfixed by this, glad that he'd seen it right at the beginning of his tour, before he became punch-drunk, sated and oblivious.

What rocks Jeff's slowly sinking boat on this Venice trip is his meeting, at the first evening's first party, with Laura Freeman. This beautiful young American with the significant second name is the perfect partner for Jeff: witty, irreverent, generous, more than willing to seduce and be seduced, altogether a more promising object of desire than Aschenbach's elusive Tadzio. Laura makes her man wait just long enough to allow for the obligatory sightings between vaporetti, then takes him to bed, where, despite scores of bellinis, the lovemaking is long, lavish, and, most surprising, loving. Indeed, so perfect is the sex and so brilliant, polished, and savvily cinematic the dialogue (these two are incapable of a dull moment) that the reader quickly appreciates that Laura is hardly a character at all, more an exemplum in an essay. (Dyer has spoken of preferring essays to fiction, and it is precisely his didactic vocation that obliges him to seek disguise in flippancy.) Laura will bring Junket Jeff to the point where he yearns to be with her always. Initially reflecting that "life, at its best, was about wanting never to go home," he will soon be wanting Laura to be his home. However, an encounter on his second morning warns him of what is to come.

Commissioned by *Kulchur* magazine to interview a famous artist's ex-wife ("an old has been," Jeff thinks, or rather a "never was") and if possible wrest from her a drawing that the artist is known to have made of her in her prime, he meets a "slovenly posh" lady in her fifties who shares a joint with him and distinguishes herself for her complete lack of the ugly craving for attention that drives on artists and journalists. Here at last is someone who does not fret about never having written a book, is sufficient to herself. Eventually the woman fetches the drawing. Executed with evident passion, it shows her naked, legs apart, genitals freely revealed, but with an expression on her face indicating "absolute indifference" to the yearning of the man drawing her. "One only needed to look at the picture for a few moments to know that the relationship was not going to endure," Jeff observes.

So it is with Jeff and Laura. The three days are perfect but, sensing she isn't eager to talk about an afterward, he is unable to press for more, commenting with regret that it has become "easier to lick someone's ass than to ask when you might see them again." After Laura leaves for the airport, Jeff returns to a bar where the two had enjoyed some time together, only to find that the biennale crowd has drunk it dry. The transition to the second, penitential, or purificatory, part of the novel, where Varanasi substitutes for Venice and "Death" for "Jeff," has already begun:

Like parched locusts, they had descended on this bar, drunk
it dry, squeezed every last drop of alcohol from it and then

moved on elsewhere. . . . It was still, ostensibly, a bar but it was a place, now, of abandoned meaning. The atmosphere was woebegone, an architectural equivalent of a fearful hangover. It was as if an atrocity had been committed, something shameful that no one cared to remember but which permeated the walls, the floors and all the fixtures. It seemed quite possible that a curse had now fallen on the place, that it would never again enjoy the dizzy heights of the last few days when the booze flowed and flowed and then ran out, leaving in its wake an emptiness that could never be filled, an after-taste of waste and pointlessness.

The second half of the book flips Dyer's romantic coin, moving straight from Eros to Thanatos, eliding in the process all that makes up most ordinary lives (and that rarely finds a place in Dyer's writing): work, family, routine, the slow accretion of shared life that might have been if Jeff and Laura had got together. Much has been made of Dyer's repeated portrayal of the would-be writer who fails to write his book, or even to start it, but this is perhaps only emblematic of a deeper failure truly to embark on any life project, no doubt out of fear that to give oneself to one book, one woman, one career, is to close down other opportunities, forgo immediate pleasures. Again and again Dyer's alter egos are attracted to people deeply engrossed in what they are doing, people who are not forever scratching themselves out of one itch into another, but not dull either. Watching musicians play together, for example, he finds it "difficult not to envy their absorption." Shortly after leaving the bar that was drunk dry, Jeff runs into an Italian family whose young daughter is bouncing along on a space hopper shaped like a kangaroo and complete with a little pouch. He finds this image of domestic bliss "completely adorable"—here are people combining pleasure and long-term project—and if possible "would have climbed right in there, into the pouch, and gone bouncing along with them."

Just as *Jeff in Venice* frequently alludes to Mann's *Death in Venice,* so it also looks forward to *Death in Varanasi.* An opening quotation from Allen Ginsberg explicitly compares the two cities; Laura speaks of going to live in the Indian town; at a party Jeff's friends quote the Buddha and refer to their champagne glasses as renouncers' begging bowls. Yet as the second part of the book begins, again with a journalist being commissioned to make a trip, this time to Varanasi, we have no explicit reference back to the first part. Is our new narrator Jeff Atman, or not? Is this the same story? Visiting an exhibition of photographs, disconcertingly bereft of captions, the narrator remarks:

> There was nothing to help you get your bearings and then, after a while, once you accepted the idea, you realized that you didn't need these things that you so often relied on, that there were no bearings to get. A given picture had no explicit or narrative connection with the one next to it, but their adjacency implied an order that enhanced the effect of both.

So it is with the adjacent halves of the book, they call to each other. If our narrator isn't Jeff, he is someone very like him, and since Varanasi with its death pyres, mysticism, and sheer weight of raw humanity is a place for shedding rather than affirming identity, the loss of name is appropriate. After all, the Sanskrit *ātman* does not correspond to the Christian notion of the individual soul, but can mean the consciousness we all share. One life can easily be superimposed on another. There is much talk of reincarnation.

Our nameless narrator arrives for five days but, without apparent purpose, decides to stay. For months. He is fascinated by the Indian city's combination of seething vitality and unending funeral procession. His time is spent exploring the ghats and temples, having himself rowed up and down the river by the ever-available, poverty-stricken boatmen (there are echoes of Aschenbach's dealings with gondoliers), and dining and conversing with the other guests in his hotel.

Dyer's style is more meditative now, but still determinedly comic, still recognizably Dyer, always ready to throw in a hip word or bizarre analogy when the writing risks taking itself too seriously. It is possible, he remarks at one point "to be a hundred per cent sincere and a hundred per cent ironic at the same time."

The narrator befriends a young man and woman at the hotel where he is staying and as the two fall in love finds himself able to observe their growing intimacy with pleasure; he no longer needs to be the one involved. Likes, dislikes, and even his sex drive fall off him like discarded clothes. Not that he renounces drink and drugs (how dull that would be), but the urgent appetite of *Jeff in Venice* is behind him. Nor does he submit himself to some spiritual discipline or embark on a serious study of the intense religious life all around him. However eager to "bust out of the prison of the ego," no self-respecting Dyer hero would do such things. True, he has his head and eyebrows shaved, begins to dress in a *dhoti,* and eventually bathes in the filthy Ganges, but this is neither from a desire for spirituality nor in response to some program of purification. "It was more as if I knew that one day I would bathe in the river and so there was no point in not doing so." He has accepted that he is caught up in a larger process, not a single Jeff Atman but an infinitesimal part of the universal *ātman.* "I had taken myself out of the equation," he tells us.

There is much excellent travel writing in these pages and, alongside the obvious and ironic references to *Death in Venice,* much allusion to Lawrence's travel writing, as if Dyer had found, in the notion that our lives are interchangeable, another frame for putting himself in relation to Lawrence. A hilarious account of a last flare-up of self-assertion, when the narrator fights to keep his place in line at a cash machine, loudly echoes Lawrence's description in *Sea and Sardinia* of a struggle to buy ferry tickets in the port of Naples. When the narrator sits face to face with a bearded holy man so that the two can look into each other's otherness, we are reminded of the extraordinary scene in *Twilight in Italy* where Lawrence watches an old woman spinning in a mountain village above Lake Garda. Like Lawrence, Dyer realizes that there can be no affinity between a modern and a premodern consciousness, but that "what distinguished us from each other was that he had no interest in [my world] whereas I was intensely curious about his." Lawrence wrote: "That I had a world of my own, other than her own, was not conceived by her. She did not care."

Unwilling to find himself a guru, Dyer's narrator relies on illness to complete the erosion of his identity. A bout of dysentery prevents him taking his antimalaria pills, and the mosquitoes get him, the fevers begin. Again, though the obvious parallel is with Thomas Mann's sickening Aschenbach, there is once more a deeper affinity with Lawrence. In 1927, his tuberculosis irreversible, Lawrence, as though to prepare himself for death, visited the underground Etruscan tombs in malaria-stricken Tuscany and wrote the book published posthumously as *Sketches of Etruscan Places.* Visiting the funeral pyres of Varanasi and catching malaria, Dyer's narrator is "in mourning for [himself]." But while Lawrence set his distinctive, combative style aside for some stretches of this work, bringing the calm of acceptance right into his prose, Dyer's hallucinating narrator finishes his tale with an intensely Dyerish, determinedly comic tour de force. Having previously joked with friends about adding a kangaroo to the variegated Hindu pantheon, he hallucinates the arrival of a huge kangaroo on the Varanasi ghats. When the creature is greeted and garlanded by the locals, the narrator climbs into its pouch, at last "letting go, leaning on nothing."

Thus the novel, or essay, ends on a note of surreal comedy with the dissolution of the alter ego's ego. Dyer, however, is far from leaning on nothing, and his identity even farther from dissolution. Not only does the scene remind us of the moment at the end of *Jeff in Venice* when Jeff wanted to jump into the pouch of the child's toy kangaroo, it is also stacked (like the whole book, for that matter) with cross-references and allusions, offering a powerful affirmation of Dyer's authorial control, literary ambitions, and trademark balancing act between seriousness and flippancy. Our author is a long way from taking himself out of the equation; we look forward with pleasure to another virtuoso performance to relieve our routine dullness.

Peter Stamm

Swiss novelist Peter Stamm's daunting project is to entertain us with an ordinary emptiness, lives without coherence or direction, stories that never take off, a style that shuns the emphatic or any local intensity of evocation, emotion, or climax. For all that, he is not an absurdist; there is comedy in these books, but never the loud comedy of Beckettian desperation. And if Stamm owes something to Camus, his work is free from the atmosphere of scandal that informs *L'étranger*. Rather, as we turn the opening pages of his stories, we have the impression of a novelist whose main resource is to describe, with quiet patience, a reality we can't help but recognize. Only as we venture further do we become aware how subversive Stamm is of the way we see novels and indeed life, and only as we approach the end of the tale do we understand that he is making fun of the way we insist on thinking about life in terms of the novels we have read.

The balance between content and rhythm is all important. Paragraphs in which a character's routine is described with attentive but directionless detail alternate with others where it seems something important is happening, perhaps a rapid sequence of events unfolds, only for the little surge of excitement to exhaust itself almost before it started. Here is Andreas in *On a Day Like This* (2006):

> From the Gare du Nord, Andreas took the suburban train out to Deuil-la-Barre. He took the same train every day.

He studied the faces of the other passengers, ordinary, unremarkable faces. An elderly man sitting across from him stared at him with expressionless eyes. Andreas looked out the window. He saw rails, factories and storage facilities, an occasional tree, electricity towers or lampposts, brick or concrete walls spattered with graffiti. He has a sense of seeing only colors, ocher, yellow, white, silver, a dull red, and the watery blue of the sky. It was a little after seven, but time seemed not to matter.

Andreas is a high school teacher, who, when asked what emptiness means to him, reflects: "Emptiness was his life in this city, the eighteen years in which nothing had changed, without his wishing for anything to change." When something does happen, it is very soon as though nothing had happened; the tone remains unchanged:

Andreas spent his spring break in Normandy. Once again, he had intended to read Proust, but he ended up sitting around in the hotel, watching TV or reading the newspapers and magazines he bought at the station newsstand every morning. He spent a night with an unmarried woman teacher he had met on one of his long walks along the beach. He had been fascinated by her large breasts, and invited her to supper. It took a lot of effort to talk her into going up to his room, and then they talked for a lot longer while they emptied the minibar. While they made love, the woman kept moaning his name out loud, which got on his nerves. He was glad to be alone when he woke up late the following morning. She had left him a note, which he glanced at briefly before balling it up and throwing it way.

Andreas has two lovers but neither is planning to build her life on him. He enjoys the fact that each year he faces a new group of children to teach: he will not grow attached to them nor they to him. Free of moral concerns, he is disturbed by only two things: life's intensity and the idea that other people lead more exciting, "real" lives than himself. That is, he is both drawn to and afraid of anything that could provoke deep feeling: when he drops a girlfriend, he doesn't answer the phone for a week; when a colleague who is dying with cancer retires, he finds a lame excuse to avoid the farewell party. He will not visit his parents' grave, nor get close to his brother or nephews. Though he remembers fondly, even obsessively, a girl he once loved and to whom he never had the courage to declare himself, he makes no effort to seek her out.

The opening fifty or so pages of *On a Day Like This* revel in the description of this aimless life, with the author apparently taking as much pleasure as Andreas in "the empty mornings when he would stand by the window with a cup of coffee in one hand and a cigarette in the other, and stare down at the small, tidy courtyard, and think about nothing except what was there in front of him." But it is of the nature of novels that sooner or later they must conjure up the drama that will sweep such complacency aside. All the same, Stamm seems as lacking in enthusiasm as the heavy-smoking Andreas as he steers him and his chronic cough to the hospital for a tomography scan of his lungs. Inside the scanner Andreas "shut his eyes, and tried to imagine he was lying on the beach in the sun, but the clattering of the machine kept bringing him back to reality."

What does reality mean for Andreas? Any unavoidable truth that brings with it intensity, urgency, feelings of freedom and fear, exposure, unprotectedness. It could be the beauty of the girl he loved and cannot forget. It could be news of incurable cancer. How to respond?

Denial. Andreas senses he will one day have to do something about his old love, but postpones a decision. Once he wrote a letter but did not send it. Invited urgently to the hospital to discuss the results of his tomography, he turns back on the threshold. He doesn't want to go there.

Another resource is diversion: choose a lesser intensity and explore that in order to hold the greater at bay. Andreas's life has been a series of unimportant girlfriends to keep the one who matters at a distance. His job has been just about interesting enough to prevent him from throwing himself into some bolder adventure. But to hold off the fear of imminent death, more radical diversions will be necessary. It is the end of the term. The summer holiday deprives him of his protective routine. Andreas starts an affair with Delphine, a colleague much younger than himself, a loving woman in search of a husband. It is not enough. He sells his apartment, his furniture, quits his job, buys a car, decides to drive to Switzerland, to his home village, his brother, his parents' grave, and above all Fabienne: the girl of his life about whom he knows so little.

The car is an instrument of escape, but Andreas contrives to make it an emotional protection. He buys an ancient Dyane such as people used to drive around the time he met Fabienne. It is a source of nostalgia. And though traveling toward an old love, he takes the new with him; Delphine is invited along. It's not clear here which girl is protection from which. There is a disquieting stop-start to Andreas's relationships. Earlier, he spent a wonderful evening with Delphine, then packed her off home in the middle of the night. Now, heading at last for the obsession that is Fabienne, he is glad to have the lesser intensity of Delphine beside him. And he will use his attachment to Fabienne to warn Delphine that he is not a man to marry. Stamm's achievement in all this is to align the tone and movement of his own narrative very closely with the ambiguous wanderings of his main character; it is as though he appreciates that a writer must deal with the great questions of love and death, but would far rather be talking about the car, the journey, the landscape. There is a fine moment during the drive from Paris to Switzerland when Delphine, who is learning German, slips a cassette of listening exercises into the car's audio player:

> Andreas wanted to take the cassette out, but Delphine put her hand over his and they listened to the woman slowly and clearly speak the examples.
>
> Tomorrow I shall see you again. Tomorrow you will see me again. Tomorrow we will see you again. Tomorrow you will see us again. The parents see their children again. The children see their parents again.
>
> Then a man's voice, equally warm, intoned:
>
> My day. I get up at half past five in the morning. I always get up at that time, because I have to be in the office by eight. It is only on weekends that I can sleep in. After getting up, I go to the bathroom, clean my teeth and shower, first warm, and then cold at the finish. After that, I feel thoroughly awake, and well. Then I get dressed and comb my hair. I go to the kitchen to have breakfast. I make myself some coffee, eat bread with jam or cheese or sausage . . .
>
> The man's voice had something strangely cheerful about it. It sounded as though he had yielded completely to the course of such days and years. A destiny without subordinate clauses.

It is a teasing parody of the earlier part of the novel, a rapid recall of the swaddling clothes of routine and repetition, before we face the imperatives of intensity: the encounter with Fabienne, the show-down with Delphine, the visit to his parents' grave—in short, the obligatory dramas to which both Andreas and Stamm seem to move as sheep to the slaughter, or assassins to a murder. After Andreas finally makes love with Fabienne, we hear that

> she seemed very naked and vulnerable. Andreas was put in mind of police photographs of crime scenes, pale, lifeless bodies by the side of the road in forests or rushes.

Stamm's earlier novel *Unformed Landscape* (2001) also features a journey that the traveler, in this case a woman, presents to herself as a move toward an intensity she both fears and desires and away from a situation she can no longer face. Still in her twenties, with a child from a first marriage, Kathrine is a customs officer in northern Norway. She has never been south of the Arctic Circle. Marooned in a sexless second marriage, she chooses to flee when she discovers that the supposed achievements of her husband Thomas—his being a champion swimmer and skier, inventor of a successful computer game—are the merest fictions. He is a compulsive liar. Although we later hear that "her favourite days had been the ones where every-thing was exactly as always," Kathrine is so shaken by this discovery that she sets off south to a warmer world and a man she met some time ago, a Dane whom she eventually tracks down in Boulogne. She could hardly have chosen a safer adventure: Christian, a trustworthy email correspondent, had never shown any desire to make love to her. All the same, she feels obscurely that "There was something to be done." The need to be living and doing, to have a story, is felt as a burden imposed from elsewhere: "She was even more afraid of a new life than she was of her old one." This fear helps Kathrine understand her husband: one invents stories to construct an illusion of intensity without taking risks.

Storytelling is also important in *On a Day Like This,* when a friend tells Andreas about a love affair that consisted only in fantasizing sexual adventures, not having them. Stamm uses these anecdotes, no doubt, to question his own storytelling vocation, its place in the world, and to invite us to examine our own expectations from reading. But it would be a mistake to think that he sees storytelling as mere evasion. It is essential to the mental world of his characters, who are constantly telling themselves stories, whether to spur themselves on or to allay their fears. Leaving her lying husband, Kathrine too makes up an exciting life for herself when she shares a couchette with a young man. However, her glamorous fantasy doesn't solve the problem of feeling that something is wanted of her. There must come a point, Stamm seems to suggest, at which the stories we tell ourselves engage with reality and push us in this direction or that. Deep down, Kathrine knows that she will have to seduce someone.

In Stamm's first novel, *Agnes* (1998), a writer is invited by his girlfriend to write a story about her, but what he eventually puts down diverges sharply from their real relationship. In reality he is angry about her pregnancy; they split up and get back together only after she has miscarried. In his story, instead, the couple have a happy family. Yet he can't help finishing the tale with the girl's death, something that, in the novel's ambiguous ending seems to have prompted the real Agnes to leave him. In short, there is a traffic between imagination and reality such that it is hard to understand what importance to attribute to longings on the one hand and events on the other. At the core of Stamm's work is the story of our attempts to get to grips with this process.

The blurb for Stamm's 2014 book *Seven Years* tells us that "Alexander is torn between two very different women." This is not the case. A man there is, and a wife and a mistress of sorts, but Stamm's characters are never "torn." Rather, they oscillate, they act and they retreat from action. To be "torn" would imply greater intensity and perhaps a moral dimension, a sense of guilt. There are puritans and moralists in Stamm's books: Kathrine's father-in-law in *Unformed Landscape;* Alexander's mistress and her friends in *Seven Years.* But their moral interpretations of events only provoke the hero's incomprehension. He cannot take their rhetoric of right and wrong seriously. Imprisoning oneself in a moral code comes across as just another strategy for avoiding life.

If *On a Day Like This* shows its maturity by moving away from the foregrounded literary tropes of the earlier novels (the writer at work in *Agnes,* the blatant use of Arctic geography in *Unformed Landscape*), *Seven Years* marks another departure by offering a first-person narrative with a far longer time span—not seven years, in fact, but twenty, from Alexander's graduation as an architect to his separation from his wife, Sonia, after eighteen years of marriage. The sense of the title is given to us by a certain Hartmeier, a landlord who, having befriended Alexander's long-term mistress, Ivona, one day demands that Alexander meet him.

> She loves you, he said, and sighed deeply. I shrugged my shoulders. With all her heart, he added. She's waited for you for seven years, the way Jacob waited for Rachel. I only vaguely remembered the story, but I remembered that at the end of seven years, Jacob had gone off with the wrong woman. Leah, Hartmeier said. And then he had to wait another seven years. I didn't understand what he was driving at. . . .

But the Lord saw that Leah was less beloved, and he opened her womb, said Hartmeier, and then I understood. . . . He didn't speak, and it was as though I caught a glimpse of secret triumph in his face. . . .

Ivona is pregnant, said Hartmeier.

As a paradigm, the story is comically inappropriate. In love, Jacob worked seven years for the father of his beautiful Rachel, only to be tricked into marrying her plain sister Leah and forced to work another seven years for Rachel. For his part, seven years before this conversation with Hartmeier, Alexander married, of his own choice, his beautiful, intellectual architect wife, Sonia, but has nevertheless continued to visit his plain, uneducated Polish mistress, Ivona, without ever being in love with either. The only real parallel element is the seven years of dull routine, something that in Stamm's world means a relatively happy time. Alexander remarks:

My relationship with Ivona had been from the start, nothing other than a story, a parallel world that obeyed my will, and where I could go wherever I wanted, and could leave when I'd had enough.

Ultimately, however, that story produces the reality of a child. How can Stamm avoid melodrama now?

In his forties, Alexander tells his tale to an older friend of his wife's, Antje, a painter, on the occasion of her visit to their Munich home. Flashbacks and reflections alternate with the moment of telling, and this, together with Stamm's decision to mix dialogue and narrative without clear punctuation, means the reader is constantly struggling to establish the chronology and status of the events told, a condition that mirrors Alexander's perennial uncertainty, especially when it comes to women. In fact, the novel opens with his watching his wife through the window of an art gallery where Antje's paintings are showing: "Like the paintings on the walls, to which no one paid any attention . . . [Sonia] seemed somehow not there, or only superficially there."

What Alexander tells Antje, perhaps because he senses that the story of his marriage is approaching its end, is that shortly before his graduation, while sitting in a Munich beer garden, a friend invited a "completely unattractive" Polish girl to join their party. Without conversation or art, the girl ruins the evening. "From the very outset, Ivona was disagreeable to me," Alexander tells us. "I felt sorry for her, and at the same time I was irritated by her docile and long suffering manner." All the same he tries to have sex with her. Religious, modest, Ivona does not allow herself to be undressed. Alexander is inexplicably excited. He spends the night with her. She tells him she loves him "like the statement of an immutable fact." For the rest of his life, sometimes on a regular basis, sometimes after long intervals, he will seek her out, but only for the briefest of encounters and without any communication between their meetings; for her part, Ivona will always be available, she will never have any other lover.

For a man who has two women, Alexander gets precious little sex. Sonia, who at the time he met Ivona was dating another architecture student, "was the absolute opposite of Ivona. She was lovely and smart and talkative and charming and sure of herself." But not loving. "I always found her presence somewhat intimidating," Alexander tells us. He entertains "the idea of falling in love with Sonia," but it is some time before their discussions about architecture finally lead, with Antje's encouragement, to their becoming a couple.

Stamm distinguishes the two by their architectural preferences. Cerebral to the exclusion of all animal warmth, Sonia is a fan of

Corbusier, of buildings that "improved people," encouraging decorous rational behavior. Alexander favors structures that would grow "like a plant," "sculptures of light and shade," yet the buildings that actually give him a sense of well-being are enclosed spaces, even the prison cells of an old castle: "Oddly I had a sensation of shelter and protection rather than confinement." Arguing against Sonia's ideas, he insists: "A living room is first and foremost a place of refuge. It has to offer protection from the elements, the sun, hostile people, and wild animals. Sonia laughed and said, well, I might just as well go to the nearest cave in that case."

Ivona is that cave, or rather Ivona's room: "stuffed full of junk, faked memories of a life that hadn't happened. . . . The pokiness, the untidiness, and the absence of aesthetic value only seemed to intensify my desire." With Ivona Alexander feels "a mixture of freedom and protectedness" such as "I hadn't had from childhood." On the other hand, when he first kisses Sonia, "it was not out of some whim. . . . The kiss was a decision we had come to together." Everything is reasoned. Everything is planned. The first lovemaking, after extended ablutions and discouraging interruptions to purchase contraceptives, is a comedy of frigidity. Alexander has been chosen, but as part of Sonia's career. Before they marry she makes him an architect's model of their future home.

The originality of Stamm's novel is to have taken one of the oldest plots in the world and made it new, convincing, even urgent. Sonia is so much the right woman for a middle-class Alexander aspiring toward the more sophisticated world she moves in. But she is "incapable of passion." So far we might be in a story by D. H. Lawrence or a hundred other authors. It is Ivona, and all that is implied by Alexander's attachment to her, that is the novelty. This is no Fabienne, not a woman to dream on, not a lusty lover, not a good companion, never an alternative to Sonia. But to a man exhausted by a purpose-driven, achievement-obsessed world, her submission and quietly animal existence are irresistible. Alexander is "beside [himself] with lust." It comes as no surprise that while Sonia's carefully laid plans to have a child come to nothing, when Alexander finally penetrates Ivona she conceives at once.

When Stamm's characters—Kathrine, Andreas, Alexander—meet the disasters they fear, their paradoxical reaction is relief. The doubleness of their lives, the tension between seeking and fleeing intensity, is wearisome. Now they can be like men who go "freely to their graves to protect themselves from death." So on hearing Hartmeier's news of Ivona's pregnancy, Alexander "felt a great feeling of calm and a kind of relief. I would have to talk to Sonia." There will be a showdown, everything will be simpler.

Not at all. Sonia is not a woman for showdowns. They don't suit her plans. So Stamm can quickly defuse the melodrama he has set up. Sonia agrees to take the child herself. It will save her the animal trouble of pregnancy. And Ivona will again be utterly submissive to Alexander's requirements, surrendering her child without protest. So the story can go on more perversely than before with the brilliant sterile wife bringing up the child of the dumb but fertile mistress. The genius of Stamm's book is its perfect meshing of three characters, each of whom in quite different ways uses the others to strike a precarious balance between mental world and practical existence.

A word about Peter Stamm's Swissness and Michael Hoffman's excellent translations from the original German. On opening the promotional material accompanying a recently published German novel, *Funeral for a Dog,* I read: "Thomas Pletzinger is German, but you wouldn't know it from his debut, which is both wise and worldly," the implication being that the last thing the American reader wants is to be bothered with foreignness. People must be "worldly" but not from some elsewhere in the world.

Stamm is one of a growing group of authors—one thinks of the Norwegian Per Petterson or the Dutch author Gerbrand Bakker—who, whether consciously or otherwise, have evolved styles to suit the requirements of a global literary market. None of these authors writes exclusively, or even first and foremost, for the country he lives in. Nor do they write about those countries, in the way, say, that Roth or Franzen writes about America. Stamm keeps culture-specific detail to a minimum, while his prose is lexically and syntactically spare to an extraordinary degree. This does not mean that translation was easy; good translation is always difficult, and Hoffman's rhythm and tone are impeccable. But it means such a translation was possible, something that is not always the case with more elaborate writing.

What we are seeing, then, is the development of styles of writing that are to be understood no longer in relation to the literary tradition the author grew up in but as part of the new world of international fiction, books translated no sooner than written into a dozen languages. Stamm's cleverness is to align a spareness that works in translation with his characters' instinctive fear of all things rich and intense. Lean as it is, his prose is wonderfully "literary" in its fine integration of voice and story. The constant disorientation of his characters, their sense that their lives are interchangeable with any number of other lives, seems peculiarly suited to this era of globalization.

Graham Swift

Perhaps the finest piece of storytelling in Graham Swift's *Wish You Were Here* has to do with the death of a dog. Three characters are involved: Michael Luxton, a taciturn dairy farmer; Jack, his elder son, aged twenty-six; and Tom, his much younger son, approaching his eighteenth birthday. The old sick dog, named Luke, was originally just a farm dog, then for many years Jack's close companion, but now more recently Tom's. The events are remembered by Jack, from whose point of view, albeit in third person, most of the novel is narrated.

The men are not a happy threesome. It is only five years since Michael's wife and the boys' mother, Vera, chief source of warmth and affection in the family, died; it was after the mother's death that the dog mysteriously shifted his loyalty from Jack to Tom. Since then the Devonshire farm has been devastated by mad cow disease, or rather by the government reaction to it, the Luxtons' healthy herd having been slaughtered and incinerated in the great cull. Inevitably, the old dog's long illness reminds the men of Vera's death, the misery of the cull, the possible end of a great phase of their lives, bankruptcy, loss of the land.

One heavy, sullen August morning Michael drove the pickup into the yard, fetched a spade from the lean-to and put it in the back, then went into the house, unlocked the gun cabinet between the kitchen and the stairs and carried the shotgun out to the pick-up too. Jack and Tom were both in the yard at the time, but felt from the way their father was looking and moving that they shouldn't speak. Then Michael went into the kitchen where Luke was by now confined to his blanket in a corner—beyond even padding his way to the door—and lifted him up and carried him out and put him in the back of the pick-up along with the spade.

Michael is going to shoot the dog. He tells the boys he doesn't want help, then changes his mind and invites Tom to come along. From that moment, everything Jack remembers is what he heard from Tom: how the father drove to the corner of a field, laid the dog down, loaded his shotgun, then offered it to Tom to do the killing; how Tom refused, or tells Jack he did, claiming that had he accepted the gun he would have shot not the dog but his father, who had taken him out of school at sixteen, forcing him to work on the doomed farm; and how then the farmer blew the dog's brains out from close range, dug the grave together with his young son, and finally went off to wash his hands while Tom heaped earth on the animal.

Jack is excluded. Jack lost the loyalty of the dog to his brother and now he misses its death. He hasn't even said good-bye. All he hears is the shot, but that comes through "clearly enough like something hitting his own skull." Jack suffers, but without acting, without even making an effort to act. Jack would never have thought of setting the family free from the dying dog in this way or indeed of freeing the animal from its agony. Unlike Tom, Jack would never contemplate hurting his father to free himself from the farm and its now inevitable failure.

This incident, which so neatly captures the positions of the three men in respect to one another and the world, is somewhat overshadowed by the melodramatic frame in which Swift sets his novel. The opening pages give us an older Jack gazing from a window through heavy rain at a seaside view, a shotgun on the bed beside him. His thoughts are of the mad cow cull, of 9/11, the war on terror, and the whereabouts of a certain Ellie. Emotionally charged allusions to intolerable recent events alert us that Jack is very likely about to shoot himself, or Ellie, or both. Swift will let us know whether he actually does so or not only 350 pages later. Meantime, he unpacks Jack's biography. Or rather: Jack, while waiting, as we said, to kill himself, to kill Ellie, or both, recalls his past, all of it, right back to earliest childhood, in some detail and employing many clever delaying effects that keep us on the edge of our seat. Various hints in the dog scene, for example, tell us that this was not the last ugly drama from which Jack was to be excluded.

Nor is this the first time that Swift has given us a man who feels unable to assert himself. As early as 1980 the main character of his first novel, *The Sweetshop Owner,* was a husband bossed into nullity by his oppressive wife and as a result rejected by his beloved daughter. In *Ever After* (1992) the protagonist Unwin occupies an academic post he is not fit for, provided for him by his charismatic stepfather, his feelings of inadequacy compounded by the contempt of the academic community, which excludes him. His natural father shot himself when he, Unwin, was eight. Again there is a drama from which the main character is not only cut out but left to deal with the aftermath. In *Waterland* (1983), Tom Crick is one who lives in the shadow of a complex cluster of dramatic events, leaving him with an obsession for explaining the unsatisfactory present by constant reference to the past, something that animates the man's idiosyncratic history lessons.

Childlessness is a constant theme, a state that compounds the inadequacy of sterility with exclusion from the ongoing process of history: in *Waterland* Crick, whose wife cannot bear children after an early abortion, spends his life teaching other people's children but risks exclusion even from this surrogate fatherhood since history is no longer appreciated as a school subject; Crick is obsolete. Unwin opens *Ever After* with the warning, "These are . . . the words of a dead man." Who is more excluded from the living than the dead? The whole of *Tomorrow* (2007) is a wife's monologue preparatory to a confession to her twin children that they were conceived by artificial insemination, that their father is not their natural father, something that, as she sees it, is a deep flaw in their otherwise happy lives. Now, in *Wish You Were Here,* Jack and Ellie—for she is his lifelong partner and wife—are again childless, albeit for a different reason. Jack feels Ellie has manipulated him, denied him the initiative; he feels he is always left to pick up the pieces of other people's more intense lives; he feels excluded.

In short, Swift has spent his whole writing career—it is hardly unusual—digging around the same distressed psychology, seeking simultaneously to understand, express, dramatize a certain cluster of negative emotions, a particular behavior pattern. Freedom is always an issue. To act would be to be free. In the short story "Learning to Swim" (1982), a fearful but proud young boy pushes away from his parents into the water and a terrifying life that is nevertheless "all his own." In the main, however, the gesture of cutting loose is fatally associated in Swift's writing with disappearance and in some cases death. Even the positive note struck at the end of *Last Orders* confirms the equation of death with freedom: the friends scattering Jack Dodd's ashes hold "their hands out cupped and tight like they've each got little birds to set free."

Wish You Were Here offers three examples of people making a break for freedom. Ellie grew up on the farm neighboring Jack's. When she was sixteen, her mother walked out with a "mystery man" and was never heard from again. Only after she, the mother, and her third husband are dead will Ellie receive a letter informing her that she has inherited a trailer park on the Isle of Wight.

A few months after Michael Luxton shoots the dog, Jack's younger brother Tom slips out of the farmhouse in the early hours of his eighteenth birthday to join the army. He will never be in touch again, and Jack, beyond writing three brief letters, will never do anything to contact him. The possibility of emails or social networks is never mentioned. There are no half measures in Swift's world; when someone goes, he goes. Inevitably this sudden and total absence has a profound effect on those left behind, who feel at once more isolated in their small, enclosed world and more afraid of what escape might entail. Ellie has suffered all her life from her mother's departure; Jack suffers Tom's silent absence. And how can Jack and Ellie themselves ever break free now, when to do so would mean depriving their respective fathers of all remaining company and support? Fear of the risks of escape is compounded by guilt. Whatever he does, whenever he is in any way exposed to public view, Jack feels cripplingly guilty, is obsessed by a need to efface himself. To act, for Jack, is to give offense; freedom is an imperative, but to seize it would be unspeakably cruel.

The third and most dramatic escape occurs when, once again, Jack hears a shot ring out: on the night after Remembrance Sunday, the first on which Tom is absent, Michael Luxton has left the house, gone to sit down under the farm's big oak tree, and blown his brains out. Freedom, death, and cruelty are superimposed. Excluded, Jack picks up the pieces. He feels guilty. He should have done something to prevent this.

Remembrance Sundays are important. Although Swift is frequently described as writing about "ordinary," nonintellectual, noncharismatic characters—butchers, sweetshop owners, farmers— perhaps precisely because these would seem to be people who have not freed themselves from their destiny (in this regard there is much that is Hardyesque in Swift's writing), and although he often tells his stories from their apparently "humble" point of view, nevertheless his novels are determinedly, even relentlessly "literary": foreshadowing events, clever parallels, symbols, and meaningful names abound. The cross-referencing is abundant to the point of suffocation, as if Swift were creating, in literary form, the mental prison in which his characters are trapped.

For Jack Luxton, Remembrance Sunday is part of that prison. He grows up hearing from his mother, Vera, the story of his two great-uncles, George and Fred Luxton, who died on the same day in the Battle of the Somme, one of the two—their commanding officer wasn't sure which—having accomplished an act of bravery for which, at random, George rather than Fred was awarded, posthumously, the Distinguished Conduct Medal. Every November throughout Jack's childhood, Vera, "like some diligent curator," polishes up this medal so that it can be taken to the Remembrance Sunday Service, where the Luxtons, with their two names on the village war memorial, enjoy a certain celebrity. In a rare moment of conviviality afterward, Michael Luxton will pull the medal from his pocket while standing neighboring farmers a drink and say a few words about George's heroism.

This is the burden of expectation that hangs over Jack. But of the two brothers, it seems far more likely that the younger Tom, who excels Jack in all manly pursuits, hunting and womanizing in particular, but also in certain traditionally feminine activities (cooking

and ironing), will be the more likely hero. Swift goes to considerable
lengths to draw parallels between the two sets of two brothers. Vera
tells Jack that had his great uncles survived the Somme, George
would surely have broken his medal in two and shared it with Fred.
When Jack and Tom go hunting, Tom shoots two pigeons to Jack's
none, but gives Jack one as they return home to protect him from
their father's scorn. In return he expects Jack to cover his back when
he escapes the farm for the army.

One can only admire the patience and resourcefulness with
which Swift constructs all his interconnections (the frequent parallel
between culled cattle and slaughtered soldiers is another), but the
regular chime of internal reference can grow obtrusive. The narration
is more effective when straightforward. Even the scene where the dog
is shot is weakened to the extent that the reader feels it has been
worked hard to fit into a pattern of events. After the dog is shot, Tom
will remove the filthy blanket from its basket, wash it, and fold it,
and this blanket will later appear on the bed of the father the night
he shoots himself with, needless to say, the Distinguished Conduct
Medal in his pocket. Then, of course, Jack will remove the medal and
make sure to have it in his pocket on a later dramatic occasion.

Still, the core of the story, the relationships between its main
characters, is convincing. Brought together very young by the simple
fact of being neighbors, Jack and Ellie find it hard to feel that they
consciously chose each other. It's "as if they'd been born together."
After the disappearance of Ellie's mother and the death of Jack's, the
two widowers, each of whom needs his child to work his farm, allow
the teenage couple a furtive sexual freedom, but only so as not to
concede the real freedom of leaving to set up a home together. Perhaps Ellie would break out with Jack, if Jack showed sufficient initiative or cruelty toward his father to grasp his freedom. He doesn't.

The two become marooned in an adolescence prolonged into their late twenties, each at once the salvation and the jailer of the other.

After Michael Luxton kills himself and Ellie's father dies of cancer, the couple is hopelessly tied up in debt. At this point Ellie produces a six-month-old letter announcing the inheritance of the trailer park in the Isle of Wight. Hence when Jack sells the farm and moves to the coast, it is on Ellie's bidding and part of a manipulative strategy, he feels, to persuade him to start a family with her. Having failed to take the initiative, Jack refuses to father a child.

Trailers fit the pattern. At once a home, but mobile and temporary, the trailer offers a compromise between domestic imprisonment and unconditional freedom. Jack remembers with great fondness the two brief trailer vacations he enjoyed in his early teens with his mother and younger brother. It was on one of these that, with great effort, he wrote a postcard to Ellie: "Wish you were here." The title of the book recalls the ambiguous pleasure of desiring someone's presence while being happily away from her, of simultaneously having and not having a relationship. Again and again we are told that Jack feels one thing and its opposite too. Such mental states can be hard to handle. "Death was a kind of shelter" is one of Jack's more dangerous apprehensions.

So having lost his "birthright," the farm, Jack becomes a herder of trailers; he thinks of them as cattle. He is protective in their regard. He "milks" them. He feels guilty when he leaves them. And he protects the vacationers; when they get drunk and argue, he calms them down. Protection and mediation are the two actions possible to a man like Jack, who remembers with unhealthy intensity rocking his younger brother's cradle. Running the trailer park, he has brought together routine and evasion, found a role in the world that doesn't leave him feeling trapped or guilty. Once a year Ellie drags him off for a vacation of their own in Santa Lucia. Jack learns to wear brightly colored shirts;

he is in danger of enjoying life. Then news arrives that Tom has been killed in Iraq. There will be the harrowing business of recovering and burying the body. Inevitably, the past comes back; old tensions surface. Above all Jack senses that Ellie, now in her late thirties, will use this liberation from the last member of his family to insist on starting a family of her own. The relationship cracks. All too soon the last remaining Luxton will be in the bedroom with a loaded shotgun. True to pattern, the house, once a lighthouse, is called the Lookout. "And it was lookout time now all right," Jack, or Swift, tells us.

Reading *Wish You Were Here* one frequently wonders whether the author isn't dressing a fine story in the wrong clothes. It is not only the obtrusive patterning of imagery and the loud mechanics of melodrama; there is also Jack's remorseless lucubration. Here is a man of no special education, so little that he is unfamiliar with the word "hypocrisy," one whose recall of events nevertheless involves, at every point, highly verbal and nicely nuanced distinctions of behavior and motivation. About the farm itself and the deep nature of his attachment to it, we hear little and feel less. There is nothing of the intimacy with cattle that emerges from, say, Nell Leyshon's fine play *The Farm,* nothing of the engagement with land and with labor on the land that so wonderfully comes through in Gerbrand Bakker's novel *The Twin.* And though Swift has a great descriptive talent, we never get that extraordinary placing of figure in landscape that one finds in Hardy's novels. It is rather as if Swift were interested in the farm only insofar as it represents tradition and unrelenting routine and hence constitutes a setting in which to place a man who is to be torn between loyalty and the fear that he has been imposed upon and is missing life. Even the following fine introductory description of the farm immediately tilts us to concerns with subjugation and courage.

It was deep, steep, difficult but good-looking land, with small patchy fields that funnelled or bulged down to the woods in the valley. They had one field up on the ridge where they grew occasional wheat and autumn feed, otherwise it was down to grass and like almost every farm for miles around: sheep or dairy, and they'd always been dairy—beef calves for sale, and dairy. It was hard work for the softest, mildest thing in the world. It was all about turning the land into good white gallons, as many as possible. And it was all about men being slaves to the female of the species, so Michael Luxton had liked to say, with a sideways crack of his face, when Vera had still been around, especially in her hearing. They were all bloody milksops really.

This passage is excellent, but rare. Far more often—and it is this that stretches the novel to 350 pages—we have Jack's anxiously intricate analyses of his own and others' behavior. Here he is at thirteen writing the famous postcard to Ellie from the trailer:

When he sat down at the tiny pale-yellow Formica topped table in the caravan and wrote his postcard to Ellie it was with a mixture of honesty and guilt. Yes he really did wish she was there. But if he really wished that, how could he be so happy in the first place? Wishing she was there was like admitting he was happy without her. It was like saying he was writing this postcard because he'd betrayed her.

Avowedly "poor with words," Jack is constantly reflecting on language. Here he is on the phone discussing the "repatriation" of his brother's coffin:

Major Richards had explained that Jack and Mrs Luxton would be sent further, full details of the ceremony. And of course a formal invitation. To Jack, the word "invitation" didn't seem like a word that went with the army, though in this case it didn't seem like the right word anyway. Major Richards had said that meanwhile he'd continue to "liaise" (which seemed a real army word) by phone and even, if convenient, by a further visit and that Jack shouldn't hesitate if there was anything he wished to ask.

After Major Richards visits the house, Ellie leaves Jack in the living room to make tea in the kitchen.

He heard the gush of water in the kitchen. It would have been a good inducement and a good moment to shed a few more tears while Ellie wasn't looking. And an opportunity—if that's how it was—for Ellie to do a bit of private gushing herself. But he didn't think so. He only imagined how her hand might be grasping the tap a bit more tightly and for longer than was necessary.

Jack, who doesn't know "hypocrisy," casually deploys "inducement." He plays with the word "gushing." He does the novelist's work, or perhaps film director's, imagining Ellie's hand on the tap. And he is supposedly recalling all this in an aberrant state, contemplating suicide with a gun beside him. During one highly charged argument, Ellie accuses Jack of being responsible for his father's death, and we have:

He hadn't expected that. He wasn't sure if it further complicated or only clarified the situation. If it was even the nub of the matter.

Complicated or clarified. It seems Jacks poverty of language applies only when he has to communicate with others; meantime, his internal prevarication weaves a web of fine distinctions that distances him from tough decisions. Since this is a very special, highly controlled, and verbal mindset, you would expect the voice to change significantly when Ellie, an entirely different kind of person, takes over the narrative. It does, a little, but not much. Here is Ellie's consideration on whether to cry over Tom:

> So when that letter had arrived . . . saying, with deepest regret, that Tom was dead, Ellie had felt her hopes fly up once again. Though she hadn't shown it. It wasn't so difficult to disguise the feelings she'd always disguised. On the other hand, she wasn't going to disguise them now to the extent of shedding false tears.

As she hurries to meet Jack in one dramatic occasion we have:

> Haste, in this case, would have been quite inappropriate, though so too would have been lateness, or any hint of evasion.

When the dead Tom takes over the story for a single short section two-thirds through the book, his contribution simply confirms all we already know about him: conveniently, he remembers the same experiences, holidays, girlfriends, and letters that Jack has mentioned. This section gives Swift a chance to describe getting blown up in an armored vehicle as a strangely dreamy, even positive experience, and, again, one that fits in with what we already know:

He could think about being in a caravan with just Jack and Mum. . . . But he was lying in Barton Field more or less where Luke had been shot and had known all along it was coming.

Most curious of all, toward the end of the novel, Swift inserts a long section from the point of view of the wife of the family that bought the Luxtons' farm when Jack sold it. Unaware of old Luxton's suicide, she describes her spooky feelings around the oak tree. She also tells about her husband's affair and her sense that he has used the farm purchase to send her off for the summer and exclude her from his real life. Aside from making us wait a little longer for the closing melodrama and suggesting that the same behavior patterns can be found everywhere, it is really not clear what this section adds to the book.

Jack is constantly of two minds. Perhaps it is Swift's intention to create the same ambivalence in the reader; at times, however great my attachment to plot, the literary web he weaves was so oppressive that I was tempted, like Jack, to make some drastic bid for escape and abandon ship. But then I would have missed all Swift's undoubted achievements (the fine account of the repatriation of the body, to mention but one), just as Jack will miss so much if he really does blow his head off.

In this regard it occurred to me: if Jack needs his interminable lucubration to hold at bay the conflict between loyalty and freedom, does Swift's writing habit have a similar function? Could it be that he can write about his own mindset only if he imagines it in people as different from himself as possible, these "ordinary" folk, at the risk then of the story's not feeling entirely authentic? But perhaps stories are actually safer, more protective, when they don't feel a hundred percent authentic? Did anyone, after all, ever really believe the plot of *Tess of the D'Urbervilles*? There is so much that Hardy and Swift have in common: the humble, vulnerable characters whose parents die young, or thrust their children too young from the nest; the pleasure in rootedness and the yearning for escape; the submission to an oppressive destiny that gets mixed up with social inequality and dense literary patterning; the apprehension that any decisive initiative will end in catastrophe; the frequently expressed idea that only death will solve the dilemma, when, as Hardy has the uneducated Tess so beautifully put it, we shall all at last be "grassed down and forgotten."

Forced to take a break in my reading when yet another connection clanged (this time a "wind-hurled seagull" is a "whizzing missile" so that Jack's seaside drama can link with Tom's Iraq destiny), I found myself wondering whether that sacred literary imperative "only connect" isn't merely a product of neurosis, a desire to throw up a barrier between ourselves and reality and to make awfulness reassuring by giving it form? "I don't care what you call it," says Crick in *Waterland,* "explaining, evading the facts, making up meanings, taking a larger view, putting things into perspective, dodging the here and now, education, history, fairy-tales—it helps to eliminate fear."

If Crick is right, there are perhaps two ways a writer can deal successfully with the patterning habit: expose it, laugh at it, drawing pathos from our need for it; or create the pattern so subtly and seductively that the reader is not aware he is being manipulated. To fall between these two stools is fatal.

Dave Eggers

The title of Dave Eggers's memoir, *A Heartbreaking Work of Staggering Genius* (2000), brings two assumptions into sharp relation: that we want to read about suffering and that writerly genius manifests itself in the evocation of suffering. With comic hyperbole, the reader is promised someone to sympathize with and someone to admire; in this case, the same person. Meantime, we are reminded that the book is born into a world of hackneyed hype and anxiously constructed celebrity. If our genius chose this puff for a title, Eggers seems to ask, can his motives be pure, is his ego under control?

There are four hundred very full pages but the outline is quickly sketched. Aged twenty-one, Dave loses both parents to cancer. The family wrecked, he takes over the parenting of his eight-year-old brother Christopher, or Toph, and moves from Illinois to California to be near his elder sister Beth and brother Bill. No longer under stern parental control, Dave, excited, liberated, quickly understands that society feels somehow guilty in regard to orphans like themselves, offering generous subsidies and recognizing their victim status as a form of celebrity. The more society expresses this guilt, the more self-righteous Dave feels in his efforts to be an ideal guardian for Toph. Drawn toward journalism, blessed or cursed with a manic energy, sometimes constructive, sometimes destructive, frequently both, Dave hungers for visibility. He starts up a satirical magazine,

Might, on the side of youth and liberal rectitude and considers turning his parents' sickness and death into a blockbuster memoir.

Dave is given to wild exaggeration. He loves to tell tales, forgivable because hilarious, endearing because so obviously the product of a youthful desperation to achieve. The exaggeration seeps into the memoir itself; an interview where Dave explains to a TV producer why he should be on a reality show becomes a fifty-page tour de force. Much of what he tells the producer beggars belief, while the length and elaborate nature of the interview suggest Eggers is exaggerating for us what exaggeration there may have been at this encounter, assuming it took place.

Despite our amused skepticism, the technique works as memoir; this is the kind of person Dave is. We have not so much his life as his constant retelling of it. All is performance and persuasion, with the present state of Dave's mind the only topic on offer. Long conversations with Toph, for example, allow the younger boy to deconstruct, with sophistication beyond his years, the self-serving, pseudo-ethical positions Dave takes in the magazine. Rather than giving an accurate picture of Toph, it seems that Dave is aware of his brother mostly insofar as he offers a foil to explore his own misgivings. After Toph lands one particularly eloquent blow, Dave protests: "You're breaking out of character again."

Is Eggers's memoir actually *about* celebrity, or is it that a thirst for celebrity is the form that a certain kind of youthful vitality inevitably takes in the United States? "You feel deep down," Toph says, "that because there is no life before or after this, that fame is, essentially, God." Fame, as it were, puts order into chaos; life doesn't make sense without it. "These are people," says Dave of applicants to a reality show "for whom the idea of anonymity is existentially irrational, indefensible." But of Adam Rich, who had agreed to be given out by

Might as murdered in an attempt to ridicule the public obsession with celebrity, Dave wonders:

> Could he really be doing all this for attention? Could he really be milking his own past to solicit sympathy from a too long indifferent public?
>   No, no. He is not calculating enough, cynical enough. It would take some kind of monster, malformed and needy. Really, what sort of person would do that kind of thing?

Indeed. The cleverness of the memoir is to make Dave's agonized concern about his possibly dishonorable motives for seeking celebrity another form of suffering with which to sympathize, and another performance to admire. The puzzle for the reader is that what we most like about Dave is precisely this lively, supremely slippery self-regard.

Two years later, in his first novel, *You Shall Know Our Velocity!* (2002), Eggers invents a charmingly schematic collision between monomania and altruism: two young Americans try to get round the world in a week, giving away thirty-two thousand dollars in cash to anyone whose poverty might make them a worthy recipient.

The difference in tone between fiction and memoir is not as great as you might suppose; we have a first-person narrator, Will, who constitutes the only real character and consciousness for most of the novel, his close friend Hand being essentially a sidekick whose recklessly confrontational style is bound to make things happen around Will. It is thanks to Hand's provocation of a group of louts that Will has had his face so seriously rearranged that he is embarrassed to appear in public; he will not be seeking the limelight.

Yet Will has already achieved celebrity of a kind. A photograph of him installing a lightbulb was picked up by an advertising agency, which paid eighty thousand dollars to use it in silhouette on lightbulb packaging. "I felt briefly, mistakenly, powerful," remembers Will: "*My outline burned into the minds of millions!* But then came back down, crashing. It was an outline, it was reductive. It was nothing." In *A Heartbreaking Work*, Dave had remarked that the stories you tell about yourself to gain attention are no more than "snake skins" that cease to be you as soon as shed. It's exciting to be known to millions, but disappointing that what is known is not really you. Celebrity is not the way forward. Giving away money, Will hopes, may offer a more real relationship with the world.

What precipitates the decision to make the trip, however, is a death. This is a frequent motif in Eggers's stories: someone dies, a family or community is shattered, and narrative kicks off from a sense of grief and scandal. The victim here is the twenty-six-year-old Jack, who with Will and Hand completes a threesome of friends, each balancing the other: Jack "had calm where I had chaos and wisdom where Hand had just a huge gaping always-moving mouth." With the group's force for stability gone, Will sets out with Hand to combine a week's exotic tourism with some impulsive and random charity.

There is a *Dumb and Dumber* hilarity to the opening pages of *You Shall Know Our Velocity!*: the young men's ignorance and presumption as they plan their flights; their indignation when some bizarre itinerary (Greenland-Rwanda) proves impossible, their embarrassment approaching people (in Senegal) to give away money, the disruptive consequences of their capricious gifts, some as careless as tossing banknotes out of a car window or taping them to animals.

We found a group of boys working in a field. . . . They were perfect. But I couldn't get my nerve up. . . .

—"This is predatory," I said.

—"Yeah but it's okay."

—"Let's go. We'll find someone better."

We drove, though I wasn't sure it would ever feel right. I would have given them $400, $500, but now we were gone. It was so wrong to stalk them, and even more wrong not to give them the money, a life-changing amount of money here, where the average yearly earnings were, we'd read, about $1,600. It was all so wrong and now we were a mile away and heading down the coast.

Finally, someone states the obvious:

—You do more harm than good by choosing the recipients this way. It cannot be fair.

—How ever is it fair? . . .

—You want the control money provides.

—We want the opposite. We are giving up our control.

—While giving it up you are exercising power. . . . You want its power.

In 2005, in collaboration with other writers, Eggers published two extended polemical essays: *Teachers Have It Easy: The Big Sacrifices and Small Salaries of America's Teachers* and *Surviving Justice: America's Wrongfully Convicted and Exonerated*. In his three following full-length works, *What Is the What* (2006), *The Wild Things* (2009), and *Zeitoun* (2009), he chose to tell borrowed stories, rather than invent his own. All three have to do with the struggle between chaos and order. Expanding Maurice Sendak's classic children's story, *The Wild Things* gives us a Max who seems very much a younger version of Dave in Eggers's memoir, a boy who would like to be good but whose childish energy leads him to wild misbehavior. Sendak's vision closely matches Eggers's, and in developing it into a full-length novel, Eggers has the advantage that he cannot be accused of promoting himself: there are, as Max likes to observe, "other people to blame."

The other two books are more radical departures. *What Is the What* gives the true, though novelized, story of a Sudanese refugee who escapes genocide to emigrate to the United States, while *Zeitoun,* labeled nonfiction, tells of a Syrian house painter, Abdulraham Zeitoun, who remained in New Orleans to help during the flooding that followed hurricane Katrina only to find himself arrested on terrorist charges, brutally mistreated, and imprisoned for a month. They are tales of heartbreaking suffering, but with the staggering genius of an author now free from suspicion of "milking his past" to achieve celebrity. It is as if, in penitential response to the fertile tension between renunciation and self-indulgence that energized the earlier books, or simply to the fact that his celebrity was predicated on his parents' early death, Eggers were trying to eliminate anything self-regarding in the act of writing, imposing an indisputably constructive content and purposefulness.

The premise behind this exercise is that a writer's talent can simply be switched away from his own concerns to write up, after long interviews and much research, the instructive experiences of others. The books do not bear this out. *What Is the What* opens with its hero, Valentino Achak Deng, being mugged and held hostage in his apartment in Atlanta. Bound and gagged, Valentino recounts in extended flashback the story of his infancy in Sudan, the destruction of his happy family in civil strife, and the terrifying vicissitudes of his escape. Doing so, he imagines addressing his words to his assailants, first a black man and woman, then their young son who watches TV while Valentino is bound on the floor.

TV Boy, you are no doubt thinking that we're absurdly primitive people, that a village that doesn't know whether or not to remove the plastic from a bicycle—that such a place would of course be vulnerable to attack, to famine and any other calamity. And there is some truth to this. In some cases we have been slow to adapt. And yes, the world we lived in was an isolated one. There were no TVs there, I should say to you, and I imagine it would not be difficult for you to imagine what this would do to your own brain, needing as it does steady stimulation.

This device, of flashback and indignant address, is tediously labored over many pages; suddenly Eggers seems a much less talented author.

The situation improves in *Zeitoun,* where Eggers uses a third person and keeps the chronology fairly straight, bar long flashbacks that paint an idealizing picture of Zeitoun's Syrian childhood and of the family he has formed with his American but Muslim wife, Kathy. The description of Katrina, the ensuing flood, Zeitoun's attempts to help those stranded, his arrest and mistreatment all make fascinating reading, but again Eggers undoes much that is good with labored dramatic filler: "It was growing ever more apocalyptic and surreal," he tells us at one point." Some days after the flood begins, Zeitoun, in his canoe with a friend, sees a corpse.

Zeitoun had never imagined that the day would come that he might see such a thing, a body floating in filthy water, less than a mile from his home. He could not find a place for the sight in the categories of his mind. The image was from another time, a radically different world. It brought to mind photographs of war, bodies decaying on forgotten battlefields. Who was that man? Zeitoun thought. Could we have saved him? Zeitoun could only think that perhaps the body had traveled far, that the man had been swept from closer to the lake all the way to Uptown. Nothing else seemed to make sense. He did not want to contemplate the possibility that the man had needed help and had not gotten it.

It is hard to believe this rhetoric. Zeitoun is caught up in a devastating flood that he knows has caused victims; he knows that for days the TV has been speaking of lootings and shootings. Disturbing as it is, a corpse would be far from unexpected or hard to categorize. But Eggers is determined to present Zeitoun as a paragon of decency, stability, and generosity—"Could we have saved him?" he wonders—this, presumably, in order to increase the sense of grievance when he is arrested; but the scandal of arbitrary arrest would be the same however pleasant or unpleasant the arrested man.

Later, when Zeitoun and his friends are questioned, then imprisoned in a large outside cage, we hear that the situation "surpassed the most surreal accounts he'd heard of third world law enforcement." Clearly Zeitoun had not read *What Is the What*. Cruel, stupid, unnecessary, and illegal his arrest certainly is, but Zeitoun does, thank heaven, come out of jail after a month in one piece.

One aspect of the story seems to interest Eggers more than others. Imprisoned, Zeitoun wonders whether he isn't being punished for having believed himself chosen by God to save people from the flood. Again constructive actions are suspected of containing a germ of destructive self-regard. Perhaps there is simply no way of getting away from this ambiguity when acts of goodness draw attention to those who perform them. Has Eggers himself, for example, achieved a complete separation between promoting himself and promoting his cause? If he wanted to lend his pen to Zeitoun and Achak Deng, someone might ask, could these books not have been ghostwritten and published under the protagonists' names? Or would that have impeded their success? "All author proceeds from this book go to the Zeitoun Foundation, dedicated to rebuilding New Orleans and fostering interfaith understanding," we are told at the beginning of *Zeitoun.* This is extremely generous, and certainly in this way more donations will be raised, but to achieve that goal Eggers lays himself open to the suspicion that he is drawing attention to himself along with the foundation. We are far away here from Will and Hand's random charity in *You Shall Know Our Velocity!* yet once again we realize how hard it is to perform an act of public charity without equivocation.

And, as with Will and Hand, how hard to predict the consequences. If you seek to encourage a liberal attitude by offering an idealized view of an ongoing real-life narrative, you risk the eventuality that a new twist in that story, after your book is finished, could undermine all your persuasion. Rereading now the happy picture of Syria painted in *Zeitoun,* it is hard not to think of events there today. Hearing the recent news that Zeitoun, after castigating his daughters for their non-Islamic dress habits, today stands charged with hiring a killer to murder his now estranged wife, some hard hearts will not only feel confirmed in their prejudices but will suppose that Eggers is a sucker. These are not the kinds of considerations that would normally fall within a reviewer's brief, but the radical form of writing Eggers has chosen here makes them inevitable. It is with some relief, then, that one opens *A Hologram for the King* to find that it is an absolutely ordinary novel.

Alan Clay (as in "feet of"), fifty-four, failing in every department—work, home, health, romance—arrives in Saudi Arabia with a last chance to turn his life around: a usually idle private consultant, he is fronting a small team from the giant information technology company, Reliant, which is bidding to be a major supplier for King Abdullah Economic City (KAEC), a vast development on the coast of Saudi Arabia. If Reliant gets the deal, Alan will be solvent again.

Eggers gets the ball rolling with great confidence and dispatch. On the trip over, Alan met a woman he would have liked to know better, but failed to get her contact details; our subject is inadequacy, missed opportunity. Oversleeping on his first night in Riyadh, he misses his transport out to KAEC, and finds on late arrival that the city so far comprises just three buildings in a desert and that the king, who is to assess their presentation, is not scheduled to put in an appearance any time soon. To make matters worse, his team of three young technicians, Rachel, Cayley, and Brad, has been relegated to a large tent without adequate air-conditioning or Wi-Fi, the latter being essential for their plan to impress King Abdullah by projecting a hologram of a Reliant executive in London who will explain the details of the company's bid. Every attempt by Alan to get information about the king's movements or to improve conditions in the tent is fobbed off. This situation remains static for several days.

Alan is the book. Like previous Eggers heroes, he swings between defeatism and wild optimism. One moment he thinks of running away from his American life and reneging on the debts that shamefully prevent him from paying for his daughter's college; at others he feels he could "stride the world, a colossus, enough money to say fuck *you,* and *you,* and *you.*" But where Dave and Will in earlier books were on the excited brink of adulthood and full of energy, Alan is fading fast. He built a career selling for Schwinn bicycles, manufactured in Chicago, but lost his job when production was moved to Asia. His consequent decline is made emblematic of the decline of American manufacturing, American power, American confidence in the world. Alan had drawn a lot of his energy from his conflicted relationship with his ex-wife Ruby, but eventually they fell apart; similarly, tensions in the once fertile relationship between unions and management destroyed American enterprise. These are the two broken families behind our narrative. Meantime, Alan has a growth on the back of his neck that he fears is cancerous; he hasn't had sex for years.

Eggers stays remorselessly on theme. Conversation after conversation, flashback after flashback fill in the steps that brought Alan's life and America to this. Alan phones his father, an erstwhile union leader in shoe manufacturing, and is mocked for his naïveté when, to save Schwinn, he betrayed their traditional workers and relocated production. An acquaintance tells of losing a contract to provide quality glass for the Ground Zero development to a Chinese manufacturer. A close friend of Alan's who has sought to free himself from materialism in Emersonian transcendentalism has killed himself by walking into a Massachusetts pond. Rachel, Cayley, and Brad, Reliant's team, are youngsters who have no knowledge of manufacturing and do nothing but stare at their computers; they seek no relationship with Alan, or he with them; rather, he is afraid that they will see him, rightly, as utterly impotent.

Here is a problem for the novel. We never believe that a man like Alan would be fronting a crucial bid by a major IT company. He knows nothing of IT, nor gives any indication of having done much homework. He was chosen because he once had a brief acquaintance with a nephew of the king; Arab royalty, however, is famous for its multitudinous families, and this particular nephew is known to be a loser. Could Reliant be so inept? Out at KAEC Alan mooches about the site musing over his stalled life, frequently stumbling and hurting himself. Back at the hotel he gets drunk on the ferocious liquor provided for him by a bored Danish ex-pat eager for sexual pleasure he can't offer; drinking, he writes letters to his daughter Kit in which he seeks and fails to offer her useful wisdom. Eventually he takes a serrated knife to the growth on his neck in a gesture of self-harm that always seems to lie just below the surface of those characters closest to Eggers, men frustrated by the impossibility of turning their natural energy to good use. The problem with America's decline, for Alan, is that it has left him without a harness to work in, taken away any reason for not drinking himself sick; only drunkenness gives him an illusion of vitality and purpose.

Mightn't KAEC itself provide such a reason? Eggers's characters like to form purposeful groups who build things together. In the memoir Dave has his magazine. Zeitoun looks forward to rebuilding New Orleans. Eggers himself has his publishing house, McSweeney's. As his bibliography suggests, he likes collaborations, individual energy subsumed in the communal will. His books carry long lists of acknowledgments, as if he were eager to convince us that he is not the only person responsible for what we are reading. So in *A Hologram* Alan is intensely drawn to the vision of the future KAEC. "He wanted to believe that this kind of thing, a city rising from dust, could happen." He imagines staying in the city and becoming part of the project. Alas, as its name suggests, the development of King Abdullah Economic City depends entirely on the caprice of an absent king.

Alan's one meaningful contact with Saudi Arabia is his driver, Yousef, who he immediately imagines might be his son, someone he can help. A source of comedy, the savvy young Yousef is concerned that he might be murdered by the man who married the girl Yousef himself was in love with and who now continues to send him erotic text messages at great risk to both their lives, given Saudi laws on adultery. In keeping with Eggers's focus on the tension between constructive and destructive energies, what fascinates Alan in Saudi Arabia is the gap, everywhere evident, between a rigidly ethical Islamic facade and people who seem to be doing whatever the hell they want. But this world is too puzzling and alien for Alan to have any useful part in it. In the end he is happiest when, in the country with Yousef, he sees some men building a wall and, to the bewilderment of his driver, persuades them to let him help.

Cleverly set up, the novel falters. The references to American decline and Saudi duplicity begin to weary. Everything is a little too schematic, symbolic, and significant. Alan has what proves to be a lipoma removed by a Saudi woman surgeon aided by a Chinese, a German, an Italian, and a Russian, with an Englishman "observing." Afterward he manages to start a romance with this surgeon, who invites him to her home by the sea, where they swim together, she, in her late fifties, wearing only her bikini bottoms in order to appear, to any distant snooper, as another man. Such scenes are not easy to get right.

> He had never seen anything more beautiful than her hips rising and falling, her legs kicking, her naked torso undulating. She swam out farther and paused where the floor dropped precipitously into deepest blue.

Finally Alan has found someone he can connect with. However, as the couple are about to make love, he is blocked by memories of his wife, thoughts of the mess his life has become. If Eggers's earlier books are fired with the tension between selfish energy and constructive goodness, chaos and order, Alan has neither the energy that would generate chaos nor a framework—family, business, nation—in which to construct. This is a melancholy performance, but so much more alive than the true stories that preceded it.

Haruki Murakami

Considering the life and work of Haruki Murakami it's as well to keep a sharp eye on the relationship between individual and community, on questions of inclusion and exclusion, belonging and abandonment. Grandson of a Buddhist priest, his father a teacher of Japanese literature, Murakami has made a point of writing outside the Japanese tradition, against it almost, drawing to a large extent on tropes, images, and cultural references from Western literature, classical music, and pop culture. In this respect he has been praised for, but also accused of, pioneering a new global literature whose stories, whether real, surreal, or "magical," are not radically located in any place or culture precisely in order to appeal to a worldwide audience.

Murakami denies this. While admitting that as a child he "wanted to escape from [Japanese] culture . . . felt it was boring, too sticky," on the other hand he insists, "I don't want to write about foreigners in foreign countries; I want to write about us. I want to write about Japan, about our life here. That's important to me. Many people say that my style is accessible to Westerners; it might be true, but my stories are my own, and they are not Westernized."

So, for Murakami, his rejection of traditional culture has meaning primarily within the context of Japan; any international payoff is coincidental. That said, a writer in conflict with his own culture and sympathetic to material that circulates in the international space is bound to appeal to those in other countries who see themselves in similar positions. The appeal is all the stronger in Murakami's case, thanks to a fluid prose style that remains syntactically and lexically straightforward however strange the content. Translation may not be easy, but it is certainly possible.

In interviews Murakami insists on being an outsider: "I'm a loner. I don't like groups, schools, literary circles." In each novel, he says, he wants his main character to be "an independent, absolute individual . . . a type of man who chooses freedom and solitude over intimacy and personal bonds." On the other hand, from 1974 to 1981 Murakami and his wife ran a coffeehouse and jazz bar, as does his hero in *South of the Border, West of the Sun*. So this is by no means a man averse to community, on his own terms. "I made the cocktails and I made the sandwiches," he tells us. "I didn't want to become a writer—it just happened. It's a kind of gift, you know, from the heavens. So I think I should be very humble."

With the same kind of humility Murakami insists, "I am just like the people who read my books." Thus if one culture and community is abandoned because "sticky," another is nevertheless formed: the clients in the jazz club, the readers of his fiction; it's a more fluid, easygoing culture, but also one where Murakami himself is now controlling rather than compliant, thanks to that gift from above. Talking about the phenomenal worldwide success of his writing, he remarks: "It's incredible. I write a novel every three or four years, and people are waiting for it. I once interviewed John Irving, and he told me that reading a good book is a mainline. Once they are addicted, they're always waiting." This begins to sound like another form of stickiness, perhaps as much for the pusher as the addict. But no doubt any community requires some kind of glue.

Becoming a loner has its price. Within a family, a community, one has a position in relation to others and life has a visible drama, tragic or comic, that makes sense inside the terms of the dominant culture. To fall outside that network of relationships or deliberately withdraw from it is to be thrown entirely onto one's own resources, to become prey to bizarre thought processes, dreams, hallucinations, perhaps to sink into a deep well of depression. Wells are a recurring image in Murakami's work, holes one falls down, but also bubbling with strange psychic life.

To survive one must become strong. "You've got to be the world's toughest 15-year old," the young hero of *Kafka on the Shore* is told as he prepares to abandon his father's home. In many of Murakami's novels the main character will find himself torn between two women, one tormented and "spiritual," drawing him into a rich but potentially fatal alternative world, the other easygoing, practical, with a sense of humor, and ready to give him not just sex but traditional family, even tribe: "I'd make a pile of babies for you as tough as little bulls. And we'd all live happily ever after, rolling on the floor," says Midori in *Norwegian Wood*.

It sounds attractive. But any reconstitution of family and community will involve loss. In *Hardboiled Wonderland and the End of the World*, we hear that in order to join a certain walled community, would-be residents are obliged to leave their shadows outside; they cannot keep their intimate individuality if they wish to join the group. "The protagonist's mind," Murakami comments, "is split between these totally different worlds and he cannot choose which to take." The author himself has no children and is on record as saying he couldn't imagine himself as a father.

In the event, the pattern of the novels is that the hero chooses first one woman and then the other, as indeed Murakami's writing itself has oscillated between an extravagant surrealism outside the mainstream and a straightforward lyrical realism that appeals directly and easily to the broadest of publics. That said, each novel contains elements of both approaches, the lead character shuttling back and forth between the two sides, before returning, or preparing to return, to some more recognizably traditional community. Thus after the many bizarre adventures that do indeed make the young Kafka (a Japanese boy, it should be stressed) "the toughest 15-year-old in the world," he nevertheless sets out for home as the story closes. For all the surreal adventure of the loner's alternative world, it is the world we are familiar with that reassuringly reasserts its dominance. In that sense these stories are perhaps less revolutionary than they might seem.

Now, in his sixties and with the expectations of a huge community of fans weighing on him, Murakami has reached a point in his career when it would be all too easy to sink into mannerism. *Colorless Tsukuru Tazaki and His Years of Pilgrimage* attempts to avoid that trap by reformulating the author's familiar tropes in the realism of a spare third-person voice describing a character who, rather than abandoning a world he is dissatisfied with, finds himself brutally and inexplicably thrust out of the happiness of peer group friendship into a pit of lonely depression. The opening lays it on thick.

"From July of his sophomore year in college until the following January, all Tsukuru Tazaki could think about was dying." Looking back on events sixteen years after this low point (a narrative strategy that recalls the opening of *Norwegian Wood*), Tsukuru remembers himself "teetering over the precipice"; he was "Jonah in the belly of the whale," "a person in a storm desperately grasping at a lamppost," a man confronting "an abyss that ran straight through to the earth's core."

The immediate cause of his distress is clear enough. In his adolescence Tsukuru had been one of a group of five friends, three boys and two girls, who had come together when they volunteered to tutor underperforming elementary schoolchildren. They were acting positively, for the benefit of the larger community, and they formed a tight and ideal community themselves, indeed a "unique sense of harmony developed between them—each one needed the other four and, in turn, shared the sense that they too were needed." They were "a perfect combination . . . Like five fingers." Sticky fingers, one might say.

Not that there weren't some troubling aspects to this idyll. While the other four members of the group each possessed some remarkable talent—one boy intellectually brilliant, another a fine athlete, one girl a beautiful pianist, the other rumbustiously comic—Tsukuru himself did not have "anything special about him." He thus developed an uneasy feeling that he might be inadequate, unworthy of the community, something rubbed in by his friends, when they pointed out that while all their names included colors—white, black, red, and blue—he was "colorless"; his name simply meant "maker." And in fact, right from the start Tsukuru's ambition was to build railway stations, places through which communities mix and move, not places where they stay still. Of the girls in the group, however, Tsukuru felt attracted not to the jolly and practical Kuro, but to the beautiful, rather spiritual Shiro, the pianist, who looked, rather ominously, like "a traditional Japanese doll." Fragile and static.

Some readers will find these heavily loaded schemes wearisome, but they do allow Murakami to frame his debate with dispatch.

Tsukuru's railway ambitions took him away from their home town of Nagoya to university in Tokyo while the others stayed put. For a year or so all was well and the old friendship easily picked up when he returned on vacation, the group attempting to maintain their "orderly harmonious community" with a number of "unspoken rules," mainly to "keep sexual relations out." In short, the original goal of helping the wider community had now given way to the new one of "maintaining the group itself." Nothing must change.

However, returning for a second summer vacation, Tsukuru found his friends had cut him off, irrevocably. They refused to answer the phone, refused to see him, and offered no explanation for their behavior. "Tsukuru was left feeling like an outcast, as if he were carrying some virulent pathogen that the others were desperately trying to avoid." His family, with whom he wasn't close, was unable to offer any consolation, nor did he have any other friends to fall back on. For the next sixteen years, despite professional success and the occasional casual relationship, his emotional life will be as if frozen. He has been pushed off the deck of a ship "to swim alone through the cold night sea." The pilgrimage of the title is his sixteen-year crossing of that sea.

Unusually for Murakami there is no humor or irony in this novel, nor are any of the key events dramatized. Everything is solemn and mesmerizingly slow, the similes and metaphors invariably portentous. Essentially, life throws up helpers of one kind or another who encourage Tsukuru to understand that he has a problem and to solve it. As the novel opens, he meets Sara, the first woman he has been deeply attracted to for many years. This attraction is declared in one of those mysterious moments typical of Murakami's fiction:

He wasn't normally conscious of it, but there was one part of his body that was extremely sensitive, somewhere along his back. This soft, subtle spot he couldn't reach was usually covered by something so that it was invisible to the naked eye.

But when, for whatever reason, that spot became exposed and someone's finger pressed down on it, something inside him would stir. A special substance would be secreted inside him, swiftly carried by his bloodstream to every corner of his body. That special stimulus was both a physical sensation and a mental one, creating vivid images in his mind.

The first time he met Sara, he felt an anonymous finger reach out and push down forcefully on that trigger on his back. The day they met they talked for a long time, though he couldn't recall much of what they said. What he did recall was the special feeling on his back and the indefinably thrilling sensation it brought to his mind and body. One part of him relaxed, another part tightened up. That sort of feeling. But what did it mean? Tsukuru thought about it for days, but he was not, by nature, adept at abstract thinking. So Tsukuru emailed Sara and invited her to dinner. He was determined to find out the meaning of that feeling, of that sensation.

How strange all this is: a spot on the back, invisible because covered, like most of the back for that matter (to eyes naked and otherwise), and presumably not marked in any way even when uncovered; an anonymous finger (do fingers usually have names? are they usually disembodied?) that pushes down on the spot (despite the fact that it presumably remains covered and invisible); a man who spends some days trying to decide what the consequent feelings might mean, then invites a girl to dinner not because he likes her but because he's puzzled.

Whatever it "means," the function of the "feeling" in the story is that it substitutes for any dramatization of their courtship. Neither

Tsukuru's "subtle spot" nor his special sensation will be mentioned again, but the two do make it to bed.

> Leisurely foreplay, caressing her, had been amazing, and after he came he had felt at peace, as he held her close. But that wasn't all there was to it. He was well aware that there was something more. Making love was a joining, a connection between one person and another. You receive something, and you also have to give something.

In the novel's scheme—and there is little outside the scheme—Tsukuru is being invited out of his isolation, but, as Sara soon understands, he is incapable of giving. Something holds him back. Having got out of him the story of his earlier abandonment, she tells him they cannot have a serious relationship until he sorts out what happened in the past. Sara works as a travel agent. She is another facilitator of movement. She checks up on his old friends, finds their professions and addresses, and more or less orders Tsukuru to go see them, fixing his tickets for him. The two men are still in Nagoya. The practical girl is married in Finland. The spiritual girl is long dead. The novel will be Tsukuru's search for closure with this past community that rejected him, in order to open up a new life with Sara.

Before that can happen, however, we are offered a bizarre key with which to read the story. Tsukuru, who symbolically is swimming through a dark sea, actually swims every day in the pool, five thousand feet, the same distance that Murakami says he swims on the days he doesn't run six miles (endurance sports are part of the loner's survival kit). The year after his friends abandon him he meets a man in the pool, Haida, who becomes his friend and whom he follows so closely in the water that he is constantly focused on his feet. Haida, who is younger than Tsukuru and whose name means "gray field," likes cooking and brings CDs to play in Tsukuru's apartment, including a rendering of Debussy's *Mal du pays* (homesickness), which happens to be one of the pieces the talented Shiro always played. No Murakami novel is complete without its theme tune, and it has to be said that this is a wonderfully melancholy piece to convey Tsukuru's nostalgia for the lost friendships of the past.

One night Haida tells his friend a long story that involves piano playing. In the late 1960s, his father, disgusted with the student protest movement, withdrew from the university and wandered around Japan. Another loner. In a remote spa town he met a man who claimed to be a jazz pianist and one day played for him, placing on top of the piano a bag with "a strange story behind it" that he refused to tell, saying only that its contents were a kind of "alter ego." This man went on to tell Haida's father that he was shortly to die, having accepted that his life be limited in return for special spiritual powers. "Each individual has their own unique color which shines faintly around the contours of their body"; the pianist can see those colors. If he wished to avoid death, he could pass on this power to someone with a certain aura, and Haida's father is such a person. But after experiencing this "omniscient view of the world," the man has no desire to extend his life if living means returning to the "shallow and superficial" past.

Within Murakami's vision the drift is clear enough. The person abandoning community is drawn toward artistic expression and spiritual awareness, guru status almost, but this can also lure him to death, the final exclusion. It may be that Tsukuru is one of the special people who could take this path, or, since he is colorless, maybe not.

But what was in the cloth bag on top of the piano? Later, hearing of two embalmed fingers left in a railway station, Tsukuru discovers that some people are born with six fingers and have the two extra fingers amputated in order to appear no different from the crowd. He imagines that the pianist preserved his two amputated sixth fingers, his specialness, as it were, in this bag.

The night after he hears the story, Tsukuru dreams he is making love to Shiro and Kuro, the girls in his old group, but then orgasms in his friend Haida's mouth. Shortly afterward, Haida disappears, never to return, and Tsukuru rather improbably has no way of getting in touch with him. Again he has been abandoned, this time by the man leading him through the water. Because he was unworthy in some way? Did Haida know about his dream? Or because Haida was some kind of emissary whose role had been fulfilled? We will never know. But this is how Murakami's novels work: an essentially realist story, Tsukuru's abandonment and consequent depression are made intriguing not through a close-up presentation of the characters and their interaction but by running them alongside mysteriously symbolic tales that invite elaborate interpretations. Readers are reassured that everything is extremely meaningful, if only we could understand it.

When Tsukuru finally goes to find his old friends, the "real" story is more intriguing than the dreams and fables: Shiro, the beautiful piano player, had told the others that on a trip to Tokyo, Tsukuru raped her. She was so distraught that though the others didn't exactly believe her, they agreed to exclude Tsukuru from the group to protect her fragile mental health. To an extent, for Kuro, who had been in love with Tsukuru, this was a punishment for his preferring the other girl, and for the two boys there was an element of revenge for Tsukuru's upstaging them by moving to Tokyo. Ten years later, moving alone to a distant town, Shiro was strangled. She wasn't tough enough to survive as a loner. The murderer was never found. Unsurprisingly, Tsukuru begins to worry that in some strange alternative world he may in fact have raped and murdered Shiro.

The details of what happened to Shiro are not pursued, nor are the relationships inside the group. Instead, each of the old friends is carefully placed in relation to the wider community. We learn that the athlete, Ao, has become a car salesman, a solid conventional figure. Ako, the intellectual, finding he couldn't fit in anywhere, because capitalism requires mediocrities who must surrender their individuality to the corporate cause, has set up a company that trains employees to become precisely the unthinking nobodies their bosses want, something he is perhaps doing "to get personal revenge on society." In fact, Ako speaks bitterly of his coming out as a homosexual and explains that he too felt he had been "thrown overboard, alone, into the ocean." Everything is seen in terms of inclusion or exclusion from peer groups, perhaps a very Japanese concern.

The most sentimental encounter is with Kuro, the girl with the sense of humor, who, having sacrificed many years to being the minder of the deeply disturbed Shiro, finally became a potter, married a Finnish potter, and lives happily with two children in Finland. She and Tsukuru listen to *Mal du pays* together and reflect that Shiro "lives on in so many ways." At this point, the albatross finally falls from Tsukuru's neck.

He was finally able to accept it all. In the deepest recesses of his soul, Tsukuru Tazaki understood. One heart is not connected to another through harmony alone. They are, instead, linked deeply through their wounds. Pain linked to pain, fragility to fragility. There is no silence without a cry of grief, no forgiveness without bloodshed, no acceptance without a passage through acute loss. That is what lies at the root of true harmony.

In short, the breakup of community eventually allows for a deeper connection through shared suffering. The world is painful, but pain has its sweet side; "not everything was lost in the flow of time." The pilgrimage over, it remains for Tsukuru to find out whether Sara, who we have since discovered is also seeing another boyfriend, will choose him or the other. If she chooses the other, Tsukuru thinks, "I may really die. Die in reality, or die figuratively—there isn't much difference between the two. But this time I definitely will take my last breath. Colorless Tsukuru Tazaki will lose any last hint of color and quietly exit the world. All will become a void, the only thing that remains a hard, frozen clump of dirt."

Hearing this drastic declaration, one is obliged to wonder how much progress the pilgrim Tsukuru has really made. He is thirty-six. He has seen the girl only four or five times, and anyway, she always had another man. He has just usefully reconnected with a group of old friends. Some counseling is in order.

Bookshops all over the world were opened at midnight to celebrate the publication of *Colorless Tsukuru Tazaki and His Years of Pilgrimage.* In the United States the initial print run of 250,000 swiftly sold out. In essence, the novel offers an intriguing core story of how an adolescent idyll went badly wrong. The main purpose of the narrative, however, is not to have that story unfold in all its complexity but to linger over the pathos and resilience of the victim, offer some suggestively surreal backdrop to complicate matters (some readers will think, "wow"), and mull at length, sometimes interestingly, in dialogues whose tone is solemnly static throughout, on the elusive relationship between individual and community, the strength needed to live alone, and the dangers of seeking to preserve a group by curbing the vital instincts of its members. This focus on the claims of the individual, the quiet heroism of the loner, together with Murakami's considerable narrative facility and powerful imagination, may go some way to explain his appeal. In the end this is the story of a woefully prolonged adolescence. There is talk of the Nobel.

Peter Matthiessen

In 1991 I agreed to translate from the Italian a book called *There Is a Place on Earth: A Woman in Birkenau,* by Giuliana Tedeschi. It began:

> There is a place on earth that is a vast desolate wilderness, a place populated by shadows of the dead in their multitudes, a place where the living are dead, where only death, hate and pain exist.

Giving almost no personal biography, no political history, no statistics, in short, no *relief,* Tedeschi recounts her own ten months in Birkenau, from day one to liberation, focusing on the devastating labor routines, the endless humiliations, the dread of "selection," the mutual hatreds among different national, ethnic, and religious groupings, and the daily degradation of body and psyche, particularly the female body and psyche.

Having taken on the translation as an ordinary work project, I soon found it impossible to put in the hours I normally would. How can one concentrate on style and grammatical nicety when telling such things? I recall an anecdote where a group of young women is ordered to go to the gas chambers; naturally, they imagine this is the end. On arrival, however, each is given a baby carriage to push a few hundred yards from gas chambers to recycling dump. As their hands make familiar contact with the baby carriage handles, Tedeschi reflects that the emaciated, desexualized bodies of herself and companions, most in their late teens and early twenties, will now never be able to bear children, nor is she likely to see her own two children again. As for the babies whose carriages these were, their fate is obvious.

Reduced to tears, I decided that this would be the last Holocaust book I would translate and perhaps the last I would read. Receiving the plain bound proof edition of *In Paradise,* by Peter Matthiessen, whom I know as an excellent nature writer and author of the Pulitzer-winning *Shadow Country* (2008), a novel set in Florida in the early years of the twentieth century, I simply dived straight in. I had no idea a book with such a title would be taking me to Auschwitz.

Not that this is really my first Holocaust read since Tedeschi's memoir. In the 1990s an increasing number of novelists, many with no experience of the period or the place, published "holocaust novels." The Goodreads website lists more than seventy "best holocaust novels." While the desire of the survivor to tell, in memoir or fiction, what he or she went through makes perfect sense, I have always been a little perplexed by these other narratives. Is a salutary remembering, as defense against repetition, really what they are about? How does the enjoyment we associate with fiction, our pleasure in an author's ingeniousness, mesh with the vast horror of the Holocaust? Occasionally I did overcome skepticism to tackle some of these books—Martin Amis's *Time's Arrow,* Christopher Hope's *Serenity House*—but in each case it seemed to me that the literary construct was overwhelmed by the enormity of the fact.

The one novelist I'm aware of who successfully exploits the reader's knowledge of the Holocaust without being swept away by it is

Aharon Appelfeld, whose work I was obliged to read when sitting on a jury for a literary prize. Appelfeld, however, achieves his goals by looking at the lives of victims before and after the experience of the camps, which are barely if ever mentioned. *The Immortal Bartfuss,* for example, recounts the empty middle age of a Holocaust survivor living in mute and miserable hostility with his wife and daughter; any reassuring notions that the extreme experience of the Holocaust would ennoble those who went through it are implacably dismissed; hence while immersing us in Bartfuss's arid life, Appelfeld is actually making us aware of our own assumptions about suffering and survival. In a very real sense, Bartfuss did not survive.

Matthiessen is aware of Appelfeld and intensely aware of the pitfalls involved in approaching the Holocaust. The hero of his book, Clements Olin, an American professor specializing in Holocaust literature by Slav writers, tends, we hear,

> to agree with the many who have stated that fresh insight into the horror of the camps is inconceivable, and interpretation by anyone lacking direct personal experience an impertinence, out of the question.

However, this acknowledgment only raises the question more sharply; why does a writer come to the Holocaust? " 'Bearing witness'?" Olin asks himself. "What more witness could be needed? *Vernichtungslager. Extermination camp.* The name signified all by itself a mythic barbarism and depravity."

Elsewhere, mentioning the Holocaust documentaries filmed by the Allied armies on arrival at the camps, Olin talks of the viewer's "moral duty" to "absorb more punishment." So is the fascination with Auschwitz a form of masochism, with a payoff in piety and self-esteem? Olin claims to be beyond that. He no longer watches such films; "even horror becomes wearisome," he tells us, "and by now every adult in the Western world has been exposed to awful images of stacked white corpses and body piles bulldozed into pits."

Reading the opening pages of *In Paradise,* we're not aware it's Auschwitz we're headed for. The year is 1996. Traveling from Boston, Polish-born Professor Olin, fifty-five, arrives at Kraków airport, misses his train for his onward journey, and is befriended in a gloomy café by two young Poles who first take him to visit the town and finally offer to drive him the thirty miles to his destination: Oświęcim. Initially friendly, the conversation between the three grows more and more exasperated, since Olin, who has never visited Poland since being smuggled away as a baby, nevertheless knows far more about Kraków's history than the two youngsters; in particular, though remarking that he is not Jewish, he knows everything about Polish anti-Semitism.

> Were you young people never told, he says, that after the war, when those few returning refugees made their way back home to Poland to reclaim their lives, they were reviled and driven off and sometimes bludgeoned and occasionally, when too persistent, killed? "Nearly two thousand Jews were murdered in this country *after* the war," he says. "Did you know that?"

Needless to say, they did not know, and equally inevitably, this approach hardly endears the older man to the two who are helping him. Aware of his "pedantic hectoring," Olin begins to have "misgivings as to why he has come here in the first place." Only at this point do we discover that Oświęcim is in fact the Polish name for

Auschwitz, Olin's destination nothing other than the camp itself where the infamous *Arbeit macht frei* insignia rises still in fancy wrought iron over the entrance. Together with 140 "pilgrims" from twelve countries, Olin is to spend a "fortnight of homage, prayer, and silent meditation in memory of this camp's million and more victims."

One of the things that has radically changed our experience of reading over the past decade is the ability to check any detail instantly on the Internet. So moments after discovering this, for me, bizarre idea of a meditation retreat in a concentration camp, I was able to read an article in *Corriere della Sera* about an Auschwitz Christmas meditation sleepover during which the author of the piece was convinced he had smelled burning flesh and an account by an American woman who attended a retreat similar to that described in Matthiessen's novel:

> It was pitch black inside [the crematorium]. As we focused on the space, we both began to feel more strongly the evil of this terrible place, and the unimaginable suffering that happened there over several years. We discussed whether we were simply projecting onto our experience what we already knew, but both of us felt strongly that our feelings were real.

The question immediately arises: is this, as *Corriere della Sera* would have it, "the noble tourism of suffering"? Or is it the morbid adventure of "holocaust voyeurs," as Olin at one point of *In Paradise* fears? Matthiessen, we learn from a brief article in the *New York Times,* has attended three such retreats at Auschwitz and is himself a Zen Buddhist priest. He knows the territory.

On arrival Olin claims he has come to the retreat not primarily to meditate, but to do research on Tadeusz Borowski, another who both survived and did not survive the camps. Celebrated author of *This Way to the Gas Chambers, Ladies and Gentlemen,* Borowski was reunited with his girlfriend, also a camp survivor, after the war, only to commit suicide days after their first child was born. However, it soon becomes plain that this academic project is the merest alibi; there must be deeper reasons for Olin's visit.

As the participants gather for their first meetings, Olin and others are constantly prodded as to their motivation by the loudmouthed and offensive Gyorgi Earwig, an "unaffiliated" guest determined to attack any manifestation of piety, any notion of closure or resolution or "healing of faiths." Seeing a pair of nuns lighting a candle to Maximilian Kolbe, a Polish priest canonized for reputedly giving his life to save an inmate's life, Earwig denounces this story as a monstrous Catholic myth designed to cover for a pope who "sat on his holy hands while Jews by the millions were going up in smoke." When an American woman "in a fur-lined leather coat" confesses how terrible she feels on seeing the Holocaust museum, how much she would like to "do something for those people," Earwig "rounds on her like a poked badger: 'Do something, lady?' he snarls. 'Like what? Take a Jew to lunch?'" Of Olin's "research," he demands, "You got some new angle on mass murder, maybe, that ain't been written up yet in maybe ten thousand fucking books? . . . What are all you Holocaust kibitzers really here for?" When Olin replies that he has come to listen to the "silence," Earwig is scornful: "Bullshit. You want to hear lost voices, right? Like all the rest of 'em."

In short, far from being a healing experience, initially the meditation retreat generates nothing but friction. Invited, at evening meetings, to come forward and "bear witness," first tearful Germans find that their desire to unburden themselves of national guilt is met with icy coldness, then an Israeli historian is attacked for having owned to a certain element of Jewish provocation behind anti-Semitism; an American Jew is castigated for drawing a parallel between the camps and an ugly episode of prejudice experienced at high school, while a group of Polish intellectuals are criticized for being unwilling to speak up at all. Palestinian Arabs, Buddhist monks, Anglican clergymen, Kibbutz workers, rabbis, Czech revolutionaries, as each expresses his position on the Holocaust, he merely rouses the opposition of those who think otherwise. Even the survivors present are accused of having survived at the expense of others. Some break down in tears. One refuses to speak to the Germans. Another threatens to leave. Presented in lively, all too believable dialogue, these scenes allow Matthiessen to get a broad range of angry opinion on the page without being obliged to declare a position of his own.

In the morning participants meditate in silence on the long platform where prisoners went through their first selection on arrival at the camps. Olin, it turns out, like Matthiessen, is a practiced meditator, he knows how to adjust his posture and regulate his breathing "following traditional yogic practice." Yet in the event very little is said about the meditation experience. Perhaps because, no sooner seated, people find it hard in this dramatic location to stop their minds from wandering, and almost immediately fall victim to hallucinations:

Breathing mindfully, moment after moment, his awareness opens and dissolves into snow light. But out of nowhere, just as he had feared, the platform's emptiness is filled by a multitude of faceless shapes milling close around him. He feels the vibration of their footfalls.

This brings us to the irony, the conundrum if you like, at the heart of the book, and indeed of any "pilgrimage" to sites of this kind. The practice of meditation has the effect of breaking down the ego; in hours of silence, the mind intensely focused on breath and body in the present moment, there is no place for the narrative chatter that feeds the constant construction of the self. Opinions, ambitions, resentments lose their energy. In the Zen tradition meditators focus on koans, complex issues so far beyond understanding that, unable to find a response, the ego again breaks down. Auschwitz, the death camps, might be thought of as the ultimate koan; Matthiessen quotes Appelfeld as remarking that in the face of the Holocaust, "Any utterance, any 'answer' is tiny, meaningless, and occasionally ridiculous." Of the platform where they meditate, one of the retreat's leaders says: "There's no space left on that platform for interpretation. It's just there . . . It just is." The meditator's hope is that, accepting this, in silent meditation, "we immerse ourselves and are transformed."

But the ego dies hard, and though the camps may be beyond understanding they are nevertheless a source of intense drama and contention, firing and hardening personal opinion. There is also the temptation to make of the meditative experience itself a dramatic episode in the ego's ongoing and self-regarding narrative: the story of how I went to the death camps and humbled myself before one of the most horrific facts of history. The retreat thus risks becoming an exaltation rather than a dissolution of the ego. This tussle between the drama of the self and its surrender in the shadow of the Holocaust is Matthiessen's bold subject.

Although Olin claims he plans to "listen to silence," no sooner does he start meditating than his mind fastens on the real reason for his journey to Auschwitz. His mother, whom he never knew, lived in this very town. He was an illegitimate child. His father, a Polish army officer, had helped *his* parents to leave the country before the war and fled with them, while his pregnant girlfriend was left behind. The baby Olin was smuggled out of the country to join the father. Only in adolescence did he begin to hear rumors, from his snobbish, quietly anti-Semitic paternal grandparents, that his mother may have been part Jewish. Now, albeit with the reluctance of someone anxious that his entire sense of self is about to change, he wants to see whether anyone in Oświęcim remembers his mother.

As he begins that quest and as if in reaction to the truth he already suspects he will uncover, that his mother died here in Auschwitz, Olin strikes out rather desperately on another possible change in his life story; he falls in love with the nun earlier insulted for lighting the candle in honor of Kolbe. Sister Catherine, it turns out, is actually a novice in her thirties in conflict with the church over various issues, hence someone who might perhaps abandon her vocation for Olin.

If the first half of the novel, then, is mainly ferocious debate, presumably drawn from Matthiessen's own experience of Auschwitz retreats, the second is a heady, not always convincing intertwining of narratives in which Olin's reluctance to accept the truth about his mother, his Jewishness, and his personal connection with the camps aligns with the world's general wish if not to deny then at least quietly to forget about the Holocaust. At the crematorium where he supposes his mother must have died, Olin's mind is seized and thronged with deeply disturbing images. Later, the rabbi attending the retreat advises those participants who are finding the experience difficult, "The only whole heart is the broken heart. But it must be wholly broken." At once we know that this must be Olin's fate.

Matthiessen's work has always carried a powerful moral message. Much of his nature writing, with its uncanny ability to capture landscape and weather, denounces the scandal of man's destruction of the flora and fauna he so beautifully evokes. *In the Spirit of Crazy Horse* (1983), his defense of the imprisoned American Indian Leonard Peltier and the Indian cause in general was entirely in line with this, and likewise *Shadow Country* is constantly moving us to acknowledge the shameful, unspoken truths that allow the ugly events of the novel's story to unfold. In this sense, though it may seem a departure, *In Paradise* is a logical conclusion to a long writing career, for Matthiessen, who died in 2014, aged eighty-six, had announced that this would be his last book. The Holocaust, the impossibility even today of getting a group of people to shed their selfishness and their differences in the presence of the Holocaust, is perhaps the ultimate indictment of man's perversity. But in a scene I imagine Matthiessen must have witnessed himself, since it seems too bizarre to be invented, an oddly positive note is struck. As the rabbi closes an evening meeting singing Oseh Shalom, a number of participants join hands and, spontaneously, almost unconsciously, find themselves wheeled about the room in a dance of great transport and intimacy. Olin is as grateful as he is surprised.

> What could there be to celebrate in such a place? Who cares? He is delighted to be caught up in it. . . . He moves with it, into it, and now it is moving him as the bonds of his despair relent like weary sinew and gratitude floods his heart. He feels filled with well-being, blessed. Whatever "blessed" might mean to a life-long disbeliever.

It's hard not to feel that in describing this strange moment of beatitude Matthiessen is looking for an analogy with his own bleak endeavor to conjure some positive collective spirit from torment and ugliness. Needless to say, no sooner is the dance over than it becomes an object of fierce controversy, denounced by most as sacrilege, praised by some as transcendence. Matthiessen was no doubt aware that his book would be met by the same heated disagreement.

Stieg Larsson

In *The Girl with the Dragon Tattoo,* the first part of Swedish writer Stieg Larsson's trilogy *Millennium,* a disgraced journalist, Mikael Blomkvist, retires to the remote island village of Hedeby, three hours north of Stockholm, where an octogenarian industrialist, Henrik Vanger, has invited him to solve the mystery of his great niece who disappeared forty years before, aged sixteen. The key to the puzzle would appear to lie in five names and numbers that the girl, Harriet Vanger, wrote in her diary shortly before vanishing without trace.

Magda—32016
Sara—32109
R.J.—30112
R.L.—32027
Mari—32018

Since 32 and 30 are local area codes, it seems reasonable to suppose these are phone numbers, yet the police found no correspondence between names and numbers. Perplexed, Blomkvist copies the list out and pins it up on the wall of the cabin where he is staying. After he has been on the island some months, his sixteen-year-old daughter turns up out of the blue. Blomkvist is divorced and rarely sees his daughter, who has hardly been mentioned to this point. She is heading for a Christian summer camp, and though the island is very much out of the way it just happens to be on her way. Blomkvist isn't happy about the girl's religious inclinations and admits as the two say good-bye that he doesn't believe in God. His daughter points out that nevertheless he reads the Bible; she "saw the quotes on the wall." And she adds: "But why so gloomy and neurotic?"

Blomkvist doesn't understand. The girl hurries off. Then it dawns on him: the first digit of the mysterious numbers indicates a book of the Bible, the second and third a chapter, the fourth and fifth a verse. Of course! Despite the fact that Blomkvist spends hours a day surfing the net on his computer, he now rushes off to find a Bible, strangely unaware that the holy book is freely available online in almost any language you care to mention. Sure enough, the digit 3 corresponds to Leviticus, where he finds verses like:

> If a woman approaches any beast and lies with it, you shall kill the woman and the beast; they shall be put to death, the blood is upon them.

and

> And the daughter of any priest, if she profanes herself by playing the harlot, profanes her father; she shall be burned with fire.

Now at last it's clear that the names Magda, Sara, and so on refer to the Jewish victims of a sexually perverted, anti-Semitic serial killer, something that would hardly surprise those reading the original Swedish and most European editions, which, in line with the author's wishes, more bluntly entitle the novel *Men Who Hate Women*.

At this point, however, any half-awake reader is bound to object: first, that since there are many more than ten books in the Bible, biblical references (book, chapter, verse) are never displayed with five-figure codes, hence on seeing these numbers—coming, what's more, directly after names and thus plausibly telephone numbers— no one, however great her knowledge of the Bible, would assume them to be text references;

second, that even if we imagine the girl making this connection, she would hardly be familiar with the content of these particular verses from Leviticus. I was brought up in an evangelical family that lived and breathed the Bible and where everyone was expected to know vast tracts of it off by heart, but never the darkly bureaucratic Leviticus;

third, that if an adolescent daughter did make this connection and did recognize the verses, she would surely be concerned to enquire of her father why he was associating such disquieting material with specific girls' names.

All this to suggest that Larsson's trilogy has not achieved its spectacular success thanks to the author's impeccable skills as a detective story writer or any scrupulous attention to psychological realism. Loose ends and incongruities abound, lending the trilogy an endearingly amateurish feel, emphasized by a translation that, though for the most part fluent, occasionally treats us to decidedly muddled idiom ("He is pulling the load of an ox and walking on eggshells") or very curious register shifts, as for example when we have a young, uneducated punk Swede saying things like "you chaps" and "gad around." From time to time, whether due to translation or otherwise, the imagery is plain comic; Blomkvist remarks of the Leviticus murderer that "He was a cut and dried serial killer."

Never mind. These failings pale to insignificance when one considers the sales figures. Published in 2005 in Sweden, *The Girl with the Dragon Tattoo* had by mid-2011 sold fifty million copies world-wide and was the first book to sell more than a million on Kindle. It has been on U.S. best-seller lists for years, and the other volumes of the trilogy have followed suit. What is the attraction?

One character holds our attention throughout the trilogy and dominates discussion of the work: Lisbeth Salander. From the first pages, it's evident that the journalist Mikael Blomkvist is an authorial alter ego. Like his creator, he is involved in running a left-wing magazine specializing in courageous investigative journalism; he is idealistic, committed, and of course, in the novel he assumes the central, private detective's role in a situation that sets him up to be a hero protecting vulnerable women from sadistic men. Not that Blomkvist is without his complications: he married and had a child with one woman while openly continuing an affair with another (his editorial partner Erika Berger), who in turn is happily married to a man who apparently has no problems with the arrangement. An experienced financial journalist, Blomkvist has the courage to take on big industry, and indeed as the story opens has just received a three-month prison sentence for libeling a major industrialist who deliberately fed him a false scoop in an attempt to destroy both him and his magazine. When Blomkvist decides to take time away from journalism to tackle the mystery of Harriet Vanger, we feel sure that he will be the book's main focus of interest. Then Lisbeth Salander, the girl with the dragon tattoo, moves center stage and rapidly takes over both the enquiry and the trilogy. All the real energy of the book will now come from her, to the point that it is only Blomkvist's interest in Salander that keeps us interested in him.

Lisbeth Salander is a pitifully thin young woman of twenty-five, not five feet tall, flat-chested, "a strange girl—fully grown but with an appearance that made her easily mistaken for a child." When Blomkvist first meets her, he finds her "altogether odd."

Long pauses in the middle of the conversation. Her apartment was messy, bordering on chaotic. . . . She had obviously spent half the night in a bar. She had love bites on her neck and she had clearly had company overnight. She had heaven knows how many tattoos and two piercings on her face and maybe in other places. She was weird.

How does Blomkvist know that Lisbeth maybe had piercings "in other places"? He doesn't. But that is the kind of thing that Larsson's alter ego likes to think. Blomkvist is, as we are frequently told, a ladies' man.

Needless to say, a taciturn young woman of punk appearance flaunting aggressive, antisocial behavior must have had a traumatic childhood. So it is. For reasons unrevealed until the second part of the trilogy (though the reader has no difficulty guessing sexual abuse is involved), Lisbeth was locked in a psychiatric ward at age twelve and is still under the control of a legal guardian who disposes of her income. She is thus extremely vulnerable, a "perfect victim," one character thinks of her. On the other hand, she is also a "world class hacker," a brilliant, self-taught mathematician, and "an information junkie with a delinquent child's take on morals and ethics." Working freelance for a security firm that installs sophisticated alarm systems and carries out private investigations, Salander has a magical ability to get inside anyone's computer at any time and find everything relevant there in just a few moments (something many of us can't do in our own computers); she has a photographic memory to read all she sees in a flash and recall it word for word, and, or so Blomkvist imagines, she also has "*Asperger's syndrome. . . . Or something like that. A talent for seeing patterns and understanding abstract reasoning where other people perceive only white noise.*" Finally, if push comes to shove,

Salander can be extremely violent, even sadistic. She is victim, super-hero, and torturer. To emphasize this paradoxical, almost cartoonish aspect of her character, Larsson has the anorexic-looking girl wear T-shirts with aggressive slogans: I CAN BE A REGULAR BITCH, JUST TRY ME, or KILL THEM ALL AND LET GOD SORT THEM OUT.

Salander's dealings with her new guardian, Nils Erik Bjurman—which form the first novel's main subplot—establish a pattern for the trilogy's treatment of sexuality, which is arguably its central, if some-times disguised, subject. Salander's previous guardian, who gener-ously gave her near-total freedom, has suffered a stroke, and his substitute, Bjurman, a fifty-five-year-old lawyer, decides to take advantage of his new charge and satisfy a lust for domination: "[Salander] was the ideal plaything—grown up, promiscuous, so-cially incompetent, and at his mercy. . . . She had no family, no friends: a true victim."

Bjurman tells Salander she can have access to her income only in return for sex. After compelling her to engage in oral sex in one en-counter, at the next he handcuffs and brutally rapes her.

"So you don't like anal sex," he said.
Salander opened her mouth to scream. He grabbed her hair and stuffed the knickers in her mouth. She felt him put-ting something around her ankles, spread her legs apart and tied them so that she was lying there completely vulnerable. . . . Then she felt an excruciating pain as he forced some-thing up her anus.

Salander, however, turns the tables. With access, through her work, to hi-tech security equipment, she had placed a digital camera in her bag and pointed it at the bed where Bjurman raped her. How easy, you would have thought, for her now to launch this on the net and destroy the man. But "Salander was not like any normal person," Larsson tells us. She attends the next meeting with Bjurman as promised, and when he tries to repeat the scene, stuns him with a Taser, handcuffs him to the bed, and performs the same anal abuse on him; then she forces him to watch the video of the previous rape and spends a whole night tattooing on his chest in large letters "I AM A SADISTIC PIG, A PERVERT, AND A RAPIST." From now on Bjurman must do exactly as she tells him; otherwise, the video will be made public and he will be destroyed. "*She had taken control,*" thinks Bjurman in italics. "*Impossible.* He could do nothing to resist when Salander bent over and placed the anal plug between his buttocks. 'So you're a sadist,' she said."

There is an element of the graphic novel in all this, a feeling that we have stepped out of any feasible realism into a cartoon fantasy of ugly wish fulfillment. The same comic book tone returns whenever Salander goes into retaliatory action:

Her teeth were bared like a beast of prey. Her eyes were glittering, black as coal. She moved with the lightning speed of a tarantula and seemed totally focused on her prey as she swung the club again.

Having researched Blomkvist's past for Henrik Vanger, the man who commissioned him to solve the mystery of the missing girl, Salander will eventually meet the journalist when he asks Vanger's lawyer for a researcher to help him establish the identities of the victims in the strange list of biblical texts. Meanwhile, however, Salander's unpleasant encounters with her guardian are run side by side with a developing sexual adventure of Blomkvist's. When the young Harriet

Vanger disappeared forty years before, all the many members of the extended Vanger family had been on the island to attend a shareholder's meeting of the company they jointly owned. Much aged, some of those members are still in residence and must of course be questioned as part of Blomkvist's investigation. Cecilia, a headmistress in her mid-fifties, abused in the past by her estranged husband, invites Blomkvist for coffee. When he turns up, she greets him in a bathrobe, is happy to talk about her need for an "occasional lover," and props her bare legs on his knee. Very soon:

> She sat astride him and kissed him on the mouth. Her hair
> was still wet and fragrant with shampoo. He fumbled with
> the buttons on her flannel shirt and pulled it down around
> her shoulders. She had no bra. She pressed against him when
> he kissed her breasts.

Their embraces become routine, but after Blomkvist is obliged to take time away from his investigation to serve his brief prison sentence, he learns on return that Cecilia wants to end the affair because she was becoming too attached and losing control. Shortly afterward, Lisbeth Salander is engaged to help Blomkvist with his research and comes to live with him in his cabin, sleeping in a spare room. After they have spent seven days gathering information about women raped, burned, bound, strangled, and mutilated over the previous fifty years, Salander realizes that Blomkvist "had not once flirted with her." For his part Blomkvist is concerned about being seen around with Salander, because she looks "barely legal" and hence he might appear to be "a dirty old middle-aged man," something that worries him greatly. Irritated because she knows the journalist likes women but has made no move on her, Salander goes to his bed and climbs in. Like Cecilia, she too likes to sit on top. And she doesn't mind that he has no condoms. What matters is that she has control. Again like Cecilia, she prefers separate beds once the fun is over.

The reader is thus presented with quite an array of sexual behavior, all strictly divided into the grotesquely obscene and the charmingly promiscuous: on the one hand there are Bjurman's anal sadism and the gruesome, sexually motivated murders, child abuse, and incest that lie at the heart of the investigation into Harriet's disappearance (to which, in the later parts of the trilogy, will be added prostitution rackets and sadomasochistic pedophile porn); on the other there are "transgressive" but harmless encounters between consenting individuals; Blomkvist with his married lover, Erika Berger (who, we hear, prefers sex with two men at a time), Blomkvist with Cecilia, Blomkvist with Salander, Salander with her lesbian lover, Mimmi (they play domination games), and so on. Notably, all sexual encounters in which men take the initiative are violent and pathological; all encounters in which women run the relationship (avoiding commitment) are okay. There is nothing in between and no space for the traditional, assertive male libido. One might say that the emphasized and elaborately fantasized ugliness of one kind of sex makes the softer variety the only sort possible and permissible.

The *Millennium* trilogy offers much entertainment typical of genre fiction: the puzzle of the complex crime in *The Girl with the Dragon Tattoo,* the suspense of the police investigation in *The Girl Who Played with Fire,* the drama of the political thriller in *The Girl Who Kicked the Hornet's Nest.* None of this is remarkable. What is surprising is the novels' energetic focus on ethical issues and in particular the question of retribution. Fear and courage, so often central to thrillers and suspense narratives, are hardly discussed or dramatized, nor does Larsson make more than token efforts to have us really worry for his characters. We feel he is going through the motions when he has Blomkvist with a noose round his neck at the end of part one, or when Salander is shot in the head and buried in a shallow grave at the end of part two. We know our heroes are in no real danger because Larsson is not interested in these predicaments and makes little effort to imagine them. They are comic strip material. His two protagonists themselves seem aware of this and hence are quite fearless. Half choked, apparently about to die, Blomkvist has time to reflect of his torturer who is explaining how his father abused him, "Good Lord, what a revoltingly sick family."

What matters instead is the division of the world into good and evil, a division that begins with splitting sex into positive and negative experiences, then ripples out from that in fascinating ways. On the side of rape and abuse are Nazism and anti-Semitism (the Vanger family included many Nazi sympathizers), every kind of large organization (which is always understood as conspiratorial and always at some point involved in preying on young women), government, the secret services, big business, fundamentalist religion, and so on. Even families are potentially dangerous insofar as they impose a closed world in which abuse can take place, or even be taught: Martin Vanger, the missing Harriet's brother, was initiated in rape and murder by his father, who helped him to rape and strangle a girl when he was just sixteen. Of the hugely extended Vanger family we are repeatedly told that none of its members, however unhappily married, ever divorced, as if this were an indication of a deep malaise. Investigate sex abuse and you come across a sick family and a corrupt organization. Investigate a corrupt organization and invariably someone is involved in sex abuse. Every attempt by one person to control another is evil.

On the side of cheerful promiscuity is the free individual, able to move in and out of relationships and maintain more than one in openness and honesty. Lending her apartment rent-free to Mimmi, Salander says she would like to come round for sex from time to time, but that it is "not part of the contract"; Mimmi can always say no and still keep the apartment. "What Berger liked best about her relationship with Blomkvist," we are told, "was the fact that he had no desire whatsoever to control her." Reassuringly, he "had all manner of terminated relationships behind him, and he was still on friendly terms with most of the women involved."

So concerned are the candid, free individuals when they hear of sexual exploitation or any abuse of power that they inevitably become involved in pursuing it. Indeed, Blomkvist, Salander, and their author draw most of their energy and motivation from the abuses they hate, to the point that you can no more imagine them renouncing pursuit of a sex abuser than renouncing sex itself. So while the first book turns up a sexually perverted serial killer, the second, *The Girl Who Played with Fire,* starts with a freelance investigation into sex trafficking (bringing under-age eastern European girls into Sweden as prostitutes), revealing complicity in the highest places. "Girls-victims; boys-perpetrators . . . there is no other form of criminality in which the sex roles themselves are a precondition for the crime." In this world male prostitutes do not exist.

But what power does the ordinary person have to right these wrongs? Blomkvist and his steady lover Berger use their magazine, *Millennium,* to draw attention to crime and invite the authorities to take action, often a frustrating strategy, particularly when it comes to sex trafficking, because "everybody likes a whore—prosecutors, judges, policemen, even an occasional member of parliament. Nobody was going to dig too deep to bring that business down."

Salander on the other hand, as the supreme victim (when we discover the full list of what she has been through, the mind boggles), is unimpressed by the "insufferable do-gooder" Blomkvist, who thinks he can "change everything with a book." She takes the law into her own hands and has no qualms about using violence and inflicting pain. Blomkvist, speaking for the modern liberal conscience, can't condone this; he is always ready to consider mitigating circumstances. "Martin didn't have a chance," he says of the serial killer who followed his father's footsteps. Salander's response is doggedly simplistic: "Martin had exactly the same opportunity as anyone else to strike back. He killed and raped because he liked doing it." He deserves violent punishment.

The gratification that the trilogy offers comes when, mediated through Larsson's and Blomkvist's troubled but admiring contemplation, Salander exposes herself to every kind of risk in order to mete out retribution to monstrous criminals, a retribution all the more satisfying when, in biblical fashion, it resembles the crime: an eye for an eye, a tooth for a tooth, an anal rape for an anal rape. The greatest monster of them all, it turns out, is Salander's Russian father, who beat her mother savagely and was a key man in the Russian secret services and a sex and drug trafficker to boot. The moment when, still filthy with the soil that has been heaped on her, Salander drags herself and three bullet wounds from a shallow grave to take an axe to her perverted father's head can serve as an image of the pervading spirit of the book.

However, Salander never actually kills. Not herself. Once she has reduced a victim to total vulnerability—nailing his feet to the floor with a nail gun, for example—she will anonymously contact some rival criminal eager to finish the job. It might be hard for the reader, or more pertinently her creator, to love her and the violence she perpetrates if she became a killer. As it is, we are invited to admire her ingenuity and expertise.

Not all is lurid. Food is important. Shopping. Furniture. Domesticity. Larsson invites us to identify with his heroes by filling in the ordinary moments of their single lives, the humdrum aloneness that makes colorful sexual encounters so desirable. A cookbook could be compiled from Blomkvist's efforts in the kitchen in the first novel of the trilogy. Salander prefers to get herself pizza and Coke. Both of them are used to eating alone in front of a computer screen. As independent spirits, they prefer Apple to Microsoft. Both pay more attention to technical stats than to nutritional value. Replacing her computer after an accident, Salander

> set her sights on the best available: . . . the new Apple PowerBook G4/1.0 GHz in an aluminium case with a PowerPC 7451 processor with an AltiVec Velocity Engine, 960 MB Ram and a 60 GB hard drive. It had BlueTooth and built-in CD and DVD burners.

One is reminded of the frequently cited technical specs of guns in Mailer's *Why Are We in Vietnam?* The computer is Salander's weapon. Unlike firearms, however, this is a weapon every ordinary reader handles every day.

> Best of all, it had the first 17-inch screen in the laptop world with NVIDIA graphics and a resolution of 1440 × 900 pixels, which shook the PC advocates and outranked everything else on the market.

It is through the computer screen that the free individual can hack into the evil world of the great corporation with its corrupt practices and pedophile porn rings and begin the duty or the fantasy of striking back. Not quite *Alice Through the Looking Glass* but not unrelated; when Salander goes online she is transformed, omnipotent.

Many novels have captured the global imagination by presenting modern man in thrall to a vast international conspiracy; one thinks of Eco's *Foucault's Pendulum* or Dan Brown's *The Da Vinci Code*. The hidden organization that conditions and controls us is the antithesis of individualism and its natural enemy, an evil extension of the potentially perilous family that wields such power over us from birth, or indeed the traditional marriage that restricts our sexual encounters, or the incompetent if not nakedly evil State that tangles us in a web of bureaucracy and is always complicit with organized crime. From all these things, Salander shows us how to be free, with inspired use of our laptops.

It is the ingenuousness and sincerity of Larsson's engagement with good and evil that give the trilogy its power to attract. There really is no suspicion in these books that his heroes' obsessions might be morbid. Certainly the reader will not be invited to question his or her enjoyment in seeing sexual humiliation inflicted on evil rapists. That pleasure will not be spoiled. It's not surprising, reading biographical notes, that as an adolescent Larsson witnessed a gang rape and despised himself for failing to intervene, or that in his twenties he spent time in Eritrea training guerrillas—women guerrillas, of course—and then much of his mature life investigating and denouncing neo-Nazis. Indeed, he was so active in this area that he felt it wise not to make his address public, or even his relationship with Eva Gabrielsson, his partner of thirty years. The two didn't marry, she has explained in interviews, because under Swedish law marriage would have required making their address public. Nor did they have children. As a result, when Larsson died of a heart attack, age fifty, shortly before the first part of the trilogy was published and without having made a will, his estate passed to his family of origin, the father and brother with whom he was not particularly close, leaving Gabrielsson with nothing of the vast income that was about to accrue. A man with a better eye for plot, one feels, would not have allowed such a loose end to threaten his achievement; unless these are precisely the pitfalls of remaining a free individual outside any confining social system.

E. L. James

"Touching yourself" was strictly forbidden in our family. My father was an evangelical clergyman, my mother his zealous helper. The hand mustn't stray below the belt, because such pleasures were always accompanied by evil, lascivious thoughts. Yet as Dusty Springfield memorably sang in "Son of a Preacher Man," "being good isn't always easy, no matter how hard I try," and at thirteen for this son of a preacher man it was impossible. To get round the conflict—the sexual imperative and the fear of falling into sin—I would imagine going through the entire Anglican marriage ceremony with whatever girl was the object of my desire before allowing the hand to move to its inevitable destination; in this way, I hoped, my fantasies would be conjugal rather than lecherous and any sin much diminished.

A great deal of modern narrative follows this strategy for having one's cake and eating it: a certain transgression is desired, but the moral code that deems the act a transgression must not be undermined, or even openly opposed. Nicholson Baker had much sophisticated fun with this tension in his erotic novels *Vox* and *The Fermata*. The latter imagines a man who has the power to stop the world, freezing everything in a static moment, while within this "fermata" he is able to move around and manipulate whatever he wants with complete impunity. It's an extraordinary facility, but instead of using it to accumulate wealth or change the world in some dramatic way, he merely undresses beautiful girls, fantasizes, masturbates, dresses the girls again, and removes all evidence of what has happened. As much pleasure appears to be taken from the fact that the world has not been at all changed or violated as from the secret possession of female beauty and consequent sexual pleasure.

Baker is a fine writer and remarkable stylist and invites the reader to be aware of the ironies behind his hero's adventures and indeed our engagement with them; his books offer amused reflection on the ambiguous position of wayward fantasies in a moral world. However, if one wishes to achieve huge popularity as a writer, it is perhaps as well not to make fun of these complex and for many people rather solemn negotiations. Stieg Larsson's *Millennium* trilogy was a case in point: Larsson's investigative hero Blomkvist is promiscuous but always gentlemanly. The sex he enjoys is tame to the point of tedium. In particular, he always leaves the initiative to the ladies, who invariably end up sitting on top. Yet Blomkvist spends much of his time pursuing men who indulge in brutal, violent sexual perversions and is assisted in his mission by a girl who has been the victim of such perversions and who carries out ruthless revenge of the eye-for-an-eye variety. Hence the reader can enjoy descriptions of violent rape seen as a form of just retribution for previously described violent rape, while at the same time being reassured that there is a distinct line between this sort of evil sex and the friendly promiscuity between us right-minded folks who condemn it but like to read about it. Larsson seems entirely unaware of any irony; likewise, one suspects, his many fans.

The *Millennium* trilogy has sold around seventy-five million copies worldwide. E. L. James's novel *Fifty Shades of Grey* has sold more than one hundred million—and offers an even more effective formulation of the have-your-cake-and-eat-it strategy. The underlying goal of the book would appear to be to take pleasure in describing a series of softly sadomasochistic sexual encounters, in which the female reader will be invited to identify with the submissive partner; however, this is to be done in such a way that no matter how wanton the sex may become, the heroine and indeed her spanking hero can remain essentially innocent, good, positive people who, in a better world, would never have sought such a disturbing form of intimacy. Like all really popular fiction, *Fifty Shades of Grey* is resolutely conservative: transgression is explored and enjoyed not to call moral or social codes into question but to reinforce them.

Anastasia, twenty-one, a literature student approaching her final exams, is beautiful, supposedly witty, and a virgin. No man has ever so much as held her hand, and she has never used her hands to commit any impure act. It seems she has no difficulty being good. Initially her problems with control are limited to keeping her "wayward hair" in order. She thinks a great deal, "overthinks," perhaps. In any event, her favorite occupation is "reading a classic British novel, curled up in a chair in the campus library." It is safe to identify with her.

She does not seek to meet "mega industrialist tycoon" Christian Grey. Rather, she substitutes for the friend who was supposed to interview him for a student magazine but has fallen ill. The bold questions she asks Grey—"Are you gay?"—which initially cause him to take an interest in her, are not her questions but her friend's, read from a sheet of paper. She is not responsible.

An atmosphere of innocuous comic strip informs the opening pages. Exclamations of the Holy cow! Holy crap! variety abound. Anastasia, "her blue eyes too big for her face," trips up, "falling headfirst" into Grey's office—and, of course, into love. Grey, twenty-seven, is perfection in caricature: "He's not merely good-looking—he's the epitome of male beauty, breathtaking." His gaze is "bold," "unwavering, intense," his voice "warm and husky like dark melted chocolate fudge caramel." As for his body, "Michelangelo's David has nothing on him." An obsessive achiever, he flies helicopters, airplanes, and gliders, and plays piano with impeccable expertise. After their first meeting, this immensely rich and powerful fellow who exercises "control in all things" travels from his home in Seattle to Vancouver, Washington, to visit Anastasia where she works part-time in a hardware store. Needless to say, when he contrives, while making a purchase of rope and masking tape, to touch the girl's hand, she feels the effects "all the way down to somewhere dark and unexplored, deep in [her] belly," and spends the rest of the day "a quivering mass of raging female hormones." In short, the scene is set for harmless, possibly wearisome, romantic fantasy, where the only foreseeable problems for Anastasia will be how to accept lavish gifts—a computer, a car, a wardrobe of new clothes—without being overwhelmed.

It is Grey himself who warns our heroine of possible danger. A present of an 1891 first edition of Thomas Hardy's *Tess of the D'Urbervilles*, subject of Anastasia's undergraduate thesis, is prefaced with a quote from the novel,

Why didn't you tell me there was danger? Why didn't you warn me? Ladies know what to guard against, because they read novels that tell them of these tricks.

The danger Grey alludes to is his desire to control sexual experience in a sadomasochistic framework where he is dominant and his submissive partner must subject herself, blindfolded, to his every whim; these pleasures are to take place in his Playroom:

The walls and ceiling are a deep, dark burgundy, giving a womb-like effect. . . . By the door, two long, polished, ornately carved poles . . . hang like curtain rods across the wall. From them swing a startling assortment of paddles, whips, riding crops, and funny-looking feathery implements.

"Holy fuck," remarks Anastasia, confirming a decisive shift in register.

Hardy's Tess complained to her parents that they hadn't warned her of the dangers a young girl might meet, unchaperoned, in the company of an unscrupulous man. She is seduced, perhaps raped, by Alec D'Urberville, who takes advantage of a moment of exhilaration and confusion; eroticism, in Thomas Hardy, is always accompanied by a loss of control, a fatal lapse of awareness; this is its excitement and its danger. To be excessively guarded, as is Tess's more idealistic lover Angel Clare when he rejects her after discovering that she has already had sexual experience and hence is not the person he thought she was, is to renounce erotic experience. Angel abandons Tess on their wedding night, leaving their marriage unconsummated. So both Tess's partners, frequently referred to in *Fifty Shades of Grey* as possible models for Anastasia's lover, let her down, one by forcing sex on her, one by denying her physical love. Christian Grey, as it turns out, is neither one nor the other. Rather, he is determined to have all the violent excitement he can without any danger whatsoever. He will dominate, but only once he has the assent of his submissive partner. A cautious man, he will take advantage of no one, for fear of repercussions, for fear of hurting someone. He seeks to control not only the circumstances around him, his and his partner's pains and pleasures, but also the moral significance of his actions; so if he keeps Anastasia under strict surveillance and loves to turn up when she least expects it, it is always in order to be gracious, make some generous offer, charm a parent, or save his girl from some pestering rival. In particular, before there can be any sex with Anastasia, Christian, unlike Alec D'Urberville, will let her know what she is in for and invite her to sign a long and detailed contract, in which she can indicate precisely what she is and is not willing to do. It is hard to imagine any less erotic foreplay than such labored contractual formulations as:

Does the Submissive consent to be restrained with:
Hands bound in front
Ankles bound
Elbows bound
Hands bound behind back
Knees bound
Wrists bound to ankles
Binding to fixed items, furniture, etc.
Binding with spreaderbar
Suspension

On the other hand, the purpose of the contract is evident: to allow the sex partners, and indeed the readers, to take pleasure in extreme sexual experience while remaining essentially nice, considerate people who have everything under control.

E. L. James posted early versions of *Fifty Shades of Grey* online, presenting the story as fan fiction honoring Stephanie Meyer's *Twilight*. What *Fifty Shades* has in common with that book is a narrative that is essentially the extended negotiation of a relationship, with the girl at the center of our attention seeking to enjoy the rapture of being loved and physically possessed by a fantastically beautiful, powerful, and dangerous man, while nevertheless retaining her identity and independence. Meyer's romantic male is a vampire, James's an extraordinary mortal of vast wealth and talents who on his own admission, however, is "fifty shades of fucked up." For Christian's sadomasochistic obsession has a simple and rather dull explanation: his mother, a poverty-stricken "crack-whore," died when her son was just four years old; adopted by a rich family, Christian was nevertheless insecure and hence easy prey for a friend of his adoptive mother's who seduced him into a bondage relationship when he was fifteen. This lasted six years. Now an adult, he has simply reversed the terms of that formative relationship and seeks to control his sex partners as rigorously as he does his vast multinational company, which, among other things, strives to eliminate hunger worldwide, this because Grey as a little boy had suffered pangs of hunger.

"My jaw falls to the floor," remarks Anastasia on hearing about her lover's past. "What? Christian was hungry once. *Holy crap.*" Christian, then, in reaction to being a victim is a philanthropist, but also a "strange, sad, kinky guy"; the SM sex the reader is eager to read about is not natural to him, but an anomaly brought about by evil. Precisely by coming some way to meet his perverse desires, Anastasia can perhaps cure him of them. With this narrative frame in position we can actually feel virtuous as we head for the Playroom.

In line with its comic-strip atmosphere, the writing in *Fifty Shades* rarely goes beyond the formulaic. Reading it as an ebook, one is constantly tempted to count occurrences, discovering, for example, that the combination of "holy" with "cow," "crap," "shit," or "fuck" occurs 130 times, that the heroine blushes on 37 occasions and bites her lip on 15, that mouths "drop open" 15 times, eyes "roll" 59 times, and Anastasia says "Wow" 38 times. This impression of a constant reshuffling of the same limited repertoire is particularly strong in the sex scenes, where Christian finds "his release" on 8 orgasmic occasions and we are reminded of Anastasia's "panties" on 38. There are 5 references to "just-fucked" hair. Groans beat moans by 75 to 39, while squirming is approximately three times more likely than writhing, at 22 to 8. Body parts clench on 35 occasions and quiver on 10. Orgasm comes in at 18, while climax crawls behind at 10. None of this is remotely erotic for the simple reason that nothing tactile or visually exciting is ever convincingly evoked. With no gift for description, James is often reduced simply to asserting that the mood is carnal or hedonistic. For the sake of comparison with the Thomas Hardy novel that *Fifty Shades* frequently refers back to, here is a moment in *Tess of the D'Urbervilles* when Angel Clare sees Tess milking the cows in the early morning:

> She had not heard him enter, and hardly realized his presence there. She was yawning, and he saw the red interior of her mouth as if it had been a snake's. She had stretched one arm so high above her coiled-up cable of hair that he could see its satin delicacy above the sunburn; her face was flushed with sleep, and her eyelids hung heavy over their pupils. The brimfulness of her nature breathed from her. . . .
>
> Then those eyes flashed brightly through their filmy heaviness, before the remainder of her face was well awake. With an oddly compounded look of gladness, shyness, and surprise, she exclaimed—"O Mr Clare! How you frightened me—I—"

Here are a few moments from the scene where Anastasia loses her virginity:

Suddenly, he sits up and tugs my panties off and throws them on the floor. Pulling off his boxer briefs, his erection springs free. *Holy cow* . . . He reaches over to his bedside table and grabs a foil packet, and then he moves between my legs, spreading them farther apart. He kneels up and pulls a condom onto his considerable length. Oh no . . . *Will it? How?* . . .

"I'm going to fuck you now, Miss Steele," he murmurs as he positions the head of his erection at the entrance of my sex. "Hard," he whispers, and he slams into me.

"Aargh!" I cry as I feel a weird pinching sensation deep inside me as he rips through my virginity. . . .

"Come for me, Ana" he whispers breathlessly, and I unravel at his words, exploding around him as I climax and splinter into a million pieces underneath him. . . .

"See how you taste," he breathes against my ear. "Suck me, baby." His thumb presses on my tongue and my mouth closes round him, sucking wildly. . . . *Holy fuck.* This is wrong, but holy hell is it erotic.

Nevertheless, and despite the worn-out repetitions, typical of pornography and indeed of sports journalism, or any text that substitutes mere assertion for evocation, there are good reasons for *Fifty Shades of Grey*'s special success. Both Christian and Anastasia are people who think too much, they live in their heads, not their bodies; they want to remain in control, want to believe they are good, yet want to enjoy all life's good things. In short, different and caricatured as they are—he all power, wealth, and expertise, she all innocence and spunky independence—both are representative of modern middle-class aspirations.

Relationships, particularly sexual relationships, are the territory where the not unconnected obsessions of control and independence are most urgently challenged: it is hard for both sex partners to be sovereign individuals when their bodies are locked in an embrace; perhaps one wants to do something to the other that the other doesn't want, or wants the other to do something that that person isn't eager to offer; above all, the thinking, calculating mind will find itself disturbed by sensations and emotions that may prove ungovernable. Very soon both Christian and Anastasia discover they are not the people they thought they were; their long negotiation around issues of sexual domination becomes a voyage of self-discovery that threatens—very much against the grain of James's cranked out prose—to become interesting.

The pattern is set at once when Christian, having shown Anastasia his Playroom, asks her what she is willing and not willing to do when it comes to anal, bondage, toys, masturbation, and so on, and she candidly tells him she has no idea, never having had sex at all. Her inexperience disarms him, encouraging him to "make love" to her, rather than "fuck hard." This leaves him confused and convinces the reader that he will never do Anastasia any real harm. What self-respecting villain is it who warns his victims what he is about to do and encourages them to ask him to stop him if they are not happy with proceedings?

But the author has burdened Christian with an unhappy past and SM ways to give her heroine a chance to explore her sexuality more thoroughly than might otherwise have been the case. So while Christian finds his rigid rules for conducting relationships threatened by her winsome inexperience, she discovers that being blindfolded and moderately slapped and whipped is more exciting than she could have imagined. In an email she tells him:

> You wanted to know why I felt confused after you . . . spanked, punished, beat, assaulted me. Well, during the whole alarming

process, I felt demeaned, debased, and abused. And much to my mortification, you're right, I was aroused, and that was unexpected. . . . I was shocked to feel aroused.

To which Grey replies,

So you felt demeaned, debased, abused, and assaulted—how very Tess Durbeyfield of you. . . . Do you really feel like this or do you think you ought to feel like this? Two very different things.

This is as close as the book gets to suggesting that there may be areas of desirable erotic experience that not only can't be squared with the right-thinking worldview the author eventually upholds but might also require a revision of notions of identity, individualism, and the independent modern girl.

Presented with the choice of losing her beloved if she doesn't comply and getting hurt if she does, Anastasia's mind divides; the voice of moral conscience warns her to steer clear of this disturbed man, while a more enthusiastic, uninhibited part of her character rejoices in every affirmation of her sexual hold over Christian. If the latter impulse is understandably referred to as Anastasia's "inner goddess," the former is inexplicably dubbed her "subconscious." How the subconscious can participate as a voice in a very conscious debate and why it would take the part of conventional morality is unclear. When Anastasia first considers accepting Christian's SM contract, she dramatizes her indecision thus:

You can't seriously be considering this. . . . My subconscious sounds sane and rational. . . . My inner goddess is jumping up and down, clapping her hands like a five-year-old. *Please, let's do this . . . otherwise we'll end up alone with lots of cats and your classic novels to keep you company.*

Seventy pages later Anastasia agrees:

What have you done? my subconscious screams at me. My inner goddess is doing backflips in a routine worthy of a Russian Olympic gymnast.

In the end the subconscious turns up seventy-eight times, the inner goddess fifty-seven. When at the end of the book Christian gives Anastasia six lashes with a belt, causing her such serious pain that she decides to end the relationship, we hear that "my subconscious is shaking her head sadly, and my inner goddess is nowhere to be seen." Page 514 leaves us with Anastasia weeping alone and the prospect of two further, equally long books, *Fifty Shades Darker* and *Fifty Shades Freed,* to take us through a series of improbable vicissitudes and sexual exploits on the way to the inevitable marriage and motherhood that any experienced reader will have seen at once is the only possible conclusion.

It is in this regard that E. L. James's novel is so different from *Histoire d'O,* to which it has been flatteringly compared: in Anne Desclos's work there is simply no question of dominant men being "cured" of their "perversity" by cute and wholesome students of English literature; rather, O accepts her submissive role in the sadomasochistic relationship entirely and willingly, appearing in the last scene of the book with a chain leash and an owl mask, silent and unspoken to, an object for her two dominant lovers to use as and when they will. In short, the French novel is rather more challenging.

Much debate around the *Fifty Shades* trilogy has centered on the questions: is it pornography and does it demean women? James has defended her work, declaring it a romantic fantasy written entirely for herself. It's evident that many of the sex scenes, if removed from the supporting narrative of a relationship under negotiation, would be indistinguishable from any number of texts available on websites offering pornography. But this is a novel whose extraordinary sales figures are far more interesting than anything to be found between the covers; or, rather, the content invites interest mainly insofar as one struggles to understand why such a poorly written book has been so popular. After all, there is no shortage of erotica out there.

The key would seem to be that the pornographic elements become attractive when held in a narrative frame that allows the reader to feel as innocent in this sexual journey as the novel's heroine. And as responsible as its hero: Christian never forgets to put on his condom, and when he invites Anastasia to use the pill, he organizes an appointment for her with a top gynecologist. It is this atmosphere of innocent, often infantile comedy combined with middle-class dependability that perhaps frees certain readers to indulge an appetite for pornography they would usually repress. The wedding service evoked, the hand can head south.

Acknowledgments

I'd like to extend my thanks to all staff of the *New York Review of Books* and the *London Review of Books* who worked with me on these essays over the years, and in particular to Bob Silvers and Mary Kay Wilmers, who invited me to write them. Thanks also to John Donatich and Jennifer Banks at Yale University Press, who have given me the chance to bring the pieces together in this way, and to Dan Heaton for presiding so thoughtfully over the reintegration of much material for which there was no space in the originals. The essays were written to "call to each other," and they do so more easily and comfortably in a single volume than spread across a score of magazines on both sides of the Atlantic.

Credits

These essays appeared in different form under the following titles. I am grateful to the original publishers for permission to rework them for the present volume.

Dickens: "How Does He Come to Be Mine?" *London Review of Books,* August 8, 2013

Dostoevsky: "Description of a Struggle," *Nation,* June 14, 2004

Hardy: "Bitten by an Adder," *London Review of Books,* July 17, 2014

Chekhov: "Chekhov: Behind the Charm," *New York Review of Books,* April 5, 2012

Joyce: "Joyce and Company," *London Review of Books,* July 5, 2012

Beckett: "On Needing to Be Looked After," *London Review of Books,* December 1, 2011

Simenon: "Quite a Show," *London Review of Books,* October 9, 2014

Spark: "Muriel Spark, Moral Hypnotist," *New York Review of Books,* October 9, 2014

Roth: "The Truth about Consuela," *London Review of Books,* November 4, 2010

Coetzee: "The Education of 'John Coetzee,'" *New York Review of Books,* February 11, 2010

Barnes: "Death in the Family," *Australian,* May 7, 2008

Tóibín: "Life at the Core," *New York Review of Books,* April 7, 2011

Dyer: "In the Kangaroo's Pouch," *New York Review of Books,* July 16, 2009

Stamm: "Making Fun of the Stories We Know," *New York Review of Books,*
    July 14, 2011

Swift: "Beware Remembrance Sunday," *London Review of Books,* June 2,
    2011

Eggers: "Dave Eggers Abroad," *New York Review of Books,* October 11, 2012

Murakami: "The Charms of Loneliness," *New York Review of Books,*
    October 23, 2013

Matthiessen: "The Ultimate Koan," *New York Review of Books,* April 3,
    2014

Larsson: "The Moralist," *New York Review of Books,* June 9, 2011

James: "Why So Popular?" *New York Review of Books,* February 7, 2014

Index

Adams, Henry, 166
Afternoon Men (Powell), 199
"Agatha" (Chekhov), 72–73
Agnes (Stamm), 212, 213
All That Fall (Beckett), 120
Altschuller, Isaac, 79
Amis, Martin, 21
Appelfeld, Aharon, 262
Avery, Simon, 52, 55

Bachelors, The (Spark), 138–39, 147
Baker, Nicholson, 286–87
Bakker, Gerbrand, 218, 227
Bakunin, Nikolay, 31
Ballad of Peckham Rye, The (Spark), 139
Barnacle, Nora, 88–89, 90, 93, 94–95,
    97, 99, 101
Barnes, Julian, 174–82
Barrow, Thomas, 7
Bateson, Gregory, 95, 98
Beckett, Samuel, 35, 43, 46, 101, 102–23,
    206
Belmont, George, 114
Bernhard, Thomas, 46, 196, 198
Blin, Robert, 115–16, 121
"Blunder, A" (Chekhov), 71
Blunt, Wilfrid Scawen, 184

Borowski, Tadeusz, 265
Bowker, Gordon, 82, 88, 90, 94, 96, 98
Bowles, Patrick, 119
Boyhood (Coetzee), 163–66, 167
"Brilliant Career, A" (Joyce), 86–87
Brontë sisters, 149
Brooklyn (Tóibín), 191
Brothers Karamazov, The (Dostoevsky),
    40–41, 45
Brown, Dan, 285
Bulwer-Lytton, Edward, 9
Bunin, Ivan, 79

Camus, Albert, 206
Carr, Henry, 92
Caspari, Carlheinz, 118
Céline, Louis-Ferdinand, 46
"Champagne" (Chekhov), 72
Chekhov, Alexander, 67
Chekhov, Anton, 67–80
Chekhov, Evgenia Yakovlevna, 67,
    68, 71
Chekhov, Maria Pavlovna, 67–68,
    71, 79
Chekhov, Mikhail, 68, 69, 76, 79
Chekhov, Nikolay, 67, 74
Chernyshevsky, Nikolay, 30, 32, 33

Cherry Orchard, The (Chekhov), 77

Chimes, The (Dickens), 10

Christie, Agatha, 122

Coetzee, J. M., 163–73

Collins, Charles, 18

Collins, Wilkie, 18, 23

Colorless Tsukuru Tazaki and His Years of Pilgrimage (Murakami), 250–59

Comforters, The (Spark), 140, 142–43, 144–45

Coulson, Jessie, 26–27

Craig, George, 110

Crime and Punishment (Dostoevsky), 37, 45

Crime in Holland, A (Simenon), 131–34

Curriculum Vitae (Spark), 142, 143, 144, 145, 148

David Copperfield (Dickens), vii, 7, 8, 10, 14, 15–18, 23

Dead, The (Joyce), 92–93

Death in Venice (Mann), 204

Dechevaux-Dumesnil, Suzanne, 102–4, 107–8, 113, 115–16, 120

Desclos, Anne, 297

Dickens, Alfred D'Orsay Tennyson, 1, 9, 10, 14, 15, 21

Dickens, Catherine (Hogarth), 5–6, 7–8, 18

Dickens, Catherine Macready, 8–9, 12, 14, 18, 19

Dickens, Charles, 1–23

Dickens, Charles Culliford Boz, 7, 11, 15, 18, 20

Dickens, Dora Annie, 9

Dickens, Edward Bulwer Lytton, 9, 10, 14

Dickens, Fanny, 3

Dickens, Francis Jeffrey, 9–10, 14, 21

Dickens, Henry Fielding, 9, 10, 14, 15, 19, 20, 21

Dickens, Mary Angela, 7–8, 14, 19, 21

Dickens, Sydney Smith Haldimand, 1, 9, 10, 14, 15, 20

Dickens, Walter Landor, 9, 12, 13, 14, 15

Dirty Snow (Simenon), 126–27, 130, 136

Dombey and Son (Dickens), 23

Dostoevsky, Feodor, 24–47

Dostoevsky, Mikhail, 27

"Dreary Story, A" (Chekhov), 74–75

Driver's Seat, The (Spark), 141

Dubliners (Joyce), 87, 88

Duthuis, Georges, 105, 108, 110, 111–12, 115

Dyer, Geoff, 194–205

Dying Animal, The (Roth), 152–54, 155, 156, 161, 162

Eco, Umberto, 284

Eggers, Dave, 233–46

Ego and His Own, The (Stirner), 46

Eleutheria (Beckett), 109, 110

Eliot, George, 17

Eliot, T. S., 145

Ellmann, Richard, 82, 90, 94

Empty Family, The (collection), 183–85

"Empty Family, The" (short story), 185–87

Endgame (Beckett), 122, 123

Étranger, L' (Camus), 206

Ever After (Swift), 221, 222
Everyman (Roth), 152, 155, 156
Exiles (Joyce), 93–95
Exit Ghost (Roth), 150, 152, 154–55, 161, 162

Far Cry from Kensington, A (Spark), 147, 148
Farm, The (Leyshon), 227
Fielding, Henry, 9
Fifty Shades Darker (James), 297
Fifty Shades Freed (James), 297
Fifty Shades of Grey (James), 287–96
Finnegans Wake (Joyce), 87, 92, 95, 100
First Love (Beckett), 104–5, 106, 108, 109
Flaubert, Gustave, 180
Flaubert's Parrot (Barnes), 175, 181
Forster, John, 3, 5, 8
Frank, Joseph, 33
Franzen, Jonathan, 218

Gambler, The (Dostoevsky), 37, 40
Gilbert, Stuart, 100
Ginsberg, Allen, 202
Girl Who Kicked the Hornet's Nest, The (Larsson), 279–80
Girl Who Played with Fire, The (Larsson), 279–80, 281–83
Girl with the Dragon Tattoo, The (Larsson), 271–81
Gogol, Nikolay, 35, 38
Gorky, Maxim, 80
Gottlieb, Robert, 1–5, 7, 10–11, 12, 14, 18, 19–20, 22
Great Expectations (Dickens), 19

Green, Henry, 199
Greene, Graham, 142, 144
Gregory, Lady Augusta, 87, 183, 184, 185, 187, 193
"Grisha" (Chekhov), 72
Grossman, Leonid, 40
Gunn, Dan, 100–101, 107

Haldimand, William, 9
Hardboiled Wonderland and the End of the World (Murakami), 249
Hardy, Thomas, x–xi, 151, 153, 166–67, 227, 290
Hawksley, Lucinda, 12
Hayter, Bill, 122
Heartbreaking Work of Staggering Genius, A (Eggers), 233–34, 236, 244
Hingley, Ronald, 70
History of the World in 10½ Chapters, A (Barnes), 175, 180
Hoffman, Michael, 217, 218
Hogarth, Georgina, 8, 19, 20
Hogarth, Mary, 7–8
Hogarth (Dickens), Catherine, 5–6, 7–8, 18
Holloway, Joseph, 86
Hologram for the King, A (Eggers), 242–46
Hope, Christopher, 261
Humbling, The (Roth), 150, 151, 152, 154, 155, 161
Huxley, Aldous, 91

Ibsen, Henrik, 87
In Paradise (Matthiessen), 261–70

In the Spirit of Crazy Horse
(Matthiessen), 269
Indignation (Roth), 150, 151, 152, 154,
155, 156, 159, 161
Informed Air, The (Spark), 142, 144, 148
Irving, John, 248
Isaev, Maria Dimitrievna, 27, 44

James, E. L., 286–98
James, Henry, 183, 185, 192
Jeff in Venice, Death in Varanasi (Dyer),
194–95, 197–205
Joyce, Eileen, 90
Joyce, Eva, 90
Joyce, George (brother), 90
Joyce, George (son), 90, 98
Joyce, James, 81–101
Joyce, John, 83
Joyce, Lucia, 90, 97–99
Joyce, May, 83
Joyce, Stanislaus, 87, 88, 90, 92, 96
Joyce, Stephen, 101
Jude the Obscure (Hardy), x, 48
Jung, C. G., 95

Kafka on the Shore (Murakami), 249
Kentish, Jane, 26
Knipper, Olga, 79
Kolbe, Maximilian, 265, 268

Landor, Walter, 9
Larsson, Stieg, 271–85, 287
Last Orders (Swift), 222
Lautréamont, comte de, 46
Lawrence, D. H., x–xi, 55–56, 100, 151,
196, 197, 204, 216

"Learning to Swim" (Swift), 222
Letter to My Mother (Simenon), 124,
125, 126, 130, 137
Leyshon, Nell, 227
Lindon, Jerome, 102, 117
Loitering with Intent (Spark), 145, 147

MacGreevy, Thomas, 106, 110, 118,
119, 121
Macready, William, 8–9
Mailer, Norman, 283
Malone Dies (Beckett), 109, 119
Mann, Thomas, 197–98, 202, 204
Man's Head, A (Simenon), 131
Man Who Watched Trains Go By, The
(Simenon), 136
Marnham, Patrick, 128–29
Matthiessen, Peter, 260–70
Melville, Herman, 46
Memento Mori (Spark), 141
Mercier et Camier (Beckett), 109
Metroland (Barnes), 174
Meyer, Stephanie, 291–92
Middlemarch (Eliot), vii
"Misfortune, A" (Chekhov), 72
Mitchell, Pamela, 108–9, 120, 121, 122
Mizinov, Lika, 75
Molloy (Beckett), 102, 105, 109, 117,
118–20
Montaigne, Michel de, 180
Moravia, Alberto, 150
Murakami, Haruki, 247–59
Murphy (Beckett), 104, 106, 110, 119

Nemesis (Roth), 150, 152, 154, 155,
156–62

"New Spain, The" (Tóibín), 190–91
Nicholas Nickleby (Dickens), 6
Night at the Crossroads (Simenon), 134
Norwegian Wood (Murakami), 249
Notes from the Underground
   (Dostoevsky), 25–36, 38, 43–47, 60
Nothing to Be Frightened Of (Barnes),
   174–80, 181–82

Oliver Twist (Dickens), 6, 21–22
On a Day Like This (Stamm), 206–11,
   212, 213
Only Problem, The (Spark), 147
Orsay, Alfred, Comte d', 9
Orwell, George, 12–13, 17, 23
Our Mutual Friend (Dickens), 19, 23
Out of Sheer Rage (Dyer), 196–97

Parnell, Charles Stewart, 83, 85, 91
Party Going (Green), 199
"Pearl Fishers, The" (Tóibín), 189–90
Peltier, Leonard, 269
Péron, Marie, 118, 121
Petersson, Per, 218
Pevear, Richard, 26, 36
Pichugin, Zakhar, 68, 70, 76
Pickwick Papers, The (Dickens), 6, 10
Pletzinger, Thomas, 217
Portrait of the Artist as a Young Man,
   A (Joyce), 83, 84–85, 87, 88, 91,
   93, 95
Potapenko, Ignaty, 70
Pound, Ezra, 91, 92, 97
Powell, Antony, 199
Prime of Miss Jean Brodie, The (Spark),
   143, 145–47

Proust, Marcel, 181
Pushkin, Alexander, 35

Rayfield, Donald, 70
Read, Herbert, 110
Reavey, George, 110, 114
Renard, Jules, 180
Return of the Native (Hardy), 48–66
"Robbers, The" (Chekhov), 73–74
Rosset, Barney, 119, 120, 121
Roth, Philip, 150–62, 218
Russell, Bertrand, 152

Schneider, Alan, 118
Sea and Sardinia (Lawrence), 204
Seagull, The (Chekhov), 77, 78
Sendak, Maurice, 238
Seven Years (Stamm), 213–17
Shadow Country (Matthiessen),
   261–62
Shelley, Mary, 148–49
"Silence" (Tóibín), 183–84
Simenon, Christian, 124, 126
Simenon, Denyse, 126, 128
Simenon, Désiré, 124
Simenon, Georges, 124–37, 149
Simenon, Henriette (Brüll), 124–25
Simenon, Marie-Jo, 125–26
Sketches by Boz (Dickens), 10
Sketches of Etruscan Places (Lawrence),
   204
Smith, Sydney, 9
Snitkina, Anna Gigoryevna, 40
South of the Border, West of the Sun
   (Murakami), 248
Spark, Muriel, 138–49

Speshnev, Nikolay, 24

Stamm, Peter, 206–18

Stanislavsky, Konstantin, 78

Stephen Hero (Joyce), 88

Stirner, Max, 46

Strachan, Tony, 148

"Street, The" (Tóibín), 191–93

Summertime (Coetzee), 163–64, 168–73

Surviving Justice (Eggers), 237

Suslova, Apollinaria, 28

Sweetshop Owner, The (Swift), 221

Swift, Graham, 219–32

Tarantino, Quentin, 46

Teachers Have It Easy (Eggers), 237

Tedeschi, Giuliana, 260

Tennyson, Alfred, Lord, 9

Ternan, Ellen, 19, 20

Tess of the d'Urbervilles (Hardy), x, 48, 232, 289–90, 291, 293

Three Beds in Manhattan (Simenon), 127–28

Three Sisters, The (Chekhov), 77

Tóibín, Colm, 183–93

Tolstoy, Leo, 24

Tomalin, Claire, 4, 5, 20

Tomorrow (Swift), 222

Trilogy, The (Beckett), 119–20

Trocchi, Alexander, 117

Turgenev, Ivan, 35

Twilight in Italy (Lawrence), 204

Twin, The (Bakker), 227

"Two Women" (Tóibín), 188

Ugazio, Valeria, ix, 22

Ulysses (Joyce), 87, 92, 95, 96, 97, 100

Uncle Vanya (Chekhov), 77

Unformed Landscape (Stamm), 211–12, 213

Unnameable, The (Beckett), 109, 117, 119

Velde, Bram van, 110–12

Velde, Jacoba van, 118

Vinding, Ole, 99

Volokhonsky, Larissa, 26, 36

Waiting for Godot (Beckett), 109, 110, 115, 117–18, 119, 120, 121, 123

"Ward No. 6" (Chekhov), 76

Waterland (Stamm), 221–22, 232

Watt (Beckett), 109, 110, 119

Watzlawick, Paul, 151

Waugh, Evelyn, 142

Weaver, Harriet, 91, 92, 96, 97

What Is the What (Eggers), 237, 238–39, 240

What Is to Be Done? (Chernyshevsky), 30, 32, 33

Widdowson, Peter, 196–97

Wild Things, The (Eggers), 237–38

Williams, Raymond, 18

Wish You Were Here (Swift), 219–21, 222, 223–31

"Writing Life, The" (Spark), 144

Yeats, W. B., 87, 91

Yellow Dog, The (Simenon), 135–36

You Shall Know Our Velocity! (Eggers), 235–37, 241

Youth (Coetzee), 163–64, 166, 167–68

Zeitoun (Eggers), 237, 238, 239–41, 244

Zola, Émile, 180